Charles Haddon Spurgeon

Types and emblems

Being a collection of sermons preached on Sunday and Thursday evenings at the

Metropolitan Tabernacle

Charles Haddon Spurgeon

Types and emblems
Being a collection of sermons preached on Sunday and Thursday evenings at the Metropolitan Tabernacle

ISBN/EAN: 9783337113568

Printed in Europe, USA, Canada, Australia, Japan

Cover: Foto ©Lupo / pixelio.de

More available books at **www.hansebooks.com**

TYPES AND EMBLEMS:

BEING

A COLLECTION OF SERMONS

PREACHED

ON SUNDAY AND THURSDAY EVENINGS

AT THE

METROPOLITAN TABERNACLE,

BY

C. H. SPURGEON.

NEW YORK:
SHELDON & COMPANY,
677 BROADWAY.

Works of the Rev. C. H. Spurgeon.

Mr. Spurgeon undoubtedly occupies the position of greatest celebrity at the present moment among living preachers.

Sermons of the Rev. C. H. Spurgeon, In uniform styles of binding. Nine vols. $1.50 each.

Spurgeon's Gems. Being brilliant passages from his sermons. One vol. 12mo. Price, $1.50.

Morning by Morning; or, Daily Bible Readings. Price, $1.75.

Evening by Evening; or, Readings at Eventide. Price, $1.75.

The Saint and his Saviour. Price, $1.50.

Gleanings among the Sheaves. One vol. 16mo. Price, $1.25.

John Ploughman's Talk; or, Plain Advice to Plain People. One vol. 16mo. Price, 90 cts.

Types and Emblems. Price, $1.25.

ADVERTISEMENT.

This book is called for. Not a few of Mr. Spurgeon's friends think that "none of his words should fall to the ground." They are hardly content with the issue of his Sunday Morning Sermons, but they want the Evening Sermons also. To meet this demand we propose to publish a series, of which "Types and Emblems" is the first volume. The sermons it contains have been selected from a large number preached by him on Sunday and Thursday evenings. It is hoped that the size and type will be acceptable to his admirers.

THE PUBLISHERS.

CONTENTS.

	PAGE
THE STAR OF JACOB.	7
THE BROAD WALL	22
THE ONLY DOOR	41
ROYAL EMBLEMS FOR LOYAL SUBJECTS	61
A FRAIL LEAF	78
THE HELMET	93
ONE TROPHY FOR TWO EXPLOITS	112
CHRIST THE TREE OF LIFE	134
A SILLY DOVE	148
OUR BANNER	164
OUR CHAMPION	179
THE FAINTING HERO.	194
WOMEN'S RIGHTS.—A PARABLE.	209
BLACK CLOUDS AND BRIGHT BLESSINGS	225
DAVID'S FIRST VICTORY	247
DAVID AND HIS VOLUNTEERS	270

The Star of Jacob.

"There shall come a Star out of Jacob."—NUMBERS xxiv. 17.

THIS prophecy may have some reference to David; but we feel persuaded that the true design of the Holy Spirit is to set forth an emblem of our Lord Jesus Christ. All nature, above as well as around us, is laid under contribution to set forth our Lord. All the flowers of the field and many of the beasts of the plain, and now the very orbs of heaven, are turned into metaphors and symbols by which the glory of Jesus may be manifested to us. Where God takes such pains to teach, we ought to be at pains to learn. Where he makes heaven and earth to be the pages of the book, we ought to be most ardent in our study. Oh, you who have neglected to learn of Christ, may that neglect come to an end, and may some word be spoken which shall be as the beaming of a star unto the darkness of your soul, that henceforth you may be led to know Christ, and to be found in him.

Our Lord, then, is compared to a star, and we shall have seven reasons to assign for this.

I. He is called a star as THE SYMBOL OF GOVERNMENT. You will observe how evidently it is connected with a sceptre and with a conqueror. Jacob was to be blessed with a valiant leader who should become a triumphant sovereign. Very frequently in oriental literature their great men, and especially their great deliverers, are called stars. The star has been constantly associated with monarchy, and even in our own country we still look upon the star as one of the emblems of lofty rank. Behold, then, our Lord Jesus Christ as the Star of Jacob. He is the Captain of his people, the Leader of the Lord's hosts, the King in Jeshurun, God over all, glorious and blessed for ever!

We may say of Jesus in this respect *that he has an authority which he has inherited by right.* He made all things, and by him all things consist. It is but just that he should rule over all things. As there is not a tongue that can move in heaven or earth except by his permission, it is meet that every tongue should confess that he is Lord, to the glory of God the Father. Oh, that men were just towards the Son of God! Would that their rebellious souls would give way to the force of rectitude—that they would no longer say, "Let us break his bonds asunder, and cast his cords from us!" Unconverted men, I would that you would yield to Jesus. He has a right to you. It is through his intercession that your forfeited life is still spared. It is by his divine goodness that you are where you are to-night. Through his mediatorial sovereignty it is that you are suffered to be on praying ground and pleading terms with God. Give him his due then. Rob him not of the allegiance which he so justly claims. Give not your spirit over to that exacting tyrant who seeks to compass your destruction. Bow the knee and kiss the Son, even now, lest he be angry, and ye perish from the way. Acknowledge Him to be your Lord.

Our Lord as a star *has an authority which he has valiantly won.* Wherever Christ is king he has had a great and a stern fight for it. Remember the dread conflict in Gethsemane in which he says, "I have trodden the wine press alone." When he came red with his own gore from Calvary, he had in fact there and then put to flight the hosts of Bozrah and of Edom, and stained his garments with the victor's crimson. He who, then, travelled in the greatness of his strength is mighty still to save. In every human heart where Jesus reigns he reigns through having dislodged, by the force of grace, the old tyrant who had fixed his sovereignty there. The maintenance of that sovereignty within the heart is the result of the same powerful sceptre of his love and grace. Oh, that King Jesus would put forth his power and get a throne in more hearts! Believers, do you not long to see him glorious? I know you do if you love him. You would live for this, you would die for this;—that Christ might have his own, and drive the milk-white steeds of triumph through the streets of Jerusalem, all his people bowing before him and strewing his pathway with their honors. O sinners! would to God that you would yield to him. I pray that now he may gird his sword upon his thigh, and by the power of grace constrain you to bow your willing necks to his silver sceptre. Brethren and sisters, it is a mournful fact that Christ has so small a part of the world as yet in his royal power. See, the gods of the heathen stand fast upon their pedestals. The old harlot of Rome still flaunts in her scarlet. The crescent of Mahomed wanes, but still its baleful light is cast athwart the nations. Why tarries he ? Perhaps his finger is on the latch ; it may be that he will come ere long.—Come quickly Lord! our yearning hearts beseech thee to come! Meanwhile, it is for you and for me to be fighting, each soldier in his rank, each man standing in his place, as his master has bidden him, contending with heart and soul and strength for the right and for the true, for faith, for holiness, for the cross, and all that that cross indicates among the sons of men. Blessed Star of Jacob! Thou shinest with no borrowed rays; thou shinest with a mysterious power which none gave to thee, for it is inherently thine own.

Before we leave this point, I will only say this kingdom of Christ, *wherever it is, is most beneficent.* Wherever this star of government shines, its rays scatter blessing. Jesus is no tyrant. He rules not by oppression. The force he uses is the force of love. There was never a subject of Christ's kingdom that complained of him. Those who have served him most have longed to serve him more. Why, even his poor martyrs in the catacombs of Rome, dying of starvation, or dragged up to the Colosseum to be devoured by wild beasts, never said an ill word of him. Certainly if it was hard to any it seemed to be hard to them ; but the more they were troubled the more they rejoiced, and there never were sweeter songs than those which came from dying lips when men were crackling on the faggot, or being dragged limb from limb at the heels of wild horses, or being sawn asunder. Just in proportion as the bodily pains became acute, the spiritual joy became intense; and while the outward man decayed, the inner man leaped up into newness of life, anticipating the joys of the first-born before the throne. He is a good master. Young people, I would that you would serve him! Oh! that you were enlisted in his service. It is now a good many years since I gave my heart to him, it is fast getting on for twenty years, but I cannot say a word against him. Nay, but I wish I had always served him; I wish I had served him before, and I do pray that he may use me to the fullest extent. If he will make but a door-mat for his temple of me I shall be but too glad. If he will let my name be cast out as evil and give my body to the dogs, I do not care as long as his truth does but prosper, and his name becomes great. But alas! there is so much self in us, pride and I know not what besides, that we who really know the master have reason to ask him to bring in his great artillery and blow down the castles of our natural corruption, conquer us yet again, and rule in us by main force of grace, till in every part and corner of our spirits there shall be nothing but the love of Christ and the indwelling of his gracious Spirit. By the star we understand the symbol of government.

II. In the second place, the star is THE IMAGE OF BRIGHTNESS.

When men wish to speak of brightness they talk of the stars. They who are righteous are as the stars, and they that turn many to righteousness shall shine as the stars for ever and ever. Our Lord Jesus Christ is brightness itself. The star is but a poor setting forth of his ineffable splendor. Oh! let the thought come home to you. He is the brightness of his Father's glory—unutterably bright as the Deity. He is brightness himself in his human nature, for in him there was neither spot nor wrinkle. As Mediator, exalted on high, enjoying the reward of his pains, he is bright indeed. Observe, that our Lord as a star is a bright particular star in the matter of holiness. In him was no sin. Look, and look, and look again into his starlike character. Even the lynx-eyes of infidels have not been able to discover a mistake in him; and as for the attentive eyes of critics who have been believers, they have been made to water again and again, and then to glisten and sparkle with delight as they have seen the mingling of all the perfections in his adorable character to make up one perfection.

As a star, he shines also with the light of knowledge. Moses was, as it were, but a mist, but Christ is the prophet of light. "The law was given by Moses"—a thing of types and shadows—"but grace and truth come by Jesus Christ." If any man be taught in the things of God, he must derive his light from the Star of Bethlehem. You may go as you will to the universities, to the tomes of the learned, to the schools of the philosophers, but in spiritual things you receive no light till you look up to Jesus, and then in his light you see light, for there is transcendent brightness in him. He is the wisdom of God as well as the power of God; he is the way, the truth, and the life. Divine light has found its centre in him!

His light too is that of comfort. Oh! how many have emerged from the darkness of their souls and found peace by looking up to this Star of Jacob, the Lord Jesus Christ! Well did our hymn put it—

"He is my soul's bright Morning Star,
And he my Rising Sun."

One glimpse of Christ and the midnight of your unbelief is over. But a sight of the five wounds and your sins are covered and your iniquities put away. Happy day, happy day, when first the soul beholds a crucified Redeemer, and gives herself up to him, relying upon him for eternal salvation. Shine, sweet Star—shine into some benighted heart to-night! Give thou holiness, give light, give the knowledge of God, give thou joy and peace in believing, in believing in the precious blood!

When speaking upon Christ as a star, "the Symbol of Government," I said, submit to him. Now, speaking of him as a star, the Image of Brightness, I say look to him—look to him. It is the Gospel's precept. "Look unto me, and be ye saved all ye ends of the earth," and well do we sing—

"There is life for a look at the Crucified One."

Poor sinner, delay no longer. You are not asked to do anything, nor to be anything, nor to feel anything; but you are simply bidden to look away from self to what Christ has done, and you shall live.

"View him prostrate in the garden,
On the ground your Maker lies;
On the bloody tree behold him,
Hear him cry before he dies—
'It is finished,'
Sinner, will not this suffice?"

Look to him then and live.

III. Thirdly, our Lord is compared to a star to bring out the fact, that he is THE PATTERN OF CONSTANCY.

Ten thousand changes have been wrought since

the world began, but the stars have not changed. There they remain. We dreamed at one time that they moved. Untaught imagination said that all those stars revolved around this little globe of ours. But we know better now. There they are both day and night—always the same, and we may say they have not changed since the world began, nor probably will they till like a vesture God shall roll creation up because it is worn out. It is very delightful to recollect that the same star which I looked at last night was viewed by Abraham, perhaps with some of the self-same thoughts. And when we have gone, and other generations shall have followed us, those that come after will look up to the self-same star. So with our Lord Jesus. He is the same yesterday, to-day, and for ever. What the prophets and apostles saw in him, we can see in him, and what he was to them, that he is to us, and shall be to generations yet unborn. Hundreds of us may be looking at the same star at the same time without knowing it. There is a meeting-place for many eyes. We may be drifted, some of us, to Australia, or to Canada, or to the United States, or we may be sailing across the great deep, but we shall see the stars there. It is true that on the other side of the world we shall see another set of stars, but the stars themselves are always still the same. As far as we in this atmosphere are concerned, we shall look upon some star. So, wherever we may be, we look to the same Christ. One brother here has learning, but as he looks to Christ, he sees the same Christ as the poor unlettered woman in the aisles. And you, poor man, who have not, perhaps, a sixpence in the world, you have got the same Christ to trust in as the richest man in all the world. And you who think yourself so obscure that no one knows you but your God, you look to this same star, and it shines with the same beams for you, as for the Christian who leads the van in the Lord's hosts. Jesus Christ is still the same, the same to all his people, the same in all places, the same for ever and ever. Well therefore may he be compared to those bright stars that shine now as they did of old and change not.

IV. In the fourth place, we may trace this comparison of our Lord to a star as THE FOUNTAIN OF INFLUENCE.

The old astrologers used to believe very strongly in the influence of the stars upon men's minds. Without indorsing their exploded fallacies, we meet in Scripture with expressions like this:—"Canst thou bind the sweet influences of the Pleiades, or loose the bands of Orion?"—alluding, no doubt, to the fact that the Pleiades are in the ascendant in the sweet months of spring, when the warm breath and gentle showers are bringing forth the green sprout and tender blade, the foliage and the flowers of May, with all the loveliness of the season, while Orion is in the ascendant as a wintry sign, when the bands of frost are binding up the outburst of nature. But, whether there be an influence in the stars or not, as touching this world, I know there is great influence in Christ Jesus. He is the fountain of all holy influences among the sons of men. Where this star shines upon the graves of men who are dead in sin they begin to live. Where the beam of this star shines upon poor imprisoned spirits, their chains drop off, the captive leaps to lose his chains. When this star gleams upon a burdened Christian with its light, he begins to bud and blossom, and precious fruits are brought forth. When this star shines upon the backslider, he begins to mend his ways, and to follow, like the eastern sages, its light till he finds his Saviour once more. This star has an influence upon our nativity. It is through its benign rays that we are born again, and in our horoscope it has an influence upon our death, for it is in its light that we fall asleep, believing that we shall wake up in the image of the Lord Jesus. Oh! sweet star, shine on me always! Never let me miss thy rays; but may I always walk in the light thereof, till I be found sitting in the full noontide heat of the Sun of Righteousness for ever and ever.

V. In the fifth place, the Lord Jesus Christ may be compared to a star as a SOURCE OF GUIDANCE.

There are some of the stars that are extremely useful to sailors. I scarcely know how else the great wide sea would be navigated, especially if it were not for the Polar Star. Jesus is the Polar Star to us. How the poor negro in the olden times, when the curse of slavery had not been taken away, must have blessed God for that pole star—so easy to find out. Any child with but a moment's teaching will soon know how to discover it in the midst of its fellows at night, and when the negro had once learned to distinguish the star that shone over the land of freedom, how he followed it through the great dismal swamps, or along the plains which were more dreadful still; how he could ford the streams, and climb the mountains, always cheered by the sight of that pole star. Such is Jesus Christ to the seeker. He leads to liberty; he conducts to peace. Oh! I wish you would follow him, some of you who are going about a thousand ways to find peace where you will never find it. There is never a Sunday but I try to speak, sometimes in gentler tones, and at other seasons with thundering notes, the simple truth that Jesus Christ came into the world to save sinners. I do try to make it plain to you that it is not your prayers and tears, your doings, your willings, your anything, that can save you, but that all your help is laid upon one that is mighty, and that you must look alone to him. Yet, sinners, you are still looking to yourselves. You rake the dung hills of your human nature to find the pearl of great price which is not there. You will look beneath the ice of your natural depravity to find the flame of comfort which is not there. You might as well seek in hell itself to find heaven as look to your own works and merits to find some ground of trust. Down with them! Down with them, every one of them! Away with all those confidences of yours, for

> "None but Jesus, none but Jesus,
> Can do helpless sinners good."

Just reverse that helm; and shift that sail, and tack about! Follow not the wrecker's beacon on yonder shore luring you to the rocks of self-delusion, but where that pole star guides, thither let your vessel drift, and pray for the favoring gales of the blessed Spirit to guide you rightly to the port of peace.

VI. Our Lord is compared to a star, surely, as THE OBJECT OF WONDER.

One of the first lines which full many of you ever learned to recite was—

> "Twinkle, twinkle, little star,
> How I wonder what you are;"

But that is precisely what Galileo might have said, and exactly what the greatest astronomer that ever lived might say. You have sometimes looked through a telescope and have seen the planets, but after you have looked at them you do not know particularly about them; and those who are busy all day and all night long taking constant observations, I think will tell you that the result is rather that of astonishment than of intelligence. Still it is

> "How I wonder what you are."

So to those of us who are in Christ Jesus, he is a peerless star; but oh, brethren! we may well wonder what he is. We used to think when we were little ones that the stars were holes pricked in the skies, through which the light of heaven shone, or that they were little pieces of gold-dust that God had strewn about. We do not think so now; we understand that they are much greater than they look to be. So, when we were carnal, and did not know King Jesus, we esteemed him to be very much like anybody else, but now we begin to know him, we find out that he is much greater, infinitely greater than we thought he was. And as we grow in grace, we find him to be more glorious still. A little star to our view at first, he has grown in our estimation into a sun now, a blazing sun, by whose beams our soul is refreshed. Ah! but when we get near to him, what will he be? Imagine yourself borne up on an angel's wing to take a journey to a star. Travelling at an inconceivable rate you open your eyes on a sudden and say—" How wonderful! Why, that which was a star just now has become as large to my vision, as the sun at noon-day." " Stop," says the angel; "you shall see greater things than these," and, as you speed on, the disc of that orb increases, till it is equal to a hundred suns; and now you say, " But what? Am I not near it now?" "No," says the angel, "that enormous globe is still far, far away," and when you come to it, you would find it to be such a wondrous world, that arithmetic could not compute its size; scarcely could imagination belt it with the zone of fancy. Now, such is Jesus Christ. I said he grows upon his people here, but what must it be to see him there, where the veil is lifted, and we behold him face to face? Sometimes we long to find out what that star is, to know him, to comprehend with all saints what are the heights and depths, and to know the love of Christ which passeth knowledge; but, meanwhile, we are compelled to sit down and sing—

" God only knows the love of God:
Oh that it now were shed abroad
In this poor stony heart."

We have to confess that

" The first-born sons of light
Desire in vain its depth to see;
They cannot reach the mystery,
The length, the breadth, the height."

VII. But, to conclude, the metaphor used in the text may well bear this seventh signification. Our Lord is compared to a star, as HE IS THE HERALD OF GLORY. The bright and morning star foretells that the sun is on its way to gladden the earth with its light. Wherever Jesus comes he is a great prophet of good. Let him come into a heart, and, as soon as he appears, you may rest assured that there is a life of eternity and joy to come. Let Jesus Christ come into a family, and what changes he makes there. Let him be preached with power in any town or city, and what a herald of good things he is there. To the whole world Christ has proclaimed glad tidings. His coming has been fraught with benedictions to the sons of men. Yea, the coming of Christ in the flesh is the great prophecy of the glory to be revealed in the latter days, when all nations shall bow before him, and the age of peace, the golden age shall come, not because civilization has advanced, not because education has increased, or the world grown better, but because Christ has come. This is the first, the fairest of the stars, the prognostic of the dawn.

Ay, and because Christ has come, there will be a heaven for the sons of men who believe in him. Sons of toil, because Christ has come, there shall be rest for the weary. Daughters of sorrow, because Christ has come, there shall be healing for the weak. O you whom chill penury is bowing down! there shall be lifting up and sacred wealth for you, because the star has shone. Hope on! hope ever! Now that Jesus has come, there is no room for despair.

I commend these thoughts to you, and earnestly ask you once again, if you have never looked to Christ, to trust in him now; if you have never submitted to Jesus, to submit to him now; if you have never confided in him, to confide in him now. It is a very simple matter. May God the Holy Spirit teach and guide you to disown yourselves, and to acknowledge him; cease from your own thoughts, and trust his word. This done by you all, there is proof positive that all is done for you by Christ. You are his, and he is yours; where he is shall your portion be; and you shall be like him, for you shall see him as he is. It will be a day to be had in remembrance if you are led now to give yourselves to him. I well recollect when my heart yielded to his Divine grace; when I could no longer look anywhere else, and was compelled to look to him. Oh, come ye to him! I know not what words to use, or what persuasions to employ. For your own sake, that you may be happy now; for eternity's sake, that you may be happy hereafter; for terror's sake, that you may escape from hell; for mercy's sake, that you may enter into heaven, look to Jesus. You may never be bidden to do so again. This bidding may be the last, the concluding measure which shall fill up the heap of your guilt, because you reject it. Oh! do not despise the exhortation. Let the prayer go up quietly now from your spirit, "God be merciful to me a sinner." Let your soul wrestle vehemently. Let your tongue utter its mighty resolve—

"I'll to the gracious King approach,
  Whose sceptre pardon gives;
Perhaps he may command my touch,
  And then the suppliant lives.

I can but perish if I go,
  I am resolved to try;
For, if I stay away, I know
  I must for ever die.

But, if I die with mercy sought,
  When I the King have tried,
That were to die, delightful thought,
  As sinner never died."

The Broad Wall.

"The broad wall."—NEHEMIAH iii. 8.

IT seems that around Jerusalem of old, in the time of her splendor, there was a broad wall, which was her defence and her glory. Jerusalem is a type of the Church of God. It is always well when we can see clearly, distinctly, and plainly, that around the Church to which we belong there runs a broad wall.

This idea of a broad wall around the Church suggests three things: *separation, security*, and *enjoyment*. Let us examine each of these in its turn.

I. First, the SEPARATION of the people of God from the world is like that broad wall surrounding the holy city of Jerusalem.

When a man becomes a Christian he is still in the world, but he is no longer to be of it. He was an heir of wrath, but he has now become a child of grace. Being of a distinct nature, he is required to separate himself from the rest of mankind, as the Lord Jesus Christ did, who was "holy, harmless, undefiled, and separate from sinners." The Lord's Church was separated in his eternal purpose. It was separated in his covenant and decree. It was separated in the atonement, for even there we find that our Lord is called "the Saviour of all men, especially of them that believe." An actual separation is made by grace, is carried on in the work of sanctification, and will be completed in that day when the heavens shall be on fire, and the saints shall be caught up together with the Lord in the air; and in that last tremendous day, he shall divide the nations as a shepherd divides the sheep from the goats, and then there shall be a great gulf fixed, across which the ungodly cannot go to the righteous, neither shall the righteous approach the wicked.

Practically, my business is to say to those of you who profess to be the Lord's people, *take care that you maintain a broad wall of separation between yourselves and the world.* I do not say that you are to adopt any peculiarity of dress, or to take up some singular style of speech. Such affectation gendereth, sooner or later, hypocrisy. A man be as thoroughly worldly in one coat as in another, he may be quite as vain and conceited with one style of speech as with another; nay, he may be even more of the world when he pretends to be separate, than if he had left the pretence of separation alone. The separation which we plead for is moral and spiritual. Its foundation is laid deep in the heart, and its substantial reality is very palpable in the life.

Every Christian, it seems to me, should be more scrupulous than other men *in his dealings.* He must never swerve from the path of integrity. He should never say, "It is the custom: it is perfectly understood in the trade." Let the Christian remember that custom cannot sanction wrong, and that its being "understood" is no apology for misrepresentation. A lie "understood" is not therefore true. While the golden rule is more admired than practised by ordinary men, the Christian should always do unto others as he would that they should do unto him. He should be one whose word is his bond, and who, having once pledged his word, sweareth to his own hurt, but changeth not. There ought to be an essential difference between the Christian and the best moralist, by reason of the higher standard which the gospel inculcates, and the Saviour has exemplified. Certainly, the highest point to which the best unconverted man can go might well be looked upon as a level below which the converted man will never venture to descend.

Moreover, the Christian should especially be distinguished *by his pleasures*, for it is here, usually, that the man comes out in his true colors. We are not quite ourselves, perhaps, in our daily toil, where our pursuits are rather dictated by necessity than by choice. We are not alone; the society we are thrown into imposes restraints upon us; we have to put the bit and the bridle upon ourselves. The true man does not then show himself; but when the day's work is done, then the "birds of a feather flock together." It is with the multitude of traders and commercial men as it was with those saints of old, of whom, when they were liberated from prison, it was said, "Being let go, they went unto their own company." So will your pleasures and pastimes give evidence of what your heart is, and where it is. If you can find pleasure in sin, then in sin you choose to live, and unless grace prevent, in sin you will not fail to perish. But if your pleasures are of a nobler kind, and your companions of a devouter character; if you seek spiritual enjoyments, if you find your happiest moments in worship, in communion, in silent prayer, or in the public assembling of yourselves with the people of God, then your higher instincts become proof of your purer character, and you will be distinguished in your pleasures by a broad wall which effectually separates you from the world.

Such separation should be carried, I think, *into everything which affects the Christian.* "What have they seen in thy house?" was the question asked of Hezekiah. When a stranger comes into our house it should be so ordered that he can clearly perceive that the Lord is there. A man ought scarcely to tarry a night beneath our roof, without gathering that we have a respect unto him that is invisible, and that we desire to live and move in the light of God's countenance. I have already said that I would not have you cultivate singularities for singularity's sake; yet, as the most of men are satisfied if they do as other people do, you must never be satisfied until you do more and better than other people, having found out a mode and course of life as far transcending the ordinary worldling's life, as the path of the eagle in the air is above that of the mole which burrows under the soil.

This broad wall between the godly and the ungodly *should be most conspicuous in the spirit of our mind.* The ungodly man has only this world to live for; do not wonder if he lives very earnestly for it. He has no other treasure; why should he not get as much as he can of this? But you, Christian, profess to have immortal life, therefore, your treasure is not to be amassed in this brief span of existence. Your treasure is laid up in heaven and available for eternity. Your best hopes overleap the narrow bounds of time, and fly beyond the grave; your spirit must not, therefore, be earth-bound and grovelling, but soaring and heavenly. There should be about you always the air of one who has his shoes on his feet, his loins girded, and his staff in his hand—away, away, away to a better land. You are not to live here as if this were your home. You are not to talk of this world as though it were to last for ever. You are not to hoard it and treasure it up, as though you had set your heart upon it, but you are to be on the wing as though you had not a nest here, and never could have, but expected to find your resting-place among the cedars of God, in the hill-tops of glory.

Depend upon it, the more unworldly a Christian is the better it is for him. Methinks I could mention several reasons why this wall should be very broad. *If you are sincere in your profession, there is a very broad distinction between you and unconverted people.* Nobody can tell how far life is removed from death. Can you measure the difference? They are as opposite as the poles. Now, according to your profession, you are a living child of God, you have received a new life, whereas the children of this world are dead in trespasses and sins. How palpable the difference between light and darkness? Yet, you profess to have been " sometimes darkness," but now you are made " light in the Lord." There is, therefore, a great distinction between you and the world if you are what you profess to oe. You say, when you put on the name of Christ, that you are going to the Celestial City, to the New Jerusalem; but the world turns its back upon the heavenly country, and goes downward to that other city of which you know that destruction is its doom; your path is different from theirs. If you be what you say you are, the road you take must be diametrically opposite to that of the ungodly man. You know the difference between their ends. The end of the righteous shall be glory everlasting, but the end of the wicked is destruction. Unless then you are a hypocrite, there is such a distinction between you and others as only God himself could make—a distinction which originates here, to be perpetuated throughout eternity. When the social diversities occasioned by rank and dependency, riches and poverty, ignorance and learning, shall all have passed away; the distinctions between the children of God and the children of men, between saints and scoffers, between the chosen and the castaway, will still exist. I pray you, then, maintain a broad wall in your conduct, as God has made a broad wall in your state and in your destiny.

Remember again, *that our Lord Jesus Christ had a broad wall between him and the ungodly.* Look at him and see how different he is from the men of his time. All his life long you observe him to be a stranger and a foreigner in the land. Truly, he drew near to sinners, as near as he could draw, and he received them when they were willing to draw near to him; but he did not draw near to their sins. He was "holy, harmless, undefiled, and separate from sinners." When he went to his own city of Nazareth, he only preached a single sermon, and they would have cast him headlong down the hill if they could. When he passed through the street, he became the song of the drunkard, the butt of the foolish, the mark at which the proud shot out the arrows of their scorn. At last, having come to his own, and his own having received him not, they determined to thrust him altogether out of the camp, so they took him to Golgotha, and nailed him to the tree as a malefactor, a promoter of sedition. He was the great Dissenter, the great Nonconformist of his age. The National Church first excommunicated, and then executed him. He did not seek difference in things trivial; but the purity of his life and the truthfulness of his testimony, roused the spleen of the rulers and the chief men of their synagogues. He was ready in all things to serve them and to bless them, but he never would blend with them. They would have made him a king. Ah! if he would but have joined the world, the world would have given him the chief place, as the world's Prince said on the mountain : " All these things will I give thee, if thou wilt fall down and worship me." But he drives away the fiend, and stands immaculate and separate even to the close of his life. If you are a Christian, be a Christian. If you follow Christ, go without the camp. But if there be no difference between you and your fellow-man, what will you say unto the King in the day when he cometh and findeth that you have on no wedding garment by which you can be distinguished from the rest of mankind? Because Christ made a broad wall around himself, there must be such an one around his people.

Moreover, dear friends, you will find that *a broad*

wall of separation is abundantly good for yourselves. I do not think any Christian in the world will tell you that when he has given way to the world's customs, he has ever been profited thereby. If you can go and find an evening's amusement in a suspicious place, and feel profited by it, I am sure you are not a Christian; for, if you were a Christian indeed, it would pain your conscience, and unfit you for devouter exercises of the heart. Ask a fish to spend an hour on dry land, and, I think, did it comply, the fish would find that it was not much to its benefit, for it would be out of its element. And it will be so with you in communion with sinners. When you are compelled to associate with worldly people in the ordinary course of business, you find much that grates upon the ear, that troubles the heart, and annoys the soul. You will be often like righteous Lot, vexed with the conversation of the wicked, and you will say with David:

> "Ah! woe is me that I
> In Meshech dwell so long:
> That I in tabernacles stay,
> To Kedar that belong!"

Your soul would pine and sigh to come forth and wash your hands of everything that is impure and unclean. As you find no comfort there, you will long to get away to the chaste, the holy, the devout, the edifying fellowship of the saints. Make a broad wall, dear friends, in your daily life. If you begin to give way a little to the world, you will soon give way a great deal. Give sin an inch, and it will take an ell. "Take care of the pence, and the pounds will take care of themselves," is an apt motto of economy. So, too, guard against little sins, if you would be clear of the great transgression.

Look after the little approaches to worldliness, the little givings-up towards the things of ungodliness, and then you will not make provision for the flesh to fulfil the lusts thereof.

Another good reason for keeping up the broad wall of separation is, that *you will do most good to the world thereby.* I know Satan will tell you that if you bend a little, and come near to the ungodly, then they also will come a little way to meet you. Ay, but it is not so. You lose your strength, Christian, the moment you depart from your integrity. What do you think ungodly people say behind your back, if they see you inconsistent to please them? " Oh ! " say they, " there is nothing in his religion, but vain pretence; the man is not sincere." Although the world may openly denounce the rigid Puritan, it secretly admires him. When the big heart of the world speaks out, it has respect to the man that is sternly honest, and will not yield his principles—no, not a hair's breadth. In such an age as this, when there is so little sound conviction, when principle is cast to the winds, and when a general latitudinarianism, both of thought and of practice, seems to rule the day, it is still the fact, that a man who is decided in his belief, speaks his mind boldly, and acts according to his profession—such a man is sure to command the reverence of mankind. Depend upon it, woman, your husband and your children will respect you none the more because you say, " I will give up some of my Christian privileges," or " I will go sometimes with you into that which is sinful." You cannot help them out of the mire if you go and plunge into the mud yourself. You cannot help to make them clean if you go and blacken your own hands. How can you wash their faces then? You young man in the shop —you young woman in the work-room—if you keep yourselves to yourselves in Christ's name, chaste and pure for Jesus, not laughing at jests which should make you blush : not mixing up with pastimes that are suspicious; but, on the other hand, tenderly jealous of your conscience as one who shrinks from a doubtful thing as a sinful thing, holding sound faith and being scrupulous of the truth—if you will keep yourselves, your company in the midst of others shall be as though an angel shook his wings, and they will say to one another, "Refrain from this or that just now, for so-and-so is there." They will fear you, in a certain sense ; they will admire you, in secret ; and who can tell but they, at last, may come to imitate you.

Would ye tempt God? Would ye challenge the desolating flood? Whenever the church comes down to mingle with the world, it behooves the faithful few to fly to the ark and seek shelter from the avenging storm. When the sons of God saw the daughters of men, that they were fair to look upon, then it was that God said it repented him that he had made men upon the face of the earth, and he sent the deluge to sweep them away. A separate people God's people must be, and they shall be. It is his own declaration, "The people shall dwell alone ; they shall not be numbered among the people." The Christian is, in some respects, like the Jew. The Jew is the type of the Christian. You may give the Jew political privileges, as he ought to have ; he may be adopted into the State, as he ought to be ; but a Jew he is, and a Jew he must be still. He is not a

Gentile, even though he calls himself English, or Portuguese, or Spanish, or Polish. He remains one of the people of Israel, a child of Abraham, a Jew still; and you can mark him as such—his speech bewrayeth him in every land. So should it be with the Christian; mixing up with other men, as he must in his daily calling; going in and out among them, like a man among men; trading in the market; dealing in the shop; mingling in the joys of the social circle; taking his part in politics, like a citizen, as he is; but, at the same time even, having a higher and a nobler life, a secret into which the world cannot enter, and showing the world by his superior holiness, his zeal for God, his sterling integrity, and his unselfish truthfulness, that he is not of the world, even as Christ was not of the world. You cannot tell how concerned I am for some of you, that this broad wall should be kept up; for I detect in some of you at times a desire to make it very narrow, and, perhaps, to pull it down altogether. Brethren, beloved in the Lord, you may depend upon it that nothing worse can happen to a church than to be conformed unto this world. Write "Ichabod" upon her walls then; for the sentence of destruction has gone out against her. But, if you can keep yourselves as

"A garden walled around,
Chosen and made peculiar ground."

you shall have your Master's company; your graces shall grow; you shall be happy in your own souls; and Christ shall be honored in your lives.

II. Secondly; the broad wall round about Jerusalem INDICATED SAFETY.

In the same way, a broad wall round Christ's church

indicates her safety too. Consider who they are that belong to the church of God. A man does not become a member of Christ's church by baptism, nor by birthright, nor by profession, nor by morality. Christ is the door into the sheepfold; every one who believes in Jesus Christ is a member of the true church. Being a member of Christ, he is a member, consequently, of the body of Christ, which is the church. Now, around the church of God—the election of grace, the redeemed by blood, the peculiar people, the adopted, the justified, the sanctified—around the church there are bulwarks of stupendous strength, munitions which guard them safely. When the foe came to attack Jerusalem, he counted the towers and bulwarks, and marked them well; but after he had seen the strength of the Holy City, he fled away. How could he hope ever to scale such ramparts as those? Brethren, Satan often counts the towers and bulwarks of the New Jerusalem. Anxiously does he desire the destruction of the saints, but it shall never be. He that rests in Christ is saved. He who hath passed through the gate of faith to rest in Jesus Christ may sing, with joyful confidence—

"The soul that on Jesus hath lean'd for repose,
I will not, I will not desert to his foes;
That soul, though all hell should endeavor to shake,
I'll never, no never, no never forsake."

"I will be," saith Jehovah, "a wall of fire round about thee." Salvation will God appoint for walls and bulwarks.

The Christian is surrounded by *the broad wall of God's power.* If God be omnipotent, Satan cannot defeat him. If God's power be on my side, who, then, shall hurt me? "If God be for us, who can be against us?"

2*

The Christian is surrounded by the broad wall of *God's love*. Who shall prevail against those whom God loves? I know that it is vain to curse those whom God hath not cursed, or to defy those whom the Lord hath not defied; for whomsoever he blesseth is blessed indeed. Balak, the son of Zippor, sought to curse the beloved people, and he went first to one hill-top and then to another, and looked down upon the chosen camp. But, aha! Balaam, thou couldst not curse them, though Balak sought it! Thou couldst only say, "They are blessed, yea, and they shall be blessed!"

God's law is a broad wall around us, and so is *his justice* too. These once threatened our destruction, but now the justice of God demands the salvation of every believer. If Christ has died instead of me, it would not be justice if I had to die also for my sin. If God has received the full payment of the debt from the hand of the Lord Jesus Christ, then how can he demand the debt again? He is satisfied, and we are secure.

The *immutability of God*, also, surrounds his people like a broad wall. "I am God, I change not; therefore ye sons of Jacob are not consumed." As long as God is the same, the rock of our salvation will be our secure hiding-place.

Upon this delightful truth, we might linger long, for there is much to cheer us in the strong security which God has given in covenant to his people. They are surrounded by the broad wall of *electing love*. Doth God choose them, and will he lose them? Did he ordain them to eternal life, and shall they perish? Did he engrave their names upon his heart, and shall those names be blotted out? Did he give them to his Son to be his heritage, and shall his Son lose his portion? Did he say, "They shall be mine, saith the Lord, in the day when I make up my jewels," and shall he part with them? Has he who maketh all things obey him no power to keep the people whom he has formed for himself to be his own peculiar heritage? God forbid that we should doubt it. Electing love, like a broad wall, surrounds every heir of grace.

And oh, how broad is the wall of *redeeming love.* Will Jesus fail to claim the people he bought with so great a price? Did he shed his blood in vain? How can he revive enmity against those whom he hath once reconciled unto God, not imputing their trangressions unto them? Having obtained eternal redemption for them, will he adjudge them to everlasting perdition? Has he purged their sins by sacrifice, and will he then leave them to be the victims of satanic craft? By the blood of the everlasting covenant, every Christian may be assured that he cannot perish, neither can any pluck him out of Christ's hand. Unless the cross were all a peradventure, unless the atonement were a mere speculation, those for whom Jesus died are saved through his death. Therefore he shall see of the travail of his soul and be satisfied.

As a broad wall which surrounds the saints of God is *the work of the Holy Spirit.* Does the spirit begin and not finish the operations of his grace? Ah no? Does he give life which afterwards dies out? Impossible! Hath he not told us that the Word of God is the incorruptible seed, which liveth and abideth for ever? And shall the powers of hell or the evil of our own flesh destroy what God has pronounced immortal, or cause dissolution to that which God says is incorruptible? Is not the Spirit of God given us to abide with us for ever, and shall he be expelled from that heart in which he has taken up his everlasting dwelling place? Brethren, we are not of their mind, who are led by fear or fallacy to hazard such conjectures. We rejoice to say with Paul, "I am persuaded that he who hath begun a good work in you will carry it on." We like to sing—

> "Grace *will* complete what grace begins,
> To save from sorrows or from sins;
> The work that wisdom undertakes
> Eternal mercy ne'er forsakes."

Almost *every doctrine of grace* affords us a broad wall, a strong bastion, a mighty bulwark, a grand munition of defence. Take, for instance, Christ's suretyship engagements. He is surety to his Father for his people. When he brings home the flock, think you he will have to report that some of them are lost? At his hands will they be required. Not so!

> "I know that safe with him remains,
> Protected by his power,
> What I've committed to his hands,
> Till the decisive hour."

"Here am I," will he say, "and the children whom thou hast given me, of all whom thou hast given me I have lost none." He will keep all the saints even to the end. *The honor of Christ* is involved. If Christ loses one soul that leans upon him, the integrity of his crown is gone; for if there should be one believing soul in hell, the prince of darkness would hold up that soul and say—"Aha! Thou couldst not save them all! Aha! Thou Captain of Salvation, thou wast defeated here! Here is one poor little

Benjamin, one Ready-to-Halt, that thou couldst not bring to glory, and I have him to be my prey for ever!" But it shall not be. Every gem shall be in Jesu's crown. Every sheep shall be in Jesu's flock. He shall not be defeated in any way, or in any measure; but he shall divide the spoil with the strong, he shall establish the cause he undertakes, he shall eternally conquer; glory be unto his great and good name!

Thus I have tried to show you the broad walls which are round about believers. They are saved, and they may say to their enemies, "the virgin daughter of Zion hath shaken her head at them, and laughed them to scorn! Who shall lay anything to the charge of God's elect? It is God that justifieth; who is he that condemneth? It is Christ that died, yea, rather that hath risen again from the dead; who sitteth at the right hand of God, who also maketh intercession for us! For I am persuaded that neither death, nor life, nor angels, nor principalities, nor powers, nor things present, nor things to come, nor height, nor depth, nor any other creature, shall be able to separate us from the love of God which is in Christ Jesus our Lord."

III. The idea of a broad wall, and with this I close, SUGGESTS ENJOYMENT.

The walls of Nineveh and Babylon were broad; so broad that there was found room for several chariots to pass each other. Here men walked at sunset, and talked and promoted good fellowship. If you have ever been in the city of York you will know how interesting it is to walk around the broad walls there. But our figure is drawn from the Orientals. They were accustomed to come out of their houses and walk on the broad walls. They *used them for rest* from toil, and for the manifold pleasures of recreation. It was very delightful when the sun was going down, and all was cool, to walk on those broad walls. And so, when a believer comes to know the deep things of God, and to see the defences of God's people, he walks along them and he rests. "Now," saith he, "I am at rest and peace; the destroyer cannot molest me; I am delivered from the noise of archers in the place of the drawing of water, and here I can exercise myself in prayer and meditation! Now that salvation is appointed for walls and bulwarks, I will sing a song unto him who hath done these great things for me; I will take my rest and be quiet for he that believeth hath entered into rest; there is, therefore, now no condemnation to them which are in Christ Jesus." Broad walls, then, are for rest, and so are our broad walls of salvation.

Those broad walls were also *for communion*. Men came there and talked with one another. They leaned over the wall and whispered their loving words, conversed of their business, comforted one another, related their troubles and their joys. So, when believers come unto Christ Jesus they commune with one another, with the angels, with the spirits of just men made perfect, and with Jesus Christ their Lord, who is best of all. Oh! on those broad walls, when the banner of love waves over them, they sometimes rejoice with a joy unspeakable, in fellowship with him who loved them and gave himself for them. It is a blessed thing in the Church when you get such a knowlege of the doctrines of the gospel that you can have the sweetest communion with all the Church of the living God.

And then the broad walls were also intended *for prospects and outlooks.* The citizen came up on the broad wall, and looked away from the smoke and dirt of the city within, right across to the green fields, and the gleaming river, and the far off mountains, delighted to watch the mowing of hay, or the reaping of corn, or the setting sun beyond the distant hills. It was one of the common enjoyments of the citizen of any walled city, to come to the top of the wall in order to take views afar. So, when a man once gets into the altitudes of gospel doctrines, and has learned to understand the love of God in Christ Jesus, what views he can take! How he looks down upon the sorrows of life! How he looks beyond that narrow little stream of death! How, sometimes, when the weather is bright and his eye is clear enough to let him use the telescope, he can see within the gates of pearl, and behold the joys which no mortal eye hath seen, and hear the songs which no mortal ear hath heard, for these are things, not for eyes and ears, but for hearts and spirits! Blessed is the man who dwelleth in the Church of God, for he can find on her broad walls places from which he can see the king in his beauty, and the land which is very far off!

Ah! dear friends, I wish that these things had to do with you all, but I am afraid they have not; for many of you are outside the wall, and when the destroyer comes none will be safe but those who are inside the wall of Christ's love and mercy. I would go to God that you would escape to the gate at once, for it is open. It will be shut—it will be shut one day, but it is open now. When night comes, the night of death, the gate will be shut, and you will come then and say, "Lord, Lord, open to us!" But, the answer will be—

> "Too late, too late!
> Ye cannot enter now."

But it is not too late yet. Still Christ saith, "Behold, I set before thee an open door, and no man can shut it." Oh! that thou hadst the will to come and put thy trust in Jesus; for if thou dost so, thou shalt be saved. I cannot speak to some of you about security, for there are no broad walls to defend you. You have run away from the security. Perhaps you have been patching up with some untempered mortar a righteousness of your own, which will all be thrown down as a bowing wall and as a tottering fence. Oh! that you would trust in Jesus! Then would you have a broad wall which all the battering-rams of hell shall never be able to shake. When the storms of eternity shall beat against that wall, it shall stand fast for aye.

I cannot speak to some of you about rest, and enjoyment, and communion, for you have sought rest where there is none; you have got a peace which is no peace, you have found a comfort which will be your destruction. God make you to be distressed, and constrain you by sore stress to flee to the Lord Jesus and get true peace, the only peace, for "he is our peace."

Oh! that you would close in with Christ and trust him, then you would rejoice in the present happiness which faith would give you; but, the sweetest thing of all would be the prospect which should then unfold to you of the eternal happiness which Christ has prepared for all those who put their trust in him.

The Only Door.

'I am the door: by me if any man enter in, he shall be saved, and shall go in and out, and find pasture."—JOHN x. 9.

THE Word of God tells us that in the midst of the great mass of men there are to be found a special people—a people who were chosen of God out of the common race before the stars began to shine; a people who were dear to God's heart before the foundation of the world; a people who were redeemed by the precious blood of Jesus beyond and above the rest of mankind; a people who are the especial property of Christ, the flock of his pasture, the sheep of his hand; a people over whom Providence watches, shaping their course amid the tangled maze of life; a people who are to be produced at the last, every one of them faultless before the eternal throne, and fitted for the exalted destiny which, in the ages to come, he shall reveal. All through Scripture you read about this particular and special people. Sometimes they are called a "seed," at other times "a garden," at other times "a treasure," and sometimes, as in the chapter we have read, "a flock." The common name in the New Testament for them is "the church," "the church of God which he hath purchased with his own blood." "Christ loved the church, and gave himself for it; that he might sanctify and cleanse it with the washing of water by the word."

Now, the grand question is, how to obtain admission into this church? Where is this community to be found? Who are the members of it? What is the way to become a partaker of the privileges which belong to it? Jesus Christ here tells us two things: First, *How to enter the church.* The way is through himself, as the door. Secondly, *What are the benefits we shall receive through being members of Christ's church*—we shall be saved, and shall go in and out and find pasture.

I. How a man can become a member of that church which is elected, redeemed, and will be saved is simply, briefly solved by our Lord's first assertion.

Christ tells us that *the only way to enter the Church is through himself.* He is the door, the only door. There is no other mode of admission into his church but through himself. Let it be understood, then, once for all, *that we cannot get into the church of Christ through baptism.* There are tens of thousands; ay, there have been millions, who have been baptized after a fashion; that is to say, they have been sprinkled, and thousands have been immersed, who never were admitted into the church of Christ. In consideration of the ordinance as it was administered to them, with or more commonly without their consent, they were recognized by some persons as being Christians; but let me tell you that unless they came to Christ by true faith, they are nothing better than baptized Pagans; they are sprinkled heathens still. Why, you might hold a man in an everlasting shower, but you could not make him "a member of Christ" theseby; or you might drag him through the Atlantic Ocean, and if he survived the immersion, yet still he would not be one jot the better. The door is not baptism but Christ. If thou believest in Christ thou art a member of his church. If thy trust is stayed upon Christ, who is God's great way of salvation, thou hast evidence that thou wast chosen of him from before the foundation of the world; and that faith of thine entitles thee to all the privileges which Christ has promised in his Word to believers.

If Christ be the door, then it follows that men *do not get into the church by birthright*. The Society of Friends has been one of the most useful communities in the world, and it has maintained a good testimony upon most important points for many years; but it seems to me that the great evil in it, that which has done them the most mischief, is the admission of birthright membership. Do they not receive into their fellowship the children of their members as though they were necessarily proper persons to be received into the visible church? My brethren, it is a great privilege to have Christian parents; it may prove a very great advantage, if you use it rightly; but it involves a great responsibility, and if you use it wrongly, instead of being a blessing to you, it may be a fearful curse. Though you may be one of a long line of saints, "Except a man be born again, he cannot see the kingdom of God." The most pious example, the most godly training, cannot ensure conversion, and without conversion, depend upon it, you cannot be Christ's.

"Except ye be converted and become as little children, ye shall in no wise enter into the kingdom of heaven." Through our not practising infant baptism, we do not so readily fall into this error as some denominations; still it is necessary to say even here that you have no right to gospel privileges because of your mothers and fathers. You *must* be born again yourselves. You have no right to the covenant of grace, nor to the blessings and promises thereof, except as by your own personal and individual faith you come to Christ. It is not your father nor your mother that can be the door into Christ's church for you, but Christ himself. "I," saith he, " I am the door." If you get Christ, you are in his church. If you have laid hold on him, you are a member of that secret and invisible community of his elect and his redeemed; but it is not by baptism, nor yet by birthright, that you can ever be so.

Moreover, as Christ is the door, it is evident that *a man does not come to be a member of the church of Christ by making a profession of being so.* He may prove himself to be a detestable hypocrite, but he cannot prove himself to be a genuine Christian, by mere profession. Men do not get rich in this world by a lavish expenditure, or by a profession of being wealthy. They must hold the title-deeds of their estate, and have the cash in the strong box, or else they are poor, in spite of all their pretensions. And you cannot become a Christian, by coming forward and asking to be admitted into the church, declaring that you believe, and avowing that you repent. No, verily, but you must repent truly, or you shall perish; you must believe truly, or you shall have no part nor lot in this matter. The mere saying " Yes, yes, I am willing to profess this, I am willing to say that" no more makes you a Christian than it would make cotton to be silk to call it so, or make mud to be gold by labelling it with that title. Beware of a false profession, for it is doubly hazardous. The man who has no grace is in danger, but the man who makes a profession of having it when he has not, is in double danger, for he is the least likely to be awakened, and he is certain, unless sovereign grace prevent, to make his profession a pillow for his wicked and his slumbering head, till he sleeps himself into hell.

Further, and this may touch the point, perhaps, more closely still, a man does not get to be one of the Lord's people, or to be one of Christ's sheep, by being *admitted into any visible church.* He ought not to try to get into any visible church until he is in the true church. He has no right to join the external organization, until he has first got into the secret conclave by a living faith in Christ. If he leaves the door alone and gets over the wall, and comes into the outward church without being a believer in Christ, so far from being saved, Christ will say to him, " Thou art a thief and a robber, for thou has climbed up some other way, and thou camest not in by the door." I believe we do rightly to subject the admission of members to the voice of all the church; I believe we do rightly to examine candidates to see whether they make a creditable profession, and whether they know what they are at. But our examination—oh, 'tis nothing better than skin deep. We cannot search the heart, and the best judgment of never so many Christian men, though honest, and deserving to be treated with a great respect, would be a very poor thing to rest upon. If you have not Christ, your church certificates are waste paper, and your membership with any people, however pure and apostolic they may be, is but a name to live while you are dead, for the only way, the sole way, of getting into the real, vital, living church of Christ, is by coming to Christ, who is himself the door.

The plain English of this metaphor, then, is just this —*To be one of God's people, the essential thing is a simple dependence upon Jesus Christ.* If you have not this—no matter who baptizes you, or who gives you the consecrated bread and wine, or who maudles to you about a hope of salvation for which there is no warrant—you will die in your sins, notwithstanding all your sacraments, except you come to Christ. No other admittance to heaven can there be, but by a simple dependence upon him who has bled and died on Calvary's cross; the preaching of any other system is a mere delusion, against which the warning voice went forth or ever the snare was laid to trap the unwary.

Mark you, simple faith, where it is genuine, makes it plain that you do enter by Christ the door, because such *faith leads to obedience.* How canst thou suppose that thou art a member of his church if thou art not obedient to Christ ? It is necessary that the man who trusts Christ should become the servant of Christ. Real faith never kicks at this, but rather delights in it. "If ye love me," saith Christ, "keep my commandments." Except we do keep Christ's commandments out of a principle of love to him, our religion is vain. "Without holiness no man shall see the Lord." We may talk as we will about inward experiences and believings, but "by their fruits ye shall know them." The Spirit of God is the spirit of holiness. When Christ comes into the soul, all iniquity must be purged out of the soul. You know how Malachi describes his advent. He proclaims to us the promise that the Lord whom we seek shall suddenly come to his temple: that is, seekers shall be finders; do you know what he adds? "But who may abide the day of his coming? for he shall be like a refiner's fire, and like fullers' soap." Now, the refiner's fire burns up the dross, and fullers' soap takes out the stains; and so, if Christ be in you, you will pass through a refining that will burn up your outward sin, and you will be subjected to a washing like that of the fullers' soap, which will cleanse you from all your iniquities. "Be not deceived, God is not mocked, whatsoever a man soweth that shall he also reap." If ye live after the flesh ye shall die, but if, through the grace of Christ ye are living in him, trusting in him, and serving him—service being the evidence of trust, and trust being the evidence of your election—ye have then come into the church through the door, and it is well with you.

Now, if it be so, that Christ is the door into the church, and if we have entered the church through that door, *it does not signify much to us what the old gentleman at Rome thinks of us.* He may excommunicate us. This he is very fond of doing. He is a rare hand at cursing. What does it matter? It signifies not one jot, if I be in Christ Jesus a new creature, how much the Pope may rail at me. Besides, there are plenty of revilers now-a-days who are saying, "You Nonconformists are only a pack of heretics; *we* have the apostolical succession; *we* have the sacraments and the priests." Ah! they vaunt themselves as being "Catholic," though their claim is disallowed alike by the Babylon which is here below, and by the Jerusalem which is above. Let them vaunt if they will. As long as we have Christ, they may keep their apostolical succession, and all their other rubbish; he is the door, and if we have come through him it is well enough. I like that story of the Sandwich Islanders who had been converted through some of our missionaries, and the Gospel had been preached to them for years. At last, two or three gentlemen in long black gowns landed there, and the people asked them what they had come for. They said they were come to instruct them in the true faith, and to teach them. Well, they said, they should be glad to hear it. If their teaching was true, and like the Scriptures, they would listen to them. By and by, a little diagram was exhibited to the natives after the similitude of a tree. This tree had many branches. The twigs which were farthest off were the different saints, the believers, those who do good works; then the limbs, which were a little larger, were the priests; the bigger boughs were bishops; the biggest boughs were the cardinals; and, at last, these all joined on to the trunk, which was the Pope, and that went all the way down to the bottom, till it came to Peter, who was the root, deriving his authority immediately from Christ. So the natives asked about all these twigs, and branches, and specially about certain rotten branches that were tumbling off into a fire. What were they? They were Luther, and Calvin, and other heretics who had been cut off from the true tree of the church. "Well," said one of the islanders, "and pray what is the root of the tree?" Of course, that was allowed to be Jesus Christ. So they clapped their hands at once for joy, and said, "Never mind about the branches, and stems, and twigs; we have never heard of them, but we have got the root, and that will do to grow on." In like manner, brethren, we can say to-night, if we have got Christ, we have got "the root out of the dry ground." We have got the root of the matter, the basis, the sum, the substance of it.

> "Let others trust what forms they please,
> Their hopes we'll not contest."

Let them go about their business, and rejoice in their fancies; but Christ is the door. We have Christ, we have entered by the door, we have believed in him, we have entered through him into faith, and into joy, and into peace. We will be content with this; let others clamber up some other way if they please.

Before I leave this point, a question suggests itself,—*Have we all entered by the door?* We are agreed that Christ is the door. Have we entered by the door? You who are growing old—I always feel much pleasure in seeing grey heads, the type of mellowed years, in the concourse of worshippers;—but have you all believed in Jesus? You know the truth, you would not like to hear anything but the simple Gospel preached; but, have you laid hold on the Gospel? A man may starve with bread upon the table if he does not eat, and he may perish with thirst, though he be up to his neck in water, if he does not drink. Have you trusted Christ? If not, how can you remain in a state of unbelief, for "he that believeth not is condemned already, because he believeth not on the Son of God." Men and women in middle life, struggling with the cares of business, have *you* entered into Christ? I know your thoughts are much taken up, and necessarily so, with the world; but, have you not time to think upon this question, or dare you neglect it; "Dost thou believe on the Son of God?" If not, O man, thy life hangs on a thread, and that snapped, thy ruin is certain. And, oh, you young people, what a mercy it is to see you willing to come and hear the Word! But, have you all heard it with your inward ears? Have you looked to my Master? Oh, it is sweet to come to Christ in the early morning of life, to have a long day of happiness before you! May it be the blessedness of each one of us! It is vain to look at the door unless you enter. God give you grace to come in, if you never have entered before.

II. Our Lord and Master tells us WHAT ARE THE PRIVILEGES OF ENTERING THROUGH HIM, THE DOOR.

The man who enters by Christ *shall be saved, he shall go in and out and he shall find pasture.*

He shall be saved. The man who believes in Jesus Christ shall be saved; he is saved, and he shall be saved. A man has by accident killed his fellow-man. The next of kin to the murdered man will be sure to kill the man-slayer out of revenge, if he can get at him. Therefore the poor homicide takes flight as quickly as he can towards the city of refuge. How his heart beats, how his footsteps bound, how he flies with all his might. There is a handpost with the word "Refuge" upon it, and on he continues his way. But, presently, while he is running, he turns his head, and finds that the avenger of blood is after him. He sees that he is gaining upon him, he feels that he will probably overtake him. Oh! how he picks his steps lest he should trip against a stone, how he skims the ground, swift as a doe. He runs until he can see the city gates. "That is the fair CITY OF REFUGE," saith he. But, he does not rest then, for a sight of the city will not secure him, so he quickens his speed, as if he would outstrip the wind, till he shoots through the archway, and he is in the broad street of the city. Now he stops. Now he breathes. Now he wipes the hot sweat from his brow. "Now I am safe," saith he, "for no avenger of blood dares cross that threshold; he that once escapes here is delivered." So with the sinner when sin pursues him, when he discovers that he has offended God. He hears the furious coursers of divine vengeance coming on swiftly behind him, and his conscience flies, and his soul speeds towards the cross. He gets a little hope. He hears of a Saviour; but that is not enough. He will never rest, he will never say he is at peace, until he has passed the gate of faith, and can say, "Now I do believe that Jesus died for me."

He that enters in by the door shall be saved. Noah's ark was built in the olden times to preserve Noah and his family from the great flood. It could not be said that Noah would be saved till he had passed through the door; but when he had done that, a divine hand, quite unseen, put the door to, and as Noah heard it fastened, and understood that the Lord had shut him in, he felt quite safe. If God shuts us in, the floods from beneath cannot drown us, and the rains from above cannot penetrate to injure us. He must be safe whom God shuts in. The moment that a poor sinner trusts in Christ, God shuts the door. There he is, and there he shall be, till time shall be no more. He is secure. The infernal powers shall not destroy him, and the vengeance of God cannot touch him. He has passed the door, and he shall be saved.

I read a story the other day of some Russians crossing wide plains studded over here and there with forests. The villages were ten or a dozen miles from each other, the wolves were out, the horses were rushing forward madly, the travellers could hear the baying of the wolves behind them; and, though the horses tore along with all speed, yet the wolves were fast behind, and they only escaped, as we say, " by the skin of their teeth," managing just to get inside some hut that stood in the road, and to shut-to the door. Then they could hear the wolves leap on the roof; they could hear them dash against the sides of the hut; they could hear them gnawing at the door, and howling, and making all sorts of dismal noises; but the travellers were safe, because they had entered in by the door, and the door was shut. Now, when a man is in Christ, he can hear, as it were, the devils howling like wolves, all fierce and hungry for him; and his own sins, like wolves, are seeking to drag him down to destruction. But he has got in to Christ, and that is such a shelter that all the devils in the world, if they were to come at once, could not start a single beam of that eternal refuge: it must stand fast, though the earth and heaven should pass away. Now, to every man and woman Christ says that if they have entered in by the door, they shall be saved. Do not have any doubt about it. Do not let anybody raise the question whether you may be, or you may not be; you shall be. Oh, clutch at that blessed "shall." Sir, if you have been a drunkard, yet, if you trust in Christ, you shall be saved. You shall not go back to your old drunkenness, but you shall be saved from it, if you believe in him. O woman, if thou hast stained thy character to the worst, yet, if thou believest in Christ, none of thy old sins shall ruin thee, but thou shalt be saved. Ah! though you be tempted every day of your lives, tempted as none ever were before, yet God is true, and cannot lie—if you come through Christ the door you shall be saved. Do you understand what it is to come through the door? it is to depend upon Jesus, to give ourselves to him, to rest on him. When you hang up your jugs and mugs on the nail in the cupboard, what keeps them from falling? Nothing but the nail, and if that holds well, nothing can fall that hangs on it. Now, you must trust in Christ as the vessel hangs on the nail, and if you do so, he is fastened as a nail in a sure place, and you cannot and shall not perish. That is the first privilege—he shall be saved.

He that entereth in by the door shall *go in*. The man who believes in Christ shall go into rest and peace, for there is no condemnation to them that are in Christ Jesus. He shall go in to secret knowledge. He shall become a scholar, and shall be taught by Christ as his rabbi. He shall go in unto God with holy boldness in prayer. He shall go in unto that which is within the veil, and speak to God from before the mercy-seat. He shall go in unto the child's place, and shall stand as an adopted heir of heaven,

He shall go in unto close communion with God. He shall speak with his Maker. The Lord shall lift up the light of his countenance upon him. He shall go in unto the highest attainment in spiritual things. He shall go in to the treasure-house of the covenant, and say—" All this is mine." He shall go in to the store-house of the promises, and take whatsoever his soul needeth. He shall go in, passing from circle to circle, till he comes in to the innermost place where the love of God is most graciously spread abroad.

He that enters in by the door shall be saved, and he shall go in. If you know what this means—go in; go in farther; go in more constantly. Do not stop where you are, but go in till you have got a little more. If you love Christ, come nearer to him, and nearer, and nearer still. Let your prayer be—

"Nearer, my God, to thee,
　Nearer to thee;
E'en though it be a cross that raiseth me,
　Still this my cry shall be,
Nearer to thee; nearer to thee."

But if you want to get into anything that is divine, you must get in through Christ. O you who open your bibles, and want to understand a text, the way to get into the meaning of a text is through the door, Christ. O you who want to get more holiness, come through the door; the way to holiness is not through Moses, but through Christ. O you who would have closer communion with your heavenly Father, the way to come in is not through your own efforts, but through Christ. You came to Christ at first to get salvation; you must come to Christ still to get sanctification. Never look for another door, for there is but one, and that one door will let you into life, love, peace, knowledge, and sanctification. It will let you into heaven. Christ is the master-key of all the rooms in the palace of mercy, and if you get Christ you shall go in. Nothing shall keep you out of any of the secret chambers. You shall go in, in God's name, through Christ, the door.

The next privilege is that he shall go out. Putting the two together—he shall go in and out—they signify liberty. The Christian does not come into the Church, as into a prison, but he comes in as a free man, walking in and out of his own house. But, what does it mean to go out? I think it means this, brethren. The men that trust in Christ go out to their daily business through Christ, the door. I wonder how many of you ever thought of this? You know sometimes you get up, put on your things, and go blundering out to work, and then you find yourselves very weak all day. Well, I do not wonder at it, for you do not go out through Christ, the door. Oh, suppose you had given yourselves to Christ for the day, and though you had time but for a few minutes' prayer, yet you had put it thus—" Lord, I am thine; take care of me to-day; I am going out where there will be many to tempt me and try me. I do not know what may happen, but, Lord, I am going out in thy name, and resting in thy strength; if there is anything that I can do for thee, I desire to do it. If there is anything to suffer, I wish to suffer it for thy sake, but take care of me, Lord. I will not go out and face my fellow-men until I have seen thy face, and I do not want to speak to them until I have spoken to thee, nor to hear what they have to say till I have heard what God the Lord will speak." Depend upon it, it is blessed going out, when you go through the door. You will be sure to come home happy, when you go out after this sort.

May not this going out also mean to go out to suffering? You and I are called sometimes to bear great bodily pain, or losses, or bereavements. Well, now, what a sweet thing it is to go out to suffer these things through the door, and to be able to say, "Now, my Master, this is a cross, but I will carry it, not in my own strength, but in thine. Do what thou wilt with me; I shall drink the cup because thou appointest it. Whenever you can see Christ's hand in it, it makes the bitter sweet, and heavy things soon grow light. Go to your sick-bed as you hope to go to your dying bed, through the door, that is, through Christ.

And when, as sometimes happens, we have to go out, as it were, away from fellowship with Christ, to fight with our inward sins, the right way is to go out to resist them through the door. If you ever try to fight with sin in your own strength, or on a legal footing, or because you feel that you will be condemned if you do not overcome those sins, you will be as weak as water. The manner of victory is through the blood of the Lamb. There is no killing sin, except by throwing the blood of Christ upon it. When once the blood of Christ comes into contact with the besetting sin, that sin withers straight away. Go to your spiritual conflicts through the door.

And so, beloved, we ought in all that we do for the Lord, to go out through the door. It is always sweet preaching for me when I feel that I come forth in the name of my Master, when I do not come to tell you what ideas I have woven out of my own brains, nor to put attractive figures before you, as I would like to do sometimes; but, rather, when I come to tell you just what my Lord would have you know, telling it as a message to you from your God, and cherishing in my own heart his great love towards perishing sinners. Then, indeed, to minister is joy. You Sunday school teachers will always teach well, when you go down to the school-room through the door—that is, having been with Christ, having sought and enjoyed his company. I know, my dear brethren and sisters, you who are teaching larger classes, you who are engaged in instructing or exhorting, you who go about any holy work, you always do it well, when you have God's smile upon you in the doing of it; and you shall have great success in the doing of it, if you always go to it through Christ, the door; if you serve Christ through Christ, and do it, not only for him, but through him and by him. Our own strength is perfect weakness, but the strength which comes through simple dependence upon the ever-living Christ, who has said, "Lo, I am with you alway, even unto the end of the world,"—this is the strength which wins the conquest. God give you grace not only to go in, but also to go out through the door.

Well, now, the last privilege named in the text is, "*And shall find pasture.*" I suppose this is what you come here for, you who love the Lord, you come here for pasture. It is a great blessing if when we come to hear the gospel, it becomes real pasture to us. We do know some who say that the troubles of the week become unbearable, because they have such barren sabbaths. Ah, if you are members of a church that is rent with discord, where the ministry abounds in anything but Christ, you will soon begin to cry out, and you will value the privilege of hearing Jesus Christ lifted up among you. But who are the people who get the pasture where Jesus Christ is preached? Not all who hear him, nor yet all believers; there are times when you may hear a sermon that is of no use to you, and yet your brother or sister by your side may be greatly instructed and comforted thereby. In such a case, I should not wonder if it was because your friend came in to the service through the door, and you did not.

Do you remember the story of Mr. Erskine and the good lady who went to hear him preach at the communion? It was such sweet preaching, she thought she had never heard the like. So, after service, she asked, Who the gentleman was that preached to-day; and, on being told that it was Mr. Ebenezer Erskine, she said, "I will come and hear him again next Sunday morning." She went, she listened, and she thought to herself,—"Well, this is very dry, very heavy preaching." She was not at all comforted by it; then, like a foolish woman, as I should think she must have been, she went into the vestry, and said, "Oh, Mr. Erskine, I heard you last Sabbath with much pleasure, sir; I never was so edified; and, I came again this morning, but I have been dreadfully disappointed." So the good man said, very calmly, "Pray madam, when you came to the kirk last Sunday, what did you come for?" She said, "I came to communion, sir." "To have fellowship with Christ, I suppose?" he asked. "Yes, sir." "Well, you came for it, and you had it. And pray, what did you come here this morning for?" Said she, "I came to hear you, sir." "And, you had it, woman," said he, "you had it, and you had not anything else, because you did not come for anything more than that." Well, now, when people come merely to hear a minister, or for custom's sake, or for form's sake, do they not always get what they come for? If people come to find fault, we always give them plenty of our imperfections to be entertained with, so they need not be disappointed. If others come merely out of custom, they say, "Well this is my work, I have performed my duty." Of course it is, but if you had come in through the door—that is, looking to Christ, looking for Christ, desiring not to see the preacher but the Lord, not to get the word of man but the Word of God, to your soul—I believe you would have found pasture. Brethren, the sheep want pasture. No other food will suit them. So your soul wants heavenly truth, and if you come to the house of God through Christ, you will get it. If you turn to the Bible through Christ, you will find it a rich storehouse. If you come to prayer through the door of Christ, you will find it comforting, and so you shall find pasture.

I think the text may mean, that he who rests in Christ shall have all his wants supplied. If this text does not mean so, another does:—"The Lord is my shepherd, I shall not want; he maketh me to lie down in green pastures, he leadeth me beside the still waters." Some of you are very poor, but if you have trusted in Christ, you may plead this promise—" Thou hast said I shall find pasture." Come to Christ, and tell him that he himself has said it—"No good thing will he withhold from them that walk uprightly."

I would to God that some who have never yet entered into the fold might now be drawn to Jesus. Oh, that ye would come through the door into these four choice privileges. You may never have such another opportunity. You may never feel any of the motions of the Spirit of God again. Oh! that without delay, ye would just cast your helpless souls upon the Saviour's gracious arms, who is able and willing to save, that ye might be saved now.

Royal Emblems for Loyal Subjects.

"And he shall be as the light of the morning, when the sun riseth, even a morning without clouds; as the tender grass springing out of the earth by clear shining after rain."—2 SAMUEL xxiii. 4.

EASTERN despots fleece their subjects to an enormous extent. Even at the present day one would hardly wish to be subjected to the demands of an Oriental government; but in David's time a bad king was a continual pestilence, plague, and famine—a bane to the lives of his subjects, who were under his caprice; and spoliation to their fields, which he perpetually swept clean to enrich himself with the produce thereof. Hence, a good king was a *rara avis* in those days, and could never be too highly prized. So soon as he mounted the throne, his subjects began to feel the beneficent influence of his sway. He was to them "as when the sun riseth." The confusion which had existed under weak governors gave place to settled order, while the rapacity which had continually emptied the coffers of the rich, and filched the earnings of the poor, gave place to a regular system of assessment, and men knew how to go about their business with some degree of certainty. It was to them "a morning without clouds."

Forthwith, trade began to flourish; persons who had emigrated to avoid the exactions of the tyrant came back again; fields which had fallen out of tillage, because they would not pay the farmer to cultivate them, began to be sown; and the new ruler was to the land as " clear shining after rain, which makes the tender grass spring up."

I fear we do not value, as we should, the constitutional government which it is our privilege as Britons to enjoy. Let us look where we may—we need not say to the east only but to the west also—we would not wish to change the government under which we live so happily. Let us gratefully acknowledge to God his tender mercy, and his goodness, in sparing us alike from the refractory elements of a republic, and the prodigious exactions of a despotism, and for giving us to dwell in a quiet and peaceable kingdom, wherein we can sit "every man under his own vine and under his own fig-tree, none making him afraid." We may say, I am sure, of Her Majesty who is set over us in the order of Providence, that she has been " as the sun when he riseth, as a morning without clouds." Under her generous sway our country has been verdant. As " the earth by clear shining after rain " bringeth forth the green herb, so have our institutions fostered our trade and commerce by the good-will and gracious providence of God.

But, it is not my object at present to enlarge upon the secular benefits that have fallen to our lot; though I should not think it unworthy of the Christian minister to pursue a theme which calls for so much gratitude to God, and might foster so much good feeling among ourselves. We might make one another feel that there are vast mercies we enjoy which would be more esteemed if better known. Just as the Bible speaks of Christ's unknown sufferings, so many of the bounties that we daily enjoy have become so common that we are oblivious of them; and, therefore, I might call them our unknown mercies. It well becomes us to lift up our voices and hearts to heaven, and thank God for the happy land, and for the happy age in which the lines have fallen to us. Still, I take it that David was not so much speaking of mere political rulers as of Christ Jesus, King of kings and Lord of lords, whose sway is always gracious and full of good-will. May his kingdom come! "Behold, I come quickly," he crieth from heaven; "Even so, come quickly, Lord Jesus," respond those whose love inspires their worship. His kingdom is "as the sun when it riseth, as a morning without clouds;" and, when it shall have been perfectly established upon the earth, all men shall know that the Son of David, whom once they rejected, is he by whom God would make all generations to be blessed for ever and ever. May we who have waited and watched for his glorious advent live when he standeth in the latter day upon the earth, and may we constitute a part of that glorious harvest, the fruit whereof shall shake like the cedars of Lebanon. Thus we look for the day wherein the Lord shall come in the clouds of heaven.

David says of Christ, "He shall be as the light of the morning when the sun riseth." This he is as king, already, in his church, and as the rightful monarch in the individual heart of the believer. Wherever Christ comes into a soul, it is as the light of the morning when the sun riseth. The light of the morning is joyous, then all the birds begin to sing, and the earth which is silent at night, save when its stillness is disturbed by stormy winds, or by wild beasts, or by riotous drunken people, becometh vocal with songs from many mouths; so when Christ cometh into the heart, the tuneful notes of the singing birds are heard; and the voice of the turtle welcomes the gladsome season. Where darkness had brooded before, the sunlight of Christ bringeth mirth and blessed rejoicing. Oh, what streamers are there in the town of Mansoul when Prince Emmanuel rideth through! Happy day, happy day, when Jesus comes into the heart! Save the day when we shall be with him where he is, I suppose there is no day that is comparable to the first one, when we behold Christ, and see him, as our Saviour and our King. The rising of the sun is joyous, and, besides that, it is comforting and consoling to those who have been suffering from ills which night might aggravate. "Would God 'twere morning!" has been the cry of many a languishing one tossing upon his couch: "Would God 'twere morning!" may be the cry of many a heart that is troubled exceedingly with the guilt of sin. Ah, let the morning come. Let the watchman say, "The morning cometh;" let the day dawn, and the day-star appear in our hearts, and " there is the oil of joy for mourning, the garment of praise for the spirit of heaviness." Joy to cheer and comfort the disconsolate Christ bringeth, for he is as the rising of the sun.

And, how glorious is the sun when from his pavilion he looks forth at morn! Job describes the sunrise as being the stamping of the earth with a seal; as if, when in darkness, the earth were like a lump of clay that is pervious; then, as it is turned to the light, it beginneth to receive the impress of Divine wisdom; mountain and vale all stream with it, till impressed on its surface we begin to perceive the glorious works of God. So when Christ riseth upon the heart, what a glorious transformation is wrought! Where there has been no love, no faith, no peace, no joy, none of the blessed fruits of the Spirit, no sooner does Christ come than we perceive all the graces in blossom; yea, they soon become fragrant and blooming, for we are made complete in him. The advent of Christ bringeth to the heart celestial beauty; faith in him decketh us with ornaments and clothes us as with royal apparel. Better garments than Dives had, though he wore scarlet and fine linen, doth Christ give to his people when he cometh to them; and better fare than Dives had, though he fared sumptuously every day, does Jesus bestow upon his saints when he shineth into their hearts. Oh, the glory of the sun-rise of the Saviour on the darkness of the human soul! If a man might rise every morning of the year to look at the rising sun, and yet never be tired of it, because of the sublimity of the spectacle; methinks a man might consider his own conversion every hour in the day, and every day of his life, and yet never be wearied with the thrice heavenly spectacle of Christ arising over the mountains of his guilt, to banish the dense darkness of his despair. As the sun-rising is thus joyous, and comforting, and glorious, let us remember how unparalleled it is—unparalleled because divine. By no method of illumination can we manufacture such a light as the sun exhibits by his simple rising. O ye priests, ye come, with your incantations and mysteries, to make light in men's hearts, and sometimes ye strike a spark that doth but show the darkness; it dieth too soon to be called "the light." And ye pile your deeds to heaven—your faggots of good works—ye put your van-load of superstitious observances, and vainly try to make an illumination; but ere it beginneth to blaze it dieth out, and a handful of ashes alone remains to disappoint the expectant ones. But, Christ ariseth, and with what boundless majesty he looks abroad. The joy, the peace, the comfort, the confidence, the full assurance, the blissful hope, which one ray of Christ's light gives to the heart of man is not to be equalled—nay, scarcely to be compared with anything else. It is a joy that God only giveth us, and, thank God, a joy which none can take away. And, as this sun-rise of Christ in our heart is Divine, so likewise it is irresistible. No curtains can conceal the sun from the world when he willeth to rise. No tyrant, by any law, can prevent the sun's beams from gilding the cottage of the poor. Shine he must, and will. Like a giant he cometh out of his chamber, and where is he that shall wrestle with him? Where art thou, O man, who can take the bridle of the sun, and bid his courses stay their race? Until they have climbed to heaven, and then gone down again to bathe their burning fetlocks in the Western Sea, they must, they will pursue their onward course, for none can stay them, or say to their mighty driver, "What doest thou?" So, when Jesus comes into the heart—avaunt, thou fiend! Thy time of flight is come! Away despair and doubt, and aught that can prevent the soul from having joy and peace! Thus the eternal mandate runs: "Let that man go free?" Thus saith Jehovah to Pharaoh: "Let my people go;" and go they must and shall, for the time of their light and liberty is come. Like the rising of the sun when he springs forth "as a giant strong, and as a bridegroom gay," even so is Christ Jesus when he riseth in the human heart.

The sun-rise, moreover, is very much like the coming of Christ, because of that which it involveth. Those rays of light which first forced the darkness from the sky with golden prophecy of day, tell of flowers that shall open their cups to drink in the sun-light; they tell of streams that shall sparkle as they flow; they tell of the virgins that shall make merry, and the young men that shall rejoice, because the sun shineth on them, and the darkness of night is fled. And so the coming of Christ into the heart is a prophecy of years of sweet enjoyment—a prophecy of God's goodness and long-suffering, let night reign, elsewhere, as it may—yea, and it is a prophecy of the fulness of the river of God, for ever and ever, before the throne of God in heaven. Hast thou Christ, poor soul? Christ is to thee the prophet of eternal happiness. Thou canst not be dark again if Christ hath once shone on thee. No night shall follow this blessed day; it is a day that lasts for ever.

"Doth Jesus once upon thee shine,
Then Jesus is for ever thine."

Hath Christ appeared to thee? Dost thou trust him now? Art thou reposing only upon his finished work? Then the sun hath risen upon thee, and it shall go down no more for ever. The everlasting Joshua biddeth the sun stand still, and to-day and to morrow, though the whole world revolve, that Sun of Righteousness abideth still to shine on thee with healing in his wings.

We must proceed to notice that the psalmist uses another figure : "Even as a morning without clouds." Brethren, there are no clouds in Christ when he ariseth in a sinner's heart. The clouds that mostly cover our sky come from Sinai, from the law, and from our own legal propensities, for we are always wishing to do something by which we may inherit eternal life; but there are none of these clouds in Christ. There is no cloud in Christ of angry rebuke for the past. When Jesus receiveth the sinner, he chideth not. "Neither do I condemn thee" is all that he hath to say. I thought when I came tremblingly to him, that at least he would bring all my sins before me, and chide me before he sealed my pardon with the kiss of mercy; but it was not so. The Father received the prodigal without a single word of rebuke. He did but say, "Take off his rags;" he did but command them to kill the fatted calf that they might make merry ; not a word doth he speak of his hungry looks, nor his filth, nor of the far country, nor even of the harlots with whom he had spent his substance. Christ receiveth the soul without rebuke, for he is "as a morning without clouds."

And, as there is no cloud of anger, so there is no cloud of exacting demand. He doth not ask the sinner to be anything, or to do anything. That were a cloud, indeed, if he did. A sinner by nature can do nothing, and can be nothing, except as grace shall make him be and do. If Christ did ask anything of you or me, if he did but ask repentance of us, unless he gave us that repentance, his salvation would be of no avail to us. But he asketh nothing; all he bids us to do is to take him as everything, and be nothing ourselves. So, to the empty-handed sinner, he is such a full Christ, that we may well say, "He is a morning without clouds."

And, as he is without cloud of demand, so he is without cloud of falsehood. I know that some say Christ may reject those who have put their trust in him—that after they are saved, they may yet fall from grace and perish. Surely, that were not a morning without clouds? I should see in the distance the tempest gathering that might ultimately destroy my spirit; but no, if thou trustest Christ, he will surely save thee, even to the end. If thou puttest thy soul into his hand, there is no fear that he shall be false to the sacred charge; he will undertake to be surety for thy soul; he will bring thee to his Father's face without hindrance, when the fulness of time is come. Trouble not yourselves, O ye anxious ones, concerning the future. Does faith reach only to the present? Do ye trust Christ only to save you to-day? I pray you take a larger sweep of confidence, and trust him to save you to the end. If you do so, he will be better to you than your fears would suggest, or than your faith can conceive; to the end he will love you, and in the end he will bring you to be like him, and to be with him where he is. Happy is that man who seeth Christ "as a morning without clouds." They who see any clouds in him make the clouds. The clouds are only in their vision; they are not in his person. The spots and defects are in themselves; they are not in his person nor in his work. If thou wilt only trust him fully, simply, without any admixture of thine own merit or confidence, thou shalt find him to be equal to the brightest description—a morning without a single cloud.

But, now, to the last figure. Upon this we intend to dwell at somewhat greater length. David says of Christ, the king, that his sway is like "clear shining after rain, whereby the tender grass is made to spring out of the earth." We all understand the metaphor. We have often seen how, after a very heavy shower of rain, and sometimes after a continued rainy season, when the sun shines, there is a delightful clearness and freshness in the air that we seldom perceive at other times. Perhaps, the brightest weather is just when the wind has drifted away the clouds, and the rain has ceased, and the sun peers forth from his chambers to look down upon the glad earth. Well, now, Christ is to his people just like that—exceedingly clear-shining when the rain is over.

Sorrow and sadness do not last forever. After the rain there is to come the clear shining. Tried believer, after all thy afflictions there remains a rest for the people of God; and if, just now, thou art tried and vexed by some extraordinary trial, there is a clear shining coming to thy soul when all this rain is over. Look to Christ, and thou shalt find where that clear shining is. The quiet contemplation thou shalt have of him, when this time of rebuke is over, shall then be to thee as the earth when the tempest has sobbed itself to sleep, when the clouds have rent themselves to rags, and the sun peers out, shooting forth virtue with its lustrous rays. And while sorrows, like the floating clouds, last not for ever, they do work together with the bliss, that as the clear sunshine followeth afterwards, to produce good. It is not in the sorrow, perhaps, to bring forth good alone, any more than the rain might altogether bring forth the spring blade; but when the sorrow and the joy, when the affliction and the consolation, come together, then the joy of the heart is indeed benign. None bring forth much fruit for God but those who have been deeply ploughed with affliction and deluged with grief, but even they do not bring forth much fruit till they have had the joy of Christ's presence after the affliction is over. Clear shining after rain produces an atmosphere exceedingly good for the herbs, and the joy of the soul in the presence of the Lord, after a time of sorrow, makes it able to grow in grace and in the knowledge of our Lord and Saviour Jesus Christ.

Thus, after time of great trouble, Christ becometh to his people more specially and delightfully sweet than he has ever been before. I notice this in many instances. It is manifest in conversion. What happy, happy days were our first young days in the faith. I cannot forget mine—I never shall. When talking with those who come to tell me what God has done for their souls, I notice the freshness upon their memory of every separate event on the day of their new birth; they can tell how Christ appeared unto them, and how they looked unto him and were lightened. "I can never forget that, sir, till I die," says one; "I have a very bad memory, and I forget almost everything that is good, but that I shall never forget, for it was such a joyous season." I know that many of you have had good days, but they have been like pieces of money that you received when children, very bright once; but they have passed about and worn in circulation, until they have lost the image and superscription which was once so bright to your eyes. Not so the day of your new birth, it has been like a coin, as fresh as when you laid it aside, and when you take it out again, it is as fresh as the mint delivered it, and you can read it still, and read the image of Christ which it bears. I think there is scarce such a day on earth to be had in Christian experience, as that first day when we came to Christ and knew him.

The like is true also, in its measure, after great and heavy affliction. You have been bereaved. A wife, a husband, a child, has been removed from you; or, you had a great loss in business, you were crossed in some expectation, and you were cast into the lowest depth of trouble. Friends failed you, consolation fled from you; but, after a time, you had a sweet resignation; you could say, "My soul is even as a weaned child;" your troubles somehow or other grew sweet as honey, though before they had been bitter as gall. You saw the finger of a loving Lord in all those graving lines of affliction, which the chisel had made upon your brow; you saw the great Refiner sitting at the mouth of the furnace, watching your gold that it might not be destroyed, and rejoicing over your dross, because it melted away in the flame. Do you remember it? Why, I can look back to some of the happiest seasons of my life, and see them stand in juxtaposition with the blackest times of trial. Oh, it has been, sometimes, a glorious thing to be cast down by rebuke and slander, and then go into one's chamber and lay Rabshakeh's letter before the Lord, and to go down and feel more glad than a king of a hundred kingdoms, because we have been counted worthy to suffer reproach for Christ; and there is a calm within us more deep and profound than before. And, mark you, if it has been so with us individually, it has been no less so with the church. Remember the clear shining after rain in the apostles' times. "Then had the churches rest, and walking in the fear of God, were multiplied." Those little seasons of hush and calm, between the great persecutions, have always been prolific of converts. I hope in the midst of successive controversies which darken the sky overhead, that when the rain is over, and the noise and trouble it costs some tender spirits has ceased, and the powers of darkness have been hushed to sleep once more, we may have some clear shining after rain, and brotherly fellowship once again to be renewed. The day cometh when the great battle of Armageddon shall be fought; when the powers of darkness shall be roused to frenzy's highest pitch; when hell shall be loosed, and the great dragon shall be permitted to come upon the earth, trailing its chain along in the supremacy of its hour—then, when dreadful war shall come upon the earth, when nations shall reel and stagger to and fro, the Lord himself shall descend from heaven with a shout, with the trump of the archangel and the voice of God, and there shall be clear shining after the rain. And then, when the flames shall have consumed this orb, when judgment shall have been passed, when death and hell shall have been cast into the lake of fire, when all the powers of evil shall have been utterly destroyed before the majesty of his coming who shall overturn them, that his kingdom may be established in heaven; everlasting hallelujahs, "For the Lord God omnipotent reigneth," shall bear witness that there is clear shining after the rain: for so it must be in the little as the great, in the experience of the individual as in that of the multitude; there must be a rain, and there must be the clear shining after it, and the two together shall bring forth a matchless harvest to the praise and glory of his grace, who worketh all things according to the counsel of his own will.

Ask ye, now, why is it that God giveth to his people sweet seasons just after the bitter?

One reason is to take the taste of the bitter out of their mouth. Even as to our little children, when they take their nauseous medicine, we give some sweatmeat; so doth the Lord often, when he cometh to his little ones, give them such sweet honey of his grace that they forget their sufferings in the sweet nectar which he vouchsafeth them. Another reason, no doubt, is lest they should be utterly destroyed by the terror of his judgment. "He tempereth the wind to the shorn lamb;" but, better than that, he taketh it to his bosom, and when it lieth there little doth it know that but for the rain and the tempest it had not laid in his bosom, and been fondled there so tenderly. He put it there lest it should perish.

Then, again, he doth it as a sweet reward of faith. He seeth thee in trouble bravely struggling with the tempest, and saith: "I will reward that man." He seeth thee following him in the garden, still clinging to him amidst all the darkness and temptation; and, therefore, he saith: "I will give to that soul such joy, by-and-by, that it shall be well rewarded for its faithfulness to me in the past."

Is it not to prepare you for the future, that, in looking back, you may say, "The last time I had trouble there was clear shining after the rain, and so I feel it will be next time?" Ah, thou timid one, there is a trial coming; it looms over thy head. What! and didst thou behave valiantly for thy master in former times, and wilt thou be a coward now? Ah, my brother, thinkest thou there is a time of ruin threatening thee, and thou sayest: "His mercy is clean gone for ever; he will be faithful to me no more." O, wherefore dost thou say that? Doth my Lord deserve it? Hath he been with thee in six troubles?—why should he forsake thee in the seventh? He that hath helped thee hitherto will surely help thee to the end. Wherefore hath he delivered thee in the tempest, if he means to let thee sink at last? No; by the kindness of the past, the love experienced in former days, let thy faith put out its great sheet anchor and outride the storm, for there shall again be "Clear shining after the rain."

And, surely, these changeful seasons of ours, and that constant ordinance of his, ought to make us sick of self and fond of him. He putteth gall on the world, and he putteth honey on his own lips; so that we may eschew the one and love the other. We are so fond of this world that we must be drawn away from it: and when we are drawn away from it, and enticed to him, our foolish hearts come to know his value, and we yield ourselves up to him.

I cannot tell to whom this sermon is addressed. I am sure it has a mission to fulfil. O brothers and sisters, it may be that these words may be worth a mine of gold to some of you, as a clear shining after rain. If they reach thy case, do thank my Master for it. He may have a harvest from thy soul yet. Be sure that ye give him the first-fruits of the harvest. When there is clear shining after the rain, honor him more, serve him better, give more to his cause, pray more for his people, live more in his fear, commune more with him, and walk more closely to him. Let it be true that in thy case, as in that of this round world, the rain and the clear shining after it have brought forth their abundant fruit. When you and I shall get to heaven, we will talk on its green and flowery mounts of all the showers through which we passed, and of the clear shining: and, in the sacred high eternal noon, which shall be our portion ever, we shall, with transporting joys, recount the labors of the past, and sing of the clear shining after the rain.

How sad the thought that there is no "Clear shining after rain" for some of you. There is a rain of trouble in reserve for you—that you know; there will be more troubles yet in this life; there is a heavy shower coming yet in death, and then it shall rain for ever, and there shall be a horrible tempest—that is your portion. If ye believe not that Jesus is Christ, and trust not your souls to him, all the woe you have ever known is as nothing; it is but the first spattering of the drops on the pavement; it is nothing compared with the storm which shall beat upon your head—your unsheltered head, for ever and ever. But refuge is before thee, man! The sky is dark, the tempest lowers; but the refuge is before thee. Run! in God's name, run! The storm comes hastening on, as if God were gathering up all his black artillery that he might discharge his dreadful thunders upon thee. Run! "But can I enter?" Yes, the door is open; run! "But may I enter?" Yes, he invites thee: "Come unto me, yea, come unto me—come this night—trust me," he says, "and I will save thy soul." "But I am unworthy." Well, see the tempest! Run! Let thine unworthiness put feathers to thy feet, and not stop thee in thy haste. Jesus calls thee from his throne in heaven; he invites thee: "Come unto me, all ye that labor and are heavy laden, and I will give you rest." "The Spirit and the bride say, Come; and let him that heareth say, Come." Heaven and earth say, Come. Sinner, wilt thou avoid the tempest? Wilt thou flee and find shelter in Christ? God help thee to trust Christ now, and unto him shall be the glory, for ever and ever. Amen.

A Frail Leaf.

"Wilt thou break a leaf driven to and fro?"—Job xiii. 25.

POOR Job! who could have been brought lower? He had lost his possessions, his children, his health; he was covered with sore boils, and he was aggravated by the unkind speeches of his friends. In his deep distress he turns to God, and finding no other plea so near at hand he makes a plea of his own distress. He compares himself to the weakest thing he could think of, and then he says to God, the great and the merciful, "Wilt *thou*, so glorious in power and so matchless in goodness—wilt *thou* break *me*, who am like a poor leaf fallen from the tree, sere and dry, and driven to and fro in the wind?" Thus he draws an argument out of his weakness. Because he is so low and insignificant and powerless he lays hold upon the divine strength and pleads for pity.

It is a common figure he uses, that of a leaf driven to and fro. Strong gusts of wind, it may be in the autumn when the leaves hang but lightly upon the trees, send them falling in showers around us; quite helpless to stay their own course, fluttering in the air to and fro, like winged birds that could not steer themselves, but are guided by every fitful blast that blew upon them, at last they sunk into the mire, to be trodden down and forgotten. To these Job likens himself—a helpless, hopeless, worthless, weak, despised, perishing thing; and he appeals to the awful Majesty on high, and he says to the God of thunder and of lightning, "Wilt thou put out thy power to destroy me? Wilt thou bring forth thy dread artillery to crush such an insignificant creature as I am? With all the goodness of thy great heart—for thy name is God, that is good—wilt thou turn thy Almighty power against me? Oh, that be far from thee! Out of pity upon my utter weakness and nothingness, turn away thy hand, and break not a leaf that is driven to and fro!"

The apprehension is so startling, the appeal so forcible, that the argument may be employed in a great many ways. *How often have the sick used it*, when they have been brought to so low an ebb with physical pain that life itself seemed worthless! Stricken with disease, stung with smart, and fretted with acute pangs, they felt that if the affliction continued much longer, it were better for them to die than live. They longed for the shades of death, that they might find shelter there. Turning their face to the wall, they have said, "O God, so weak as I am, wilt thou again smite me? Shall thy hand again fall upon me? Thou hast laid me very low. Wherefore again dost thou lift up thy rod? Break not, I beseech thee, a leaf that is driven to and fro!"

Not less applicable the plea *to those who are plunged into the depths of poverty!* A man is in trouble arising from destitution; perhaps he has been long out of work; bread is not to be found; the children are crying, hungering, starving; the habitation has been stripped of everything which might procure a little nourishment. The poor wretch, after passing through seas of trouble, finds himself no nearer a landing-place than before, but

"Sees each day new straits attend,
And wonders where the scene will end."

Passing through the streets he is hardly able to keep his feet from the pavement or his skin from the cold, by reason of his tattered garments. Homeless and friendless, life a leaf that is driven to and fro, he says, " O God! wilt thou continue this much longer? Wilt thou not be pleased to stay thy rough wind, mitigate the sharpness of the winter, ease my adversity, and give me peace?"

So, too, *with those who are in trouble through bereavement*. One child has been taken away, and then another. The shafts of death flew twice. Then came sickness with threatening omen upon one that was nearer and dearer still. Still did not the desolation stay its gloomy portents. It seemed at length as though the widow would be bereft of her last and only child, and then she cried, " O God! I am already broken; my heart is like a ploughed field, cross-ploughed, till my soul is ready to despair! Wilt thou utterly break me? Wilt thou spare me no consolations, no props for my old age? Must I be altogether driven away before the whirlwind, and find no rest?"

Perhaps it is even more harassing in cases of *mental distress*, for, after all, the sharpest pangs we feel are not those of the body, nor those of the estate, but those of the mind. When the iron enters into the soul, the rust thereof is poison. "The spirit of a man will sustain his infirmity, but a wounded spirit who can bear? You may be surrounded with all the comforts of life, and yet be in wretchedness more gloomy than death if the spirits be depressed. You may have no outward cause whatever for sorrow, and yet if the mind be dejected, the brightest sunshine will not relieve your gloom. At such a time, you may be vexed with cares, haunted with dreams, and scared with thoughts which distract you. You fear that your sins are not pardoned, that your past transgressions are brought to remembrance, and that punishment is being meted out to you in full measure. The threatenings rise up out of God's book, and seem to lift sharp swords in their hands with which to smite you. Time is dreadful to you, because you know it is hurrying you to eternity; and the thought of eternity stings as doth an adder, because you measure the future reckoning by the present distress. At such a time, when you are faint with longing, ready to despair, driven to the verge of madness, I can imagine your crying out, "O Lord God of mercy, I am as a leaf that is driven to and fro; wilt thou quite break me, and utterly destroy me? Have compassion, and show thy favor to thy poor broken creature!"

Many a child of God may have used this, and if he has not used it yet, still he may use it. There are times when all our evidences get clouded, and all our joys are red. Though we may still cling to the cross, yet it is with a desperate grasp. God brings our sins to remembrance, till our bones, as David puts it, "are sore broken by reason of our iniquity." Then it is that, all-broken, we can turn to the Strong for strength,

4*

and use the plea of the text, "Wilt thou break a leaf driven to and fro?" and we shall get for our answer these comforting words, "A bruised reed he will not break, and smoking flax he will not quench."

I. THE PLEA IS SUCH AS ARISES FROM INWARD CONSCIOUSNESS.

What plea is more powerful to ourselves than that which we draw from ourselves? A man may not be sure of aught that is without him, for eyes and ears may deceive; but he is always pretty well assured of anything within him, for that which he perceives in his own consciousness he is very tenacious about. Now, in this case, Job was quite certain about his own weakness. How could he doubt *that?* He looked upon his poor body covered with sores, he looked upon his friends who had perplexed and vexed him so much, and he felt that he was, indeed, just like a sere leaf. I do trust that many of us have been brought by God the Holy Spirit into such an humble frame of mind as to feel that, in a certain sense, this is true of us: "O God, if we know ourselves aright, we are all like withered leaves; we once thought ourselves fresh and green; we reckoned that we were as good as others, so we made a fine and verdant profession; but lo! thou hast been pleased to deal with us, and all the fresh verdure of what we thought to be our piety—the natural piety which we thought we possessed—has faded and withered, and now we are convinced that we are altogether as an unclean thing, and that all our righteousnesses are as filthy rags. Nay, the hope that we clung to as the leaf clings to the tree, we have had to give up. We are blown away from that. We were once upon the tree of good works; we seemed as if we had life, and should always be happy there, but the winds have taken us away, and we cannot hold on to our hope. We once thought that we could do everything; we now perceive that without Christ we can do nothing. We are cast forth as a branch separated from the vine; we are withered. What can a leaf do? What power has it to resist the wind? Just so we feel now; we can do nothing; even the sin that dwelleth in us, like the wind, carrieth us away; and we are like the leaf in the wind, subject to its power.

O, my brethren, what a great blessing it is to be made to know our weakness. To empty the sinner of his folly, his vanity and conceit, is no easy matter. Christ can easily fill him with wisdom and prudence, but to get him empty—this is the work; this is the difficulty. To make a man know that he is in himself utterly lost, ruined, and undone; this is the Spirit of God's own work. We ministers cannot make a man see that, however diligently we may point it out; only the Spirit of God can enlighten the heart to discern it; and yet, until a man does see it, he cannot enter into the kingdom of heaven, for there are none within the pearly gates who were not once broken-hearted sinners. Who could come there and sing, "Unto Him who loved us, and washed us from our sins in his blood," but those who once said, "Pardon mine iniquity, for it is great?"

While it is a confession of weakness, it is also *an acknowledgment of God's power to push that weakness to a direful conclusion.* "Wilt thou break me?" says the text—"Lord, thou canst do it. In one minute thou couldst take away hope from every one of us now in this house of prayer." Some there be who are in the house of doom, where prayer can never be answered, and where mercy's proclamation can never be heard. God could break us. It is an easy thing for him to destroy; and more, he is not only able, but he has the right to do it if he wills, for we are such worthless creatures through our disobedience, that we may say, in the words of the hymn—

> "If my soul were sent to hell,
> Thy righteous law approves it well."

When we feel this, then let us make a proper use of our own consciousness, not to despond and faint, but to arise and go to our Father, so we shall come to God and say, "Thou canst destroy me; Thou mayest destroy me justly, and I cannot resist thee. I cannot save myself from thy vengeance, nor can I merit anything at thy hand; I am as weak as water, and altogether as perishing a thing as a poor withered leaf; but wilt thou destroy me? I plead for pity. Oh! have pity upon me! O God, let thy bowels yearn towards me, and show me thy great compassion! I have heard that thou delightest in mercy; and as Ben-hadad of old, with the rope about his neck, sent in unto the king, and confessed that he deserved to die, so do I confess; and as the king forgave him, even so do thou with me—a guilty culprit trembling in thy presence!

> "Show pity, Lord; O Lord, forgive;
> Let a repenting rebel live."

II. This is also A VERY PITIFUL PLEA.

Though there is weakness, yet there is also power, for weakness is, for the most part, a prevalent plea with those who are strong and good. You could not see on your road home to-night a poor fainting woman, and pass her by, I trust. You could not have brought in before your presence a half-starved child, that could not drag its weary limbs along, without feeling that you must give relief. The mere sight of weakness draws pity. As a certain town was being sacked, one of the rough soldiery is said to have spared a little child, because it said, "Please, sir, don't kill me, I am so little." The rough warrior felt the cogency of the plea. You may yourselves just plead thus with God. "O God, do not destroy me! I deserve it, but oh, I am so little! Turn thy power upon some great thing, and let thy bowels move with compassion towards me!"

The plea gathers force *when the weakness is confessed.* If a man shall have done you some wrong, and shall come and acknowledge it, and bow down before you and confess it, why, then you feel that you cannot take him by the throat, but you say, "Rise, I have forgiven thee!" When weakness appeals to strength for protection, and confession of guilt is relied on as an argument for mercy, those who are good and strong are pretty sure to be moved with compassion.

But, best of all, going from the positive to the comparative, and from the comparative to the superlative, *how a profession of weakness touches your heart when it comes from your child.* If your child has been chastised, and has confessed his wrong, and pleads with you, how you stay your hand! Or, if the child be sick, and something be done to it which pains it, if while the operation is being performed he should look you in the face, and say, "Father, spare thy child; I can bear no more!" you have already felt more than you can make him feel; forthwith your own tears blind you, and you stay your hand. "Like as a father pitieth his children, even so the Lord pitieth them that fear him." If you have faith to bring your weakness before God with the sense of a child towards him, you surely must prevail. Come, then, you timid trembling children of your Father who is in heaven, use this plea—" Wilt thou break a leaf that is driven to and fro?"

III. This PLEA IS RIGHTLY ADDRESSED.

It is addressed to God. As I thought it over, it seemed to me as if I could use it to each Person of the Blessed Trinity in Unity. Looking up *to the great Father of our spirits*, from whom every good and perfect gift cometh down, it seemed to me that out of weakness I could say to Him, 'Wilt *thou*, whose name is *Father*, wilt *thou* break a leaf that is driven to and fro? Thou art the God that made us; wilt *thou* utterly destroy the earthen vessel which thou hast fashioned on the wheel? Thy name is 'Preserver of men;' wilt *thou* annihilate us, and break us into shivers? Hast thou not revealed thyself as delighting in mercy? Art thou not the 'Lord God, merciful and gracious, passing by iniquity, transgression, and sin'? Hast thou not said, 'Come, now, and let us reason together; though your sins be as scarlet they shall be as wool; though they be red as crimson they shall be whiter than snow?' O God the Father of heaven, wilt *thou* break a leaf that is driven to and fro?"

And then, I thought I could address myself to the *blessed Son of God*, who is also our brother in human flesh, and say to him, Wilt *thou* break—O thou "faithful High Priest, touched with a feeling of our infirmities"—" bone of our bone, and flesh of our flesh"—

Brother of our soul, by whose stripes we are healed—wilt *thou* break a leaf that is driven to and fro? Nay, by thy thorn-crowned head and thy bloody sweat, by thy cross and passion, by thy wounds and thy death-cry, thou canst not, wilt not be unmerciful and unkind. Surely, they who in confidence turn to thee, and lay hold upon thee, shall find that thy strength shall be ready to help; for though thine arm be strong to smite, it is no less strong to save.

Again, it comes across me sweetly, "O blessed *Spirit!* couldst *thou* break a leaf that is driven to and fro? Thou art no eagle; thou didst descend on Christ in Jordan as a dove; thine influences are soft and soothing. Thy name is 'The Comforter': thou takest of the things of Christ, not to blast us, but to bless us therewith; thou art not a destroying Spirit, but a quickening Spirit, not a terrifying but an enlivening Spirit; wilt *thou* break a leaf that is driven to and fro?"

Yea, I address thee, *thou Triune God*, thou who art so full of mercy, and love, and grace, and truth, that those who have known thee best have been compelled to say, "Oh, how great is thy goodness which thou hast laid up for them that fear thee! Oh, the depths of thy lovingkindness!" is it possible that *thou* canst cast away a poor, broken-hearted trembler, a poor, fearing, doubting one, who would fain be saved, but who trembles lest he should be cast away?

IV. THIS PLEA IS BACKED UP BY MANY CASES OF SUCCESS.

We will not give many, for we have not time; but there is one case which we may mention: There was a woman whose life was exceedingly sorrowful. She was an Eastern wife, and her husband had been foolish enough to have a second mistress in the house. The woman of whom we speak, a holy woman, a woman of refined and delicate mind, a poetess, indeed, of no mean order—this poor woman, having no children, was the constant butt of her rival, whose sneering spiteful remarks chaffed and chafed her. Her adversary, it is said, "vexed her sore to make her afraid." Though her husband was exceedingly kind to her, yet as with a sword that cut her bones did she go continually. She was a woman of a sorrowful spirit, her spirit being broken. Still, "she feared the Lord exceedingly," and she went up to God's house, and it was in God's house that she received, what was to her, perhaps, the greatest blow of her life. If from her rival that she received the harshest word, it was from the High Priest of God that she received this hardest blow. As she stood there praying, using no vocal sound, but her lips moving, the High Priest—an easy soul, who had brought his own family to ruin by his easiness— little knowing her grief, told her that she was drunken. A woman to whom the thought of such a sin would have been bitter as gall, it must have smitten her as with the chill blast of death, that God's priest had said she was drunken. But, as you will all remember, the Lord did not break the leaf that was driven to and fro. To her there came a comfortable promise. Ere long that woman stood there to sing. The mercy of God had made the barren woman to rejoice, and to be the joyful mother of children. The song of the Virgin Mary was modelled after the song of Hannah— that memorable poem in which she sang of the Lord who had filled the hungry with good things, while the rich he had sent empty away. In that case the Lord did not break the leaf that was driven to and fro.

In after years—to take an example of another kind—there was a king who had sinned desperately, slaying God's servants with both hands. But he was taken captive by a powerful monarch, and was thrown into prison, such a noisome prison that he was among thorns, in mental as well as in material darkness. Then, troubled in spirit, tossed to and fro, and without power to help himself, Manasseh sought unto the Lord, and he found the Lord; he prayed unto the Lord, and the Lord heard him. Out of the low dungeon, he did not break the leaf that was driven to and fro.

Take a later case, in our Saviour's time. The picture of those proud Pharisees hurrying into our Saviour's presence a poor fallen woman is even now in your mind's eye. Yes, sirs, she was taken in adultery. There was no doubt of it; she was "taken in the very act," and there she stands—nay, she kneels, all covered with blushes—before the man who is asked to judge her. And you remember his words. He never said a word to excuse her guilt: the Saviour could not and would not condone her shame; nor would he, on the other hand, lend himself to crush the woman who had sinned; but he said—"Where are those thine accusers? Go and sin no more!" Let his words come unto thee, poor leaf, driven to and fro! Oh, if there should be such a leaf as that driven here to-night, driven in, perhaps, by stress of weather! Men despise you; from your own sex you get faint pity; but, Jesus, when thou art appealed to, thou wilt not break such a leaf that is driven to and fro!

Shall I tell another story of the woman who came behind the Master in the press, and stole a cure by touching his garment? She thought she would receive a curse, but he said—"Be thou of good cheer; thy faith hath made thee whole; go in peace." It was poor faith: it is very like unbelief; but yet it was rewarded with a rich acceptance, for he will not break a leaf that is driven to and fro.

V. Once more, my text is A FAINT PLEA WHICH INVITES FULL SUCCOR.

"Wilt thou break a leaf that is driven to and fro?" O Job! there is much wrapped up in what thou hast said.

He meant this—"Instead of breaking it, thou wilt spare it; thou wilt gather it up; thou wilt give it life again." It is like that text, "A bruised reed he will not break." Oh, it means more than that; it means that he will heal its bruises. "A smoking flax he will not quench." That is good, but it means more. It means that he will stoop down to him, and that with his soft breath he will blow that smoking flax into a flame; he will not let it go out; he will preserve its heat, and make something more of it. O you, who are brought to the very lowest of weakness! use that weakness in pleading with God, and he will return unto you with such a fulness of blessing that you shall receive the pardon of sin; you shall be accepted through the righteousness of Christ; you shall be dear to the heart of God; you shall be filled with his Spirit; you shall be blessed with all the fulness of God.

My Lord is such a One that if a beggar asks a penny of him he gives him gold, and if you ask only for the pardon of sins, he will give you all the covenant blessing which he has been pleased so bounteously to provide for the necessities of his people. Come, poor guilty one, needy, helpless, broken, and bruised. Come thou by faith, and let thy weakness plead with God through Jesus Christ.

VI. WE MAY USE THIS PLEA—MANY OF US WHO HAVE LONG KNOWN THE SAVIOUR.

Perhaps our faith has got to be very low. O Lord, wilt thou destroy my little faith? I know there is sin in it. To be so unbelieving as I am is no little crime; but, Lord, I thank thee that I have any faith. It is weak and trembling, but it is faith of thine own giving. Oh, break not the poor leaf that is driven to and fro!

It may be your hope is not very bright. You cannot see the golden gates, though they are very near. Well, but your hope shall not be destroyed because it is clouded. You can say, "Lord, wilt thou destroy my hope because it is dim?" No, that he will not!

Perhaps you are conscious that you have not been so useful lately as you once were, but you may say, "Lord, wilt thou destroy my usefulness because I have been laid aside, or have not done what I ought to have done in thy service?" Bring your little graces to Christ as the mothers brought their little children, and ask him to put his hands upon them and to bless them. Bring your mustard-seed to Christ, and ask him to make it grow into a tree, and he will do it; but never think that he will destroy you, or that he will destroy the works of his own hand in you.

Oh! that I could so preach as to give the comfort to you which I felt in my own soul while musing over these words! I wish that some who feel how lost, how empty, and how ruined they are, could now believe in the great and the good heart of my Lord Jesus Christ. Little do they know how glad he will be to save them. You will be glad to be saved ; but he will be more glad to save you. You will be thankful to sit at the feast; but, of all that come to the banquet, there is no heart so glad as the heart of the king. When the king came in to see the guests, I know there were gleams of joy in his face which were not to be found in the faces of any of the guests. He has the joy of benevolence. Perhaps you have sometimes felt a thrill of pleasure when you have done some good to your poor fellow-creatures. Now, bethink ye what must be the joy of Christ, the joy of the Father, and the joy of the Holy Spirit—the joy of doing good to those who do not deserve it, the joy of bestowing favors upon the wicked and the unthankful, the joy of showing that he doeth good because he is good—not because *you* are good, but because *he* is good ; thus the Lord God will overleap the mountains of your sins and your prejudices, and the rivers of your iniquities, that he may come unto you and display the full tide of his lovingkindness and his tender mercy.

Oh! that some might be now for the first time drawn to Jesus, put their trust in him, and find pardon and peace.

The Helmet.

"And for a helmet, the hope of salvation."—1 Thess. v. 8.

THE very mention of a helmet may well serve to REMIND EVERY CHRISTIAN THAT HE IS A SOLDIER.

I. If you were not soldiers, you would not need armor; but, being soldiers, you need to be clad from head to foot in armor of proof. I suppose every Christian knows, as a matter of theory, that he is a Christian soldier, and that he has been enlisted under the banner of the cross, to fight against the powers of darkness until he wins the victory. But, we all need to have our memories refreshed upon this matter, for soldiering in time of war, at any rate, is not a very pleasant occupation, and the flesh constantly attempts to give it over. That "we have no abiding city here" is a truth we all admit, and yet the most of us try to make the earth as comfortable to ourselves as if it were to be our abiding residence. We are all soldiers, we know that; but, still, too many Christians act as if they could be the friends of the world and the friends of God at the same time. Now, Christian, recollect once for all that you are a soldier. Did you dream, young man, that as soon as you were baptized, and added to the church, the conflict was all over? Ah, it was then just beginning. Like Cæsar, you then crossed the Rubicon, and declared war against your deadly enemy. You drew your sword then; you did not sheathe it. Your proper note on joining the church is not one of congratulation, as though the victory were won, but one of preparation; for now the trumpet sounds, and the fight begins. You are a soldier at all times, Christian. You ought to sit even at your table as a soldier sits, and you should go out, especially into the world, as a soldier goes out. Never take off your armor, for if you do, in some unguarded moment you may meet with serious wounds. But, keep your armor ever about you, and be watchful, for you are always in the midst of enemies wherever you may be. Even when the persons who surround you are your friends, there are still evil spirits unseen of men who watch for your halting. You must not put up your sword, for you are to wrestle against principalities, and powers, and spiritual wickedness in high places; against these you must ever be on the watch. You are a soldier, man; remember that.

Nor are you a soldier in barrracks, or at home, but *you are a soldier in an enemy's country.* Your place is either in the trenches or else in the thick of the battle. You who are sick are like soldiers in the trenches. You are patiently hoping and quietly waiting, as it were, upon the ramparts, looking for the time to come. But, others of you, out in business and engaged in the concerns of life, are like soldiers marching in long file to the conflict, like the horsemen dashing on to the front of the battle. More or less, according to your circumstances, you are all exposed to the foe, and that at every period of life.

Where are you, let me ask, but *in the country of an enemy who never gives any quarter?* If you fall, it is death. The world never forgives the Christian; it hates him with a perfect hatred, and it longs to do him ill. Only let the world see you commit half a trip, and they will soon report and magnify it. What might be done by other men without observation, if it were done by a Christian, would be noticed, reported, and misrepresented. The world understands that you are its natural antagonist. Satan perceives in you a representative of his old enemy the Lord Jesus, and you may rest assured that he will never give you quarter if once he gets an opportunity of destroying you. Mind the enemy, mind the enemy, for he is one of a malicious spirit.

You have to fight with one too *who never yet made a truce. You* may come to terms and parley, but the powers of evil never do. *You* may hang out the white flag if you like. The foe may seem for a time as though he gave you credit, but do you never give your foe any credit. He hates you when he seems to love you best. "Dread the Greeks, even when they bring you gifts," said the tradition of old; and let the Christian dread the world most when it puts on its softest speeches. Stand, then, upon your guard, ye warriors of the cross; when least you fear, the cringing foe will come behind you, and stab you, under the pretence of friendship. Your Master was betrayed with a kiss, and so will you be, unless you watch unto prayer.

You have to do with an enemy *who never can make any peace with you, nor can you ever make any peace with him.* If you become at peace with sin, sin has conquered you; and it is impossible, unless you give up the fight, and yield your neck to everlasting thraldom, that there should ever be peace for so much as a moment. O Christian, see how guarded you ought to be. How needful to be clothed with your armor! How needful to have it of the right kind, to keep it bright, and to wear it constantly! You are a soldier, a soldier in battle, a soldier in the foeman's country, a soldier with a cruel and malicious enemy, who knows neither truce nor parley, and who gives no quarter, but will fight with you till you die. Heaven is the land where your sword should be sheathed; there shall you hang the banner high, but here we wrestle with the foe, and must do so till we cross the torrent of death. Right up to the river's edge must the conflict be waged. Foot by foot, and inch by inch, must all the land to Canaan's happy shore be won. Not a step can be taken without conflict and strife; but, once there, you may lay aside your helmet, and put on your crown; put away your sword, and take your palm-branch; your fingers shall no longer need to learn to war, but your hearts shall learn the music of the happy songsters in the skies. This then is the first thought—you are a soldier.

II. The second thought is this—BEING A SOLDIER LOOK TO YOUR HEAD.

Soldiers, look to your heads. A wound in the head is a serious matter. The head being a vital part, we need to be well protected there. The heart needs to be guarded with the breastplate, but the head needs to be protected quite as much; for even if a man should be true-hearted, yet, if a shot should go through his brain, he would not be worth much as a soldier; his body would strew the plain. The head must be taken care of. A great many Christian people never trouble themselves about defending their heads at all. If they get their hearts warmed by their religion they think that quite enough. Well; give me above everything else a good warm heart; but, oh, do have that warm heart coupled with a head that is well taken care of. Do you know that with a hot head and a hot heart together you may do a deal of mischief, but with a hot heart and a cool brain you may do a world of service to the Master. Have right doctrine in the head, and then set the soul on fire, and you will soon win the world. There is no standing in that man's way whose head and heart are both right, but to neglect the head has been a serious mischief with many Christians. They have been almost powerless for usefulness because they have not taken care of their brains. Though they have got to heaven, they have not gained many victories on the road, because their brains have been out of order. They have never been able clearly to understand the doctrines; they have not been able to give a reason for the hope that is in them; they have not, in fact, looked well to the helmet which was to cover their heads.

The text refers us to our head because it speaks of a helmet, and a helmet is of no use to any part except the head. Among other reasons why we should preserve the head in the day of battle, let us give these. The head is peculiarly liable to the temptations of Satan, of self, and of fame. It is not easy, you know, to stand on a high pinnacle without the brain beginning to reel; and if God takes a man, and puts him on a high pinnacle of usefulness, he had need to have his head taken care of. If a brother is possessed of a considerable amount of wealth, there is great danger to his soul by reason of his possessions, unless he have a wealth of grace as well as a wealth of gold. If a man is well reported of, though his sphere may not be very large, yet, if everybody praised him, he also will need to have his head well protected, for a little praise would soon make him giddy. The clapping of hands of fools would be enough for a fool to pique himself on. The fining-pot for silver, and praise for the man. If a man can stand commendation, he can stand anything. The severest trial which a zealous Christian has to bear is, probably, the trial which comes from his kind but inconsiderate friends, who would puff him up if they could by telling him what a fine fellow he is. If your friends without will not cheer you, you will probably find a friend within who will flatter you to your heart's content; and, if *you* should forget to ask for your meed, the devil will remind you that it is your due. "What a capital sermon you gave us this morning, Mr. Bunyan," said a friend, where John had been preaching. "You are too late," said Bunyan, "the devil told me that before I came out of the pulpit." Yes, and he will be sure to do so; and hence the need of having a helmet to put on the head, that when you are successful, and getting on in life, and friends are speaking well of you, you may not get intoxicated with it. Oh, to have a good, cool helmet to put on your brain when it begins to get a little hot with praise, so that you may still stand fast, and not be borne down by vanity. O Vanity, Vanity,

Vanity, how many hast thou slain! How many who seemed upon the very brink of greatness have stumbled upon this stumbling stone! Men who seemed as though they would enter heaven, but a little bit of honor, some glittering bribe, a golden boon, has turned them aside, and they fell. Take care of you heads, brethren.

And is not *the head liable to attacks from scepticism?* People who have no brains are not often troubled with doubts, but people who have brains have probably felt that, whether they resolved to use them or not, their brains would use themselves. It was very good of our good fathers to tell us not to read dangerous books, very good of them indeed; but, we do read them, for all that; and, though we tell the young folks sometimes not to read this and that heretical treatise, and we wish they would take our advice, yet, somehow or other, they do get hold of such things, and will ponder them. Brethren, I do believe that, in such times as these, when everything is so free, and when discussion is so common, we must expect that our young fellows will look at a great many things which they had better leave alone, and their heads will be endangered thereby, for the bullets of scepticism threaten to go right through their brains. Well, what then? As we cannot take Christians out of the way of the bullets, we should give them a helmet to preserve them therefrom. He who has a hope of salvation—a good hope that he is himself saved, a hope that he shall see the face of Christ with joy at last—is not afraid of any of the paltry quibbles of scepticism. He may hear them all, and for a moment be staggered by them, as a soldier might be who had a sudden shock or even a wound, but after a little while he recovers himself, and feels sound enough to enter into the conflict again. Thus the Christian in armor proof can say—

> "Should all the forms that men devise
> Assault my faith with treacherous art ;
> I'd call them vanities and lies,
> And bind the gospel to my heart."

It has been very well observed that a man is not often a very thorough democrat after he gets a little money in the savings bank. Well, I think it is very likely, so soon as a man gets a little stake in his country's welfare, he begins to be just to the merest extent conservative. And, no sooner does a man get a stake in Christianity, and feel, that he has got salvation in Jesus Christ, than he gets to be very, very conservative of the old-fashioned truth. He cannot give up the Bible then, because it is a broad land of wealth to him. He cannot give up Christ, for he is *his* Saviour, *his* salvation. He cannot give up a single promise, because that promise is so dear to his own soul. The helmet of salvation, then, will preserve the head in times of scepticism.

The head, again, is very greatly in danger *from the attacks of personal unbelief*. Who among us has not doubted his own interest in Christ? Happy for you who are free from such distractions. But, there are seasons with some of us when we turn our title-deeds over, and we are sometimes afraid lest they should not be genuine. There are times when, if we could, we would give a world to know that we are Christ's, for we cannot

> "Read our title clear
> To mansions in the skies."

Well, beloved, this is very dangerous to our heads;

but the man who has got the helmet of a right, sound, God-given hope of salvation, who has received from God the Holy Spirit such a helmet as I am going to describe by-and-by, may be of good cheer. These doubts and fears may distress him for a little while, but he knows the precautions advised for his safeguard, as he is neither timid nor rash. In the midst of Satan's accusations, the uprising of his old corruptions, the infirmities of the flesh, and the allurements of the world, he stands calm and unmoved, because he wears as a helmet the hope of salvation.

Nor are these all the dangers to which the head is exposed. *Some persons are attacked by threatenings from the world.* The world brings down its double-handled sword with a tremendous blow upon the heads of many Christians. " You will suffer the loss of all things for Christ if you are such a fanatic as to believe the Bible and consort with the saints. You will be poor yourself, your children will want bread, your wife will be worse than a widow, if you are such a fool." " Ah," says the Christian, " but I have a hope of salvation." So the blow, when it comes, does not go through his head, but just falls on the helmet, and the world's sword gets blunted. " I can afford to be poor," said Dr. Gill, when one of his subscribers threatened to give up his seat, and would not attend, if the doctor preached such-and-such a doctrine. So says the Christian, " I can afford to be poor; I can afford to be despised; I have in heaven a better and more enduring substance." So, by the use of this blessed helmet, he is protected from the threatenings of the world.

We want our young people to wear this helmet, too,

because of the errors of the times." The errors of the times are many. What with scepticism, and with superstition, they are tempted on the one side and on the other. This and that new book or old fable is cried up. "Lo here," and "Lo there." By unscrupulous authors and by designing priests there will be many misled who are not the people of God. "If it were possible, they would deceive the very elect." But the elect are not to be deceived. Their heads are not vulnerable to these errors, for they wear the hope of salvation, and they are not afraid of all the "isms" or schisms that aggrieve the professor and aggravate the profane. The man knows he is saved. Once get to know Christ personally for yourselves, to believe that he loved you and gave himself for you, and to rejoice that you are forgiven and justified through him, then, though the world will count you stupid and obstinate, you will stand firm, and be able to resist all its sarcasm and its ridicule. He who has made a refuge of Jesus Christ will stand safe whatever errors may invade the land.

They tell us that the Church of God is in great danger, because Popery will overspread the country. Peradventure it should; that it will overspread the Church of God—no; I know far better than that. The Church of God can never be in danger. Every man in whom is the life of God would be as ready to die to-morrow for the truth as our forefathers were in the Marian days. Rest assured there would be found men to stand at the burning faggot still if the times required them, and our prisons would not long be without heavenly-minded tenants of the truth needed to be defended by suffering, even unto death. There *is* danger, great danger; there never was such danger in modern times of Popery overspreading the land as now. But there is no danger to the man who has his helmet on. Let the arrows fly thick as hail, and let the foes have all the political power that they can, and all the *prestige* of antiquity that they may; a little phalanx of true-hearted Christians will still stand their ground in the very centre of the onslaught, and cut their way to glory and to victory through whole hosts, because their heads are guarded with the heavenly helmet of the hope of salvation. Soldiers of Christ, take care of your heads.

III. God has provided a covering for your heads, let us therefore now CONSIDER THE HELMET WITH WHICH HE WOULD HAVE YOUR HEADS PROTECTED.

"The hope of salvation!" This is not the hope we sometimes speak about, the hope that salvation is possible which may encourage every sinner to knock, to seek, to ask—yea, to pray importunately for mercy. This helmet is made up of an actual hope that, being already saved in Christ Jesus, you should abide unto eternal life. It is a personal hope, founded upon personal conviction, and is wrought in us by the Holy Spirit.

To begin, then, describing this helmet. *Who is its giver?* You ask our friend the soldier where he gets his regimentals from, and he answers that he gets them from the government stores. He gets his regimentals from Her Majesty, and from the monarch himself we must get our helmets. If any of you construct helmets of hope for yourselves, they will be of no use to you in the day of battle. The true helmet of hope must come from the heavenly arsenal. You must go to the Divine store-house, for unto God belongeth salvation, and the hope of salvation must be given to you by his free grace. A hope of salvation is not purchasable. Our great King does not sell his armor, but gives it freely to all who enlist. They take the bounty and accept the faith. They trust Christ, and they are enlisted, then the armor is given them gratis. From head to foot they are arrayed by grace. .

Do you ask, *who is maker of this helmet?* Weapons are valued often according to the maker. A known maker gets his own price for his articles. Armorers of old took much trouble with the ancient helmets, because a man's life might depend upon that valuable means of defence. So we have here the name of God the Holy Ghost upon this helmet. A hope of salvation is the work of God the Holy Spirit in our soul. It is the Spirit who brings us to Jesus, shows us our need of him, and gives us faith in him; and it is that same Spirit who enables us to hope that we shall endure to the end, and enter into eternal life. Be not satisfied with a hope that is natural, but have a hope that is supernatural. Rest not satisfied with that which is made in the workshop of nature; go not to those who buy and sell for themselves, but go to the blessed Spirit, who giveth freely, and upbraideth not.

Would you inquire further, *of what metal this helmet is made?* It is made of hope, we are told; but it is of the utmost consequence that it be a good hope. Beware of getting a base hope, a helmet made of paltry metal. There were some helmets they used to wear in the olden times which looked very well, but they were of no more use than brown paper hats; and when a soldier got into a fight with one of these on, the sword went through his skull. Get a good helmet, one made of the right metal. This is what a Christian's hope is made of—he believes that Christ came into the world to save sinners; he trusts Christ to save him; and he hopes that when Christ comes he shall reign with him; that when the trumpet sounds he shall rise with Christ, and that in heaven he shall have a secure dwelling-place at the right hand of the Father. This hope is made up of proper and fitting deductions from certain truthful statements. That Christ died for *sinners* is true; that he died to save all who trust in him is true; that *I* trust in him is true; therefore, that I am saved is true; and, being saved, that I shall inherit all his promises is a matter of course. Some people have a hope, but they do not know where they get it from, nor do they know a reason for it. When people die, you hear it said of one and another, " I hope he is gone to heaven." Well, I wish he may have gone; but I dare not say of some that I hope so, because hope must have a reason. An anchor is of no use without its fluke. It must be able to hold fast. It must have—at any rate, the modern anchor must have—some weight about it with which it can hold to the bottom. Hope must have its fluke, too; it must have its reason; it must have its weight. When I say I hope so-and-so, I am foolish for hoping it, if I have not a reason for hoping. If you were to say you hoped the person sitting next you would give you a thousand pounds, it would be a most absurd hope. You may wish it if you like, but what ground have you for the hope? But if somebody owes you a thousand pounds, and you have his acknowledgment of the debt, you may then very well say that you hope it will be paid, for you have a legitimate right to expect it. Such is the Christian's hope. God has promised to save those who believe. Lord, I believe it; thou hast promised to save me, and I hope thou wilt, I know thou wilt. The Christian's hope hope is not a fancy, not a silly desire. It did not spring up in the night like Jonah's gourd, nor will it wither in a night. The Christian's hope is something that will bear a hard blow from a heavy club, or a smart cut from a sharp sword. It is made of good metal. John Bunyan said of a certain sword that it was " a true Jerusalem blade," and I may call this a true Jerusalem helmet, for he that wears is need not fear.

Having shown the metal of which the helmet is made, let me now describe *the strength of the helmet*. It is so strong, that under all sorts of assaults, he who wears it is invulnerable. Recollect David, when pressed with the troubles of the world on every side. His enemies thought they had certainly ruined him. He himself half thought he should die, and he tells us that he should have fainted. And likely enough he would, only he had a bottle of cordial with him of which faith was the main ingredient. He says, "*I had fainted unless I had believed.*" But, just at the time when he thought he would faint and die, he revived. Suddenly the old hero that slew Goliath, made all his enemies fly before him as he cried, "Why art thou cast down, O my soul, and why art thou disquieted within me? Hope thou in God." And he laid about him right and left, as he should. "I shall yet praise him who is the health of my countenance and my God." "Hope thou in God," Christian. Oh, that blessed word HOPE! You know what the New Zealanders call hope; they call it in their language "the swimming thought," because it always floats and never sinks. You cannot drown it; it always keeps its head above the wave. When you think you have drowned the Christian's hope, up it comes all dripping from the brine, and cries again, "Hope thou in God, for I shall yet praise him!" Hope is the nightingale that sings in the night; faith is the lark that mounts up towards heaven; but hope is the nightingale that cheers the valley in the darkness. O Christian, be thankful that you have so strong a helmet as this, which can bear all assaults, and can keep you unscathed in the midst of the fray!

This hope of salvation *is a helmet which will not come off*. It is of main importance, you know, to have a helmet that cannot be knocked off in the first scrimmage. That is why our policemen are dressed differently from what they used to be, because their hats used to get knocked off. So it is with a commonplace hope, it fails him in an extremity; but the Christian wears a helmet that he cannot get off anyhow. There was once a good soldier of Jesus Christ—a woman—some women are among the best soldiers of Christ; his true Amazons. This good woman had been much harassed by a sceptical person; and when very much confused with some of his knotty questions, she turned round and said, "I cannot answer you, sir, but neither can you answer me, for I have a something within me that you cannot understand, which makes me feel that

I could not give up what I know of Christ for all the world." The world can neither give nor take away the hope of a Christian. It comes from God, and he will never withdraw it, for his gifts and calling are without repentance. Once let this helmet be put on, and he will never remove it, but we shall hope on and hope ever, until we shall end these struggles, see his face, and reap his promises.

I should like to go round amongst this regiment, as the commanding officers sometimes do, to have a look at you. The helmet is an old-fashioned kind of armor. In old days, the lieutenants and other officers, when they went round the regiment, used to look, not only to see that the men had their helmets, but to see that they had oiled them; for in those times they used to oil their helmets to make them shine, and to keep the various joints and buckles in good order. No rust was ever allowed on the helmets, and it is said that when the soldiers marched out, with their brazen helmets and their white plumes, they shone most brilliantly in the sun. David speaks, you know, of "anointing the shield." He was speaking of a brazen shield which had to be anointed with oil. Now, when God anoints his people's hope, when he gives them the oil of joy, their hope begins to shine bright in the light of the Saviour's countenance, and what a fine array of soldiers they are then! Satan trembles at the gleaming of their swords; he cannot endure to look upon their helmets. But some of you do not keep your hope clear; you do not keep it bright; it gets rusty and unfit for use, and then, ere long, it gets to sit uncomfortably upon you, and you get weary with the fight.

O Holy Spirit, anoint our heads with fresh oil, and let thy saints go forth terrible as an army with banners.

Do not let it be overlooked that *the helmet was generally considered to be a place of honor.* The man put his plume in his helmet, he wore his crest frequently there, and in the thick of the fight the captain's plume was seen in the midst of the smoke and dust of battle, and the men pressed to the place where they saw it. Now, the Christian's hope is his honor and his glory. I must not be ashamed of my hope; I must wear it for beauty and for dignity, and he who has a right good hope will be a leader to others. Others will see it, and will fight with renewed courage; and where he hews a lane of foes, they will follow him, even as he follows his Lord and Master, who has overcome, and sits down upon his Father's throne. I hope there are many Christians here who keep their helmets bright, and that there are many more who desire to have such helmets to protect themselves and to grace their profession.

IV. ALAS! THERE ARE SOME WHO HAVE NO HELMETS. The reason is obvious. They are not Christ's soldiers.

Of course the Lord Jesus does not provide anybody with armor but those in his own service. But Satan knows how to give you a helmet too. His helmets are very potent ones. Though the sword of the Spirit can go right through them, nothing else can. He can give, and he has given some of you, a head-piece that covers your entire skull—a thick head-piece of indifference; so that no matter what is preached, you heed it not. "What do I care?" say you, and that is your helmet.

Then he puts a piece in the front of the helmet called

a brazen forehead and a brow of brass. "What do I care?" was your cry. He takes care to fit the helmet right over your eyes, so that you cannot see; yea, though hell itself be before you, you do not see it. "What do I care?" Then, he also knows how so to fit the helmet that it acts as a gag to your mouth, so that you never pray. Though you can swear through it, you cannot pray through it. Still you keep to your old cry, "What do I care?"

Ah, it is not very likely that any sword which I wield will get at your head! Arguments will not move you, for that is a question that cannot very well be argued—"What do I care?" I pray God the Holy Spirit to get at your head, notwithstanding that horrible helmet; for, if not, God has a way of dealing with such as you are. When you come to die, you will sing another song! When you come to lie upon a bed of sickness, and the grim day of eternity is in view, you will not be able to say quite so gayly as you do now, "What do I care?" And, when the trumpet rings through earth and heaven, and your body starts up from your grave, and you see the great Judge upon his throne, you will not be able to say then, "What do I care?" Your head will then be bare to the pitiless tempest of divine wrath. Bare-headed, you must be exposed to the everlasting storm that shall descend upon you. And, when the great angel binds you up with your fellows in bundles to burn, you will feel that you are not able to say, "What do I care?" for cares will come upon you like a wild deluge, when you are banished from his presence, and all hope is gone!

Oh, I would you would take off that helmet! May

God grant you grace to unbuckle it now, never to put it on again! Do care. You are not a fool, my friend, are you? It is only a fool who says, "What do I care?" Surely you care about your soul; surely hell is worth escaping from; surely heaven is worth winning; surely that cross on which our Saviour died is worth thinking of; surely that poor soul of yours is worth caring about! Do, I pray you, think, and not go hastily on. Oh, may Jesus Christ, who died for such as you are, bring you to trust him; and then, unbuckling all that evil armor of "What do I care?" you will bow before his cross, and kiss his hands, and he will put upon you the golden helmet of a hope of salvation, and you will rise, one of the King's own soldiers, to fight his battles, and win an immortal wreath of everlasting victory. May it be so with every one of us.

One Trophy for Two Exploits.

' For by thee I have run through a troop; and by my God have I leaped over a wall."—PSALM xviii. 29.

IT sometimes puzzles the unenlightened believer to find that the Psalms often relate both to David and to David's Lord. Many a young believer has found himself quite bewildered when reading a psalm; and he has scarcely been able to make out how a passage should be true both of David and of the Lord Jesus Christ, " our Superior King." This he cannot understand. But he who is grown in grace, and has got far enough to understand the meaning of conformity to Christ, sees that it is not without a high and heavenly design that the Holy Ghost has presented to us the experience of Jesus in that model of experience through which David passed. My dear brethren, we all know as a matter of doctrine, but we have not all proved as a matter of sweet experience, that we are to be like our Head. We must be like him upon earth; like him despised and rejected by men in our generation; like him bearers of the cross. Yea, we must not shrink in any way from what is meant by being crucified with him, and buried with him, in order that we may know in after days how to rise with him, how to ascend with him, and how to sit with him upon his throne. Nay, I will go further; even in this life the believer is to have a conformity to Christ in his present glories, for we are even now raised up together in heavenly places in Christ Jesus; in him also we have obtained the inheritance, for we are complete in him who is the head of all principality and power. There is such a conformity between Christ and his people that everything that is said of Christ may, in some measure, be said of his people. Whatever Christ hath been, they should be or have been. Whatever he hath done, he hath done for them, and they shall do the like, after some fashion or another. Whatever he hath attained unto, they shall also enjoy. If he reigneth, they shall reign; and if he be heir of a universal monarchy, they shall also be kings and priests unto God, and shall reign for ever and ever. Thus the riddle becomes solved; the parable is expounded; the dark saying that was opened on David's harp shines clearly in gospel light. You can see not only how it is possible that the same psalm can relate to David and David's Lord; but you can see that there is a divine mystery, and a most rich and precious lesson, couching beneath the fact that the Holy Ghost hath chosen to set forth the doings, the sufferings, and the triumphs of Christ, under the figure or model of the doings, sufferings, and victories of the son of Jesse. You will not, therefore, be surprised to hear me remark that this text hath relation to Christ and the believer too. The doings and triumphs of Jesus must, accordingly, first engage our attention; and, in the second place, observe that we have here a picture of the wondrous doings of faith, when the believer is enabled to triumph over every earthly ill, and over every human opposition. "By thee I have run through a troop; and by my God have I leaped over a wall."

I. Let us take the first sentence with regard to Christ. "By thee have I run through a troop." How accurately Christ's enemies are here described, described by their number, they were a troop. The Captain of our salvation, although single-handed in the combat, had to fight with a legion of foes. It was not a mere duel. It is true there was but one on the victor's side, but there was an innumerable host in antagonism to him. Not only the Prince of Darkness, but all the powers and the principalities thereof, came against him. Not sin in the mass, but sin in daily temptations of every kind, and sin of every shade and form. Not only from earth a host of human despisers and human opponents, but a yet greater host from the lowest depths of hell. These, from their number, are well compared to a troop.

Nor does this expression describe their number merely, but also their discipline. They were a troop. A crowd of men is a great number, but it is not a troop. A crowd may be far sooner put to rout than a troop. A troop is a trained company that knows how to march and marshal itself, and to stand firm under the attack. It was even so with Christ's enemies. They were a crowd and a mob; but they were a troop also, marshalled by that skilful and crafty leader, the Prince of Darkness. They stood firm, and were well disciplined, and in a close phalanx; they were not broken. As though they were but one man they sustained the shock of Christ's attack, and marched against him, hoping for victory. In such character do his opponents appear. However well you might discipline a crowd of men, yet they would not become a troop unless also they have been trained in warfare. A troop means a body of well-disciplined men, all of them prepared to fight, and understanding how to make war. Thus, all Christ's enemies were well trained. There was the Archfiend of Hell, who in hundreds of battles against the Lord's elect in the olden time had gotten a thorough knowledge of all the weak points of manhood, and understood how to temper his attack, and wherein lay the greatest chances of victory. After him were all the fiends of the pit, and these were all well exercised, each of them mighty, of giant stature like Goliath—all of them mighty to do great exploits with any man less than God, however mighty that man might be. And as for sin, was it not a mighty thing? Were not our sins all of them mighty to destroy? The least one among the sins that attacked Christ would have been sufficient to destroy the human race! and yet there were tens of thousands of these, well disciplined, ranged in order, and all thoroughly prepared for battle. All these came on in dread array against our Lord and Saviour Jesus Christ. It was a troop. I have not overdrawn this, for Calvin translates this term "a wedge," for in his day it was customary in battle for the soldiers to form themselves into a wedge-shape, so that when they attacked the enemy the first man made an opening, though he fell; the next two advanced, and then after them the three, and as the wedge widened it broke the ranks of the enemy. So it seemeth as though the Holy Spirit would here describe the regular and well-directed attack which the enemy of man's soul made upon Christ. He came against him in settled order. It was no rush of some wild Tartar host against the Saviour, it was a well-arranged and well-regulated attack; and yet, glory be to his name, he broke through the troop, and ran through them more than a conqueror. Another old and eminent commentator translates the term troop by the old Greek term a phalanx, to show again how strong, how mighty, how great and powerful were the enemies of Christ. It will often be of excellent use to us for the stimulation of our faith, and for the excitement of our gratitude, if we recollect the might of the enemies of Christ. When we undervalue the strength of his enemies, we are apt to under-estimate his omnipotence. We must go through the ranks of his foes, and look the ghastly opponents in the face; we must march through the long lines of our sins, and look at the hideous monsters, and see how mighty they are, and how powerless all human strength would have been to resist them; and then shall we learn in an ample measure to estimate the might and the majesty of the glorious Son of God, when, all unarmed and unassisted, he ran through the troop and put them all to the rout. Several different eminent expositors of God's Word give divers interpretations of this sentence, each suggesting a fresh meaning, and helping to bring out that which is certainly true, if not the precise meaning of the passage. One good translator says this verse might be rendered, "By thee have I ran to a troop;" and takes this to be the sense. Our Saviour is represented to us as not waiting till his enemies came to him, but running to them, willingly and voluntarily resigning himself to their attack. He did not wait till Judas should come to the upper room and salute him in the chamber as he sat at supper; neither did he tarry on his knees in that terrible agony of his in the olive grove; but he went forth to meet Judas. Judas had come forth with swords and with staves to take him as a thief; but he sought not to make an escape. "He went forth unto them, and said unto them, whom seek ye?" Thus did he manifest both his willingness to undertake our redemption, and also his courage in facing the foe. There was at one time a human fear which seemed as if it would hold him back from the battle, when he said, "Oh, my Father, if it be possible, let this cup pass from me;" but this once expressed, the Holy One of Israel anointed him with fresh courage, and to the battle he walked with slow, majestic steps. He would not wait till they rushed on him; but he would take the initiative, and begin the fight. He had come upon them in the garden; and now already with his own blood see the conquering hero rushes to the fight, and dashes through the troop. But look what divine mercy, what holy courage is here found in the Lord Jesus Christ, that he ran to our enemies.

"Down from the shining courts above
With joyful haste he fled;
Entered the grave in mortal flesh,
And dwelt amohg the dead."

He ran *to* a troop. But our version hath it, "He ran *through* a troop;" and this is also exceedingly accurate, if you couple with it the idea which you will find in the marginal readings of your Bibles. "By thee have I *broken* through a troop." Christ made a dash at his foes. They stood firm, as if they would not flinch before him, but his terrible right hand soon found for him a way. They imagined when his hands were nailed to the cross that now he was powerless; but that nail was the very symbol of his omnipotence, for in weakness was he strong. The bowing of his head, which they perhaps thought to be the symbol of his defeat, was but the symbol of his victory; and in dying he conquered, in suffering he overcame. Every wound that he received was a death-blow to his enemies, and every pang that rent his heart was as when a lion rendeth the prey, and Christ himself was rending them when they thought that they were rending him. He ran through a troop.

It will do your souls good if you have imagination enough to picture Christ running through this troop. How short were his sufferings comparatively! Compare them with the eternal weight of punishment and misery which we ought to have endured. What a stride was that which Jesus took when he marched right through his enemies, and laid them right and left, and gained himself a glorious victory. Samson, when he grasped the jaw-bone of an ass, slew his thousand men, and said, "Heaps upon heaps with the jaw-bone of an ass have I slain a thousand men," did it all in haste, and then threw away the jaw-bone, as if it were but little he had done. And even so our mightier Samson, meeting with the hosts of sin, and death, and hell, laid them all in heaps; and then crying out "It is finished," he seemed as strong and mighty as if he had not endured the fatigues of the fight, or suffered the horrors of death, and was ready, if they required it, to meet them all again, and give them another defeat. " By thee have I run through a troop."

There is yet another version. " By thee have I run *after* a troop." After our Saviour had met and fought with his antagonists, and conquered them, they fled. But he pursued them. He must not simply defeat, but take them prisoners. There was Old Captivity. You know his name. He had been the oppressor of the human race for many and many a day, and when Christ routed him he fled. But Jesus pursued, and binding him in adamantine chains, " He led captivity captive, and gave gifts to man." He pursued the troop, and brought back old Satan in chains, bound him in fetters, slew grim death, and ground his iron limbs to powder, and left his enemies no more at large to wander where they will, but subject to his divine power and to his omnipotent sway. He ran *after* a troop, and took them prisoners.

Perhaps, however, the most striking thing in our text is the combination of those two little words, " by thee." What, did not Christ fight and obtain victory by his own innate strength ? Did not the Son of God, the Redeemer, find strength enough within himself to do all that was necessary for us? It would not be heterodox if I were to assert that it was even so. And yet in Scripture you will constantly find that the condescension of Christ is eminently pointed out to us in the fact that, as the servant of God, and as our Redeemer, he is continually spoken of as being strengthened, assisted, and animated by his Father and the Holy Spirit. Especially will you notice this in the Book of Mark. The Evangelist Mark speaks of Christ through the whole of his book as a servant. Each of the Evangelists has a distinct view of Christ. Matthew speaks of him as a king, Mark as a servant, Luke as a man, and John as God. Now, in reading through Mark, you will observe, if you take the trouble to read it carefully, the recurrence of such phrases as this—" And *immediately* the Spirit driveth him into the wilderness." This follows close on his baptism, when the Holy Ghost descended on him as a dove. And then, when he came up to Nazareth, we read that, as a servant, Christ needed anointing as well as any other; and, when he begins to preach, his text is, " The Spirit of the Lord is upon me, because he hath anointed me to preach the gospel to the poor, and hath sent me to heal the broken-hearted." Now, I take it this is a very eminent instance of the condescension of our Divine Master, that he in all things was made like unto his brethren; and, as they are utterly powerless without the Holy Spirit, and without the Father's drawing can do nothing, so Jesus Christ did, as it were, divest himself of his own Divine power, and, as our brother, he fraternized even with our infirmities. Thus he was strengthened, helped, and assisted by his Father and by the Holy Spirit. Hence, it is strictly accurate to remark that even Christ himself could subscribe to this sentence —" *By thee* have I run through a troop."

Does it seem to you, beloved, to lower your hope in the person of Christ? At first sight it may seem so. But, think again; there is much rich consolation here. O, my soul, learn that thou hast not only God the Son to be thy helper, but that thou hast God the Father and God the Spirit also! Oh, 'tis sweet to see that in redemption itself, where we are too apt with our poor blind eyes to see but one person of the Trinity—in redemption itself the triune Jehovah was engaged. If this is not the view of the work of redemption which is commonly taken, I am sure it is Scriptural. It is true that the Son paid the penalty, and endured the agony; but still it was his Father who, while smiting him with one hand, sustained him with the other; and it was the Spirit who, wrapping him about with zeal as with a cloak, and inflaming his soul with divine ardor, enabled him to dash through his enemies, and become more than a conqueror. This sweetens redemption to me. The Father and the Holy Ghost also are engaged and interested on my behalf. Our Redeemer is the Holy One of Israel—the Lord of Hosts is his name. We may say of the three persons of the Divine Trinity that each of these is our Redeemer, because they have all brought to its full completion the grand work of our redemption from the power of sin, and death, and hell. " By thee have I run through a troop." My soul, lift up thine eyes ere thou turnest from this passage, and see all thy sins forgiven in the person of Christ. Look there, and behold the old dragon's head broken; see death pierced through with one of his own shafts. See how the old serpent drags along his mangled length, writhing in his agony, for " The Lord Jehovah is our strength and our song; he also has become our salvation; " and, in him, and through him, and by him, we have broken through a troop, and are more than conquerors.

Let us now take the second sentence, " By my God

have I leaped over a wall." How is this to be understood? I think that David, if we take this as alluding to David, is here described as having stormed and taken some strongly-munitioned and well-walled city. He had by the power of God taken the strength from the inhabitants of Jebus, and so he had leaped over a wall. But we are not now speaking of David but of Christ. In what sense can we say that Jesus Christ has stormed a wall? "By my God have I leaped over a wall." I must be allowed to be figurative for a few minutes. The people of the Lord had become the slaves of Satan, and that they might never more escape from his power, he had put them into his stronghold, and had walled them round about, that they might be his perpetual captives. There was, first of all, the tremendous bulwark of sin, gathering strength from the law, with its ten massive towers mounted with ten hundred pieces of ordnance, in the shape of threatenings of destruction. This wall was so high that no human being has ever been able to scale it; so terrible, that even the omnipotence of God had to be exercised before it could be removed. Next to this there was a second rampart; it was the rampart of diabolical insinuation and satanic suggestion. Satan had not only allowed the law to stand so as to keep the soul in despair, but had added to this his own determination that he would not leave a stone unturned, might he but keep the human race in his own power. Thus hell made the second rampart, while it seemed as if heaven had built the first. Outside thereof was a deep ditch, and then another mound, called Human Depravity. This, as we must observe, was as difficult to be stormed as either of the others. Man was desperately set on mischief. He would be a sinner, let what might be said to him or done for him. He would seek greedily with both hands to work out his own destruction; and that love of destruction which was in his heart constituted one of the great barriers to his salvation. Now, Christ Jesus came, and he leaped over all these walls. He came, and in your redemption he broke through the law. Nay, he did not break through it, he mounted it, he scaled it. The law of God stands to this day as fast and firm as ever; not a stone has been taken down; not one of its castles has been dismantled; there it stands in all its awful majesty, but Christ leaped over this. He paid the penalty, endured the wrath, and so he took his people out of the first ward of the law. Whereas, after this came a second, the wall of Satan's fell determination to keep them prisoners. Christ our Lord and Master dashed this into a thousand pieces, springing the tremendous mine of his covenant purposes, and throwing the whole mass into the air, and there it was destroyed once and for ever; no more to hold the people of God in captivity and bondage. The last wall which he had to overleap, in order to get his people thoroughly free, and bring them out of the stronghold of sin and Satan, was the wall of their own depravity. This, indeed, it were hard work to storm. Many of his ministers first of all went into the stronghold and tried to storm it; but they came away defeated. They found that this was too strong for all human battering rams. They hammered at it with all their might, but there it stood, resisting the shock, and seeming to gather strength from every blow that was meant to shake it. But, at last, Jesus came, and using nothing but his cross, as the most powerful battering ram, he shook the wall of our depravity and made a breach and entered in, and let his people out into that liberty wherewith he had made them free. Oh, how sweet it is to think of Christ thus leaping over the walls. He would have his people. He came down to earth and was with them in all their misery, and took upon him all their sin. He determined to enter in, and save them from the dungeon. He made his own escape and brought them with him. He not only came himself through sin, and death, and hell triumphant, but brought all his children on his shoulders, as Æneas did his old father Anchises. The whole generation of the elect was redeemed in that hour when Christ leaped over every wall.

Thus, have I tried to expound to you the text as relating to the person of our blessed Lord and Saviour Jesus Christ. I would only repeat the remark once more, that in this verse it is said, "By my God have I done it." As mediator, in his official capacity, and in his service for our redemption, he received the strengthening assistance and aid of his Divine Father, and he could truly say, "By my God have I leaped over a wall." It will do thee good, O believer, if thou wilt often stay and look at thy Saviour accomplishing all his triumphs. O my soul, what wouldst thou have done if he had not broken through a troop, if he had not routed them? Where wouldst thou have been? Thou wouldst at this hour have been the captive of sin, and death, and hell. All thy sins would now be besetting thee, howling in thine ear for vengeance. Satan, with all the hosts of hell, would be now guarding thee, determining thou shouldst never escape. Oh, how joyous is this fact, that he had once for all routed them, and now we are secure. Then, my soul, bethink thee, what wouldst thou have done if he had not leaped over a wall? Thou wouldst have been dead this day, shut within the rampart of thine own hard heart, or within the stronghold of Satan, and with the mighty fiends of hell thou wouldst have been trebly guarded and trebly enslaved. Now thy fetters are all broken, as " a monument of grace, a sinner saved by blood." Lift up thy heart, and thy hands, and thy voice, and shout for joy and for gladness, " He hath broken the gates of brass, and cut the bars of iron in sunder." He hath leaped over a wall, and brought thee out of thy prison-house.

This brings me now to the second part of my discourse, and I must ask your patience, and pray again for the assistance of the Holy Spirit, that in this especially Christ's people may find a word of edification. We are now to regard our text as being the language of the believer. He can say, " By thee have I run through a troop, and by my God have I leaped over a wall." I shall divide my text after another fashion on this second point. I shall note, first, with regard to the believer, his trials—how varied! Sometimes it is a troop of enemies; at another time a wall of difficulties. When a man has one labor to accomplish, he soon begins to be skilful in it. If he is to be a soldier, and fight a troop, at length he learns how to get the victory. But, suppose that his labors are varied; after fighting a troop he has to go clambering over a wall, then you will see the critical situations by which he is embarrassed. Now, this aptly pictures the position of God's people; the Spirit is continually varying our trials. There is no one day's trials that are exactly like the trials of another day. We are not called to one undeviating temptation, or else it would cease to have its force; but the temptations are erratic—the darts are shot from different directions, and the stones come from quite opposite quarters. This is well set out in one of the Lord's parables. He speaks of the trials of the righteous thus:—There was a certain wise man who built his house upon a rock, and the rains descended—trials from above; and the floods came—trials from beneath; the winds blew—mysterious trials from every quarter; and they all beat upon that house, and it fell not. Trials of every shape attend the followers of the Lamb. "A Christian man is seldom long at ease; when one trial's gone another doth him seize." The archers come against us, and we receive their fiery darts; anon the company of swordsmen come, and we rebuke them; and then the slingers sling their stones against us, and then the company of spearsmen; so that we must be armed at all points, and ready for every kind of attack. Our Saviour in this was like to us. He says to us in one place, " Dogs have compassed me—that was bad enough—but the bulls of Bashan have beset me round; that was not all, they gaped upon me with their mouths, as a raving and a roaring lion." Only fancy that! A man has to fight with dogs, and then to fight with bulls, and then with lions. And yet, this is just the Christian's state. We cannot guess from the trials of the past what will be the trials of the future; we think it is to be all fighting, but we are mistaken; some part of it is to be climbing over this or that wall, and anon make way through obstructions that will not yield. Now, I have known God's people sometimes try to break through a wall, and sometimes try to climb over a troop. This is very absurd. If they have had a troop of spiritual enemies, they have tried to climb over them, and endeavor to escape them. At another time they have had a difficult trial like a wall, and they have been so headstrong they must try to go through it. Ah! we have much to learn. Some things we must fight through, others we must climb over. It is not always right for the child of God to let his courage get the better of his discretion. Let him have courage for the troop to run through them, and discretion for the wall, and not try to run through that, or he will break himself in pieces. There are exercises and trials in various ways. The believer's trials—how varied! And, next to this, notice his faith—how unflinching!

There is the troop, he runs through them; there is the wall, he is ready for that—he leaps over it. He finds that his faith is sufficient for every emergency. When his God is with him there is difficulty too great for him; he does not stop to deliberate—as for the troop, he runs through that; and then there is a wall at the other end—he takes a leap and is over that. So when God enables our faith, when the Holy One of Israel is with us, and the strength of Omnipotence girds our loins, difficulties are only the healthy exercise of our faith. God will exercise faith. There is not a single grain of faith in the breast of any living believer that is not exercised. God will not allow it to sleep—a sleeping faith, a dormant faith, I believe such a thing don't exist. If thou hast faith, my brother, expect labor; for, as sure as God gives faith, he will put it into the gymnasium and make it exercise itself; sometimes dashing at a troop, and then trying its limbs another way, no more to exercise its arm in fighting, but its knees in prayer; to climb over a hill; all sorts of exercises to keep our faith in order that we may be ready for any exercise, whatever it may be. Some men seem as if they only had to meet one form of trial. They remind me of the Indian Fakir; he holds his arm straight up; that is the triumph of his strength. Now, God does not exercise a believer's limbs till they grow stiff; but he exercises them in every way, that they may become supple, so that, come what may, he is ready to achieve any exploit.

With faith, how easy all exploits become! When we have no faith, then to fight with enemies and overcome difficulties is hard work indeed; but, when we have faith, oh, how easy our victories! What does the believer do? There is a troop—well, he runs through it. 'Tis but a matter of morning exercise. There is a wall. What about that? Does he climb over with hands and knees, as a long, hard task, putting up a ladder on one side, and pulling it over on the other? It is amazing how easy life becomes when a man has faith. Does faith diminish difficulties? Oh, no! it increaseth them; but it increaseth his strength to overcome them. If thou hast faith, thou shalt have trials; but thou shalt do great exploits, endure great privations, and get triumphant victories. Have you ever seen a man made mighty through God? But have you ever seen him in an hour of desertion? He goes out like Samson to meet the Philistines. "Oh!"

says he, "I will shake myself as at other times." But his locks have been shorn, and when the cry is raised, "The Philistines are upon thee, Samson," he shakes his limbs with vast surprise, makes feeble fight, and loses his eyes. They are put out, and he returns in blindness.

But, when God is with him, see what the believer can do. They have weaved the seven locks of his head with a web, and he takes and carries the loom away. Anon they bind him with seven green withs that have never been tried. All things are possible to him that believeth; nay, not only possible, but easy, when God is with him. He laughs at impossibilities, and says it shall be done, for faith can do all things. "By my God have I run through a troop; by my God have I leaped over a wall." And yet, though the victories of faith are thus easy, we must call to mind that these victories always are to be traced to a divine source. That man who takes the credit of his victories to himself hath no faith, for faith is one of the self-denying graces. Faith called a parliament of all the graces, and passed a self-denying ordinance. It decreed that whatever any of the graces did it should give all the glory of it to God. Christ once upon a time took the crown off his own head, and put it on the head of faith. "When was that?" say you. Why, Christ healed the poor woman, and therefore it was HE who deserved the crown; but, saith he, "Thy faith hath saved thee; go and sin no more." He thus put the crown upon faith. What was the reason? Why, because faith always puts its crown on the head of Christ. True faith never wears its own crown. It says, "Not unto me, but unto thy name, Lord, be all the glory." This is the reason why God has selected faith to achieve such mighty victories; because faith will not allow the glory or honor to cleave to its own wings, but shakes off all self-praise, just as Paul did the viper into the fire. Faith says, "No, no. Give me not thanks, or praise, or honor. I have done nothing." Faith will have it not only that it does nothing, but that Christ, which dwelleth in it, has done it all; and faith has been known to say, "I want none of your palms, ye belong to Christ, not to me." It will have nothing to do with honor, Christ must have every atom of it.

And now, my dear friends, there is one consolation with which I will close this sermon. The psalmist says, "By thee have I run through a troop; and by my God have I leaped over a wall." I think if he were here at this time he would permit me to add, "And by my God *shall* I leap over a wall, and by thee *shall* I break through many a troop." What faith has done once by its God, it can do again. We have met Satan once in the battle-field, and when he chooses to attack us once more that old Jerusalem blade that gave him a bitter blow once is ready to give him another. That shield which once caught his fiery darts is still unbroken, and still prepared to receive another portion of them when he chooses to hurl them. Martin Luther, you know, often used to defy Satan to battle. I care not to do that; but he used to say, in his queer, quaint way, "I often laugh at Satan, and there is nothing makes him so angry as when I attack him to his face, and tell him that through God I am more than a match for him; tell him to do his worst, and yet I will beat him;

and tell him to put forth his fury, and yet I will overcome him." This would be presumption if in our own strength. It is only faith in the providence of God that can enable us to say so. He that has made God his refuge need fear no storm; but just as sometimes in Christmas weather the wind and snow and storm outside make the family fire seem warmer, and the family circle seem happier, so the trials and temptations of Satan do sometimes seem to add to the very peace and happiness of the true believer while he sits wrapped up in the mantle of godly confidence.

> " Let cares like a wild deluge come,
> And storms of sorrow fall ;
> May I but safely reach my home,
> My God, my heaven, my all."

And when we know that we shall reach our home, even the storms or the tempests matter but little. Come, poor believer, pluck up thy courage. I have tried to give thee some strong meat. Feed upon it. As the Lord Jesus Christ had a troop to face, and broke through them, so shalt thou. Even as he overcame, so shalt thou overcome. Did he enter heaven, and is there a long cloud of witnesses streaming in behind him, every one a warrior? So if thou art his warrior thou shalt be one of that long stream; thou shalt also wear a crown, and wave the palm, and sing a song of victory, and talk of triumph purchased through the blood of, and achieved through faith in, the Lamb.

I must pause one moment while I address myself to those who know nothing of God, and nothing of Christ. Well, my hearers, you have a troop too, and you have your walls of difficulty; but you have no God to help you! Whatever trials the believer has, he has a God to fly to. "Look," said a poor woman to a lady who called to see her, "Look, ma'am, I'll show you all I'm worth. Do you see that cupboard, ma'am? Look in." The lady looked in, and saw nothing. "Do you see *this* cupboard?" said the woman. "Yes," said the lady, "but there is nothing in it but a dry crust." "Well," continued the woman, "do you see this chest?" "Yes, I see it; but it is empty," was the reply. "Well," said she, "that is all I am worth, ma'am; but I have not a doubt or fear with regard to my temporal affairs. My God is so good that I can still live without doubts and fears." She knew what it was to break through a troop and leap over a wall. Now, perhaps, there are some of you with cupboards just as empty as that poor woman's; but, you cannot add, "I have a God to go to." O miserable creature—miserable if you are rich, thrice miserable if you are poor—to be like a packhorse in this life, carrying a heavy burden, and then not to be unloaded at the grave, but to have a double burden laid upon you. O poor men and women without Christ—with the few comforts which you have in this life, with its many privations, with its hunger, and thirst, and nakedness, oh, that you should not have a better world to go to! Above all, it seems a miserable thing that you should go through poverty here to a place where a drop of water shall be denied you to cool your burning tongue! If Christ is precious to the rich on earth, you must think that there is a peculiar sort of relish with which the poor man feeds on the bread of heaven. But, you say,

"May I not have a hope of heaven?" Assuredly, my friend. Dost thou long for Christ this moment? Then, he longs for thee. Dost thou desire to have him? Then he gives thee that desire. Come thou to him, for the word of the gospel is, "Whosoever will, let him come and take of the water of life freely." None are excluded; none but those who do themselves exclude. The invitation is free. May the application be effectual! Oh, that some of you may be led to go to your houses now, and on your knees ask for forgiveness of sin, and seek that you may become the children of God, through faith in the precious blood once shed for many for the remission of sins.

Christ the Tree of Life.

"In the midst of the street of it, and on either side of the river, was there the tree of life, which bare twelve manner of fruits, and yielded her fruit every month: and the leaves of the tree were for the healing of the nations."—REVELATION xxii. 2.

YOU will remember that in the first Paradise there was a tree of life in the midst of the garden. When Adam had offended, and was driven out, it was said, "Lest he put forth his hand, and take of the tree, and eat, and live for ever, therefore God drove out the man." It has been supposed by some, that this tree of life in the garden of Eden was intended to be the means of continuing man in immortality, that his feeding upon it would have supported him in the vigor of unfailing youth, preserved him from exposure to decay, and imparted by a spiritual regeneration, the seal of perpetuity to his constitution. I do not know about that. If it were so, I can understand the reason why God would not have the first man, Adam, become immortal in the lapsed state he then was, but ordained that the old nature should die, and that the immortality should be given to a new nature, which should be formed under another leadership, and quickened by another spirit.

The text tells us that in the centre of the new Paradise, the perfect Paradise of God, from which the saints shall never be driven, seeing it is to be our perpetual heritage, there is also a tree of life. But here we translate the metaphor. We do not understand anything literal at all. We believe our Lord Jesus Christ to be none other than that tree of life, whose leaves are for the healing of the nations. We can scarcely conceive of any other interpretation, as this seems to us to be so full of meaning, and to afford us such unspeakable satisfaction.

At any rate, beloved, if this be not the absolute purpose of the sublime vision that John saw, it is most certainly true that our Lord Jesus Christ is life from the dead, and life to his own living people. He is all in all to them, and by him, and by him alone must their spiritual life be maintained. We are right enough, then, in saying that Jesus Christ is a tree of life, and we shall so speak of him, in the hope that some may come and pluck of the fruit, and eat, and live for ever. Our desire shall be so to use the sacred allegory that some poor dying soul may be encouraged to lay hold on eternal life, by laying hold on Jesus Christ.

First, *we shall take the tree of life in the winter with no fruit on it;* secondly, *we shall try to show you the tree of life budding and blossoming;* and, thirdly, *we shall endeavor to show you the way to partake of its fruits.*

I. And first, my brethren, I have to speak to you of JESUS CHRIST, THE TREE OF LIFE IN THE WINTER.

You will at once anticipate that I mean by this figure to describe *Jesus in his sufferings*, in his dark wintry days, when he did hang upon the cross, and bleed, and die; when he had no honor from men, and no respect from any; when even God the Father hid his face from him for a season, and he was made a curse for us, that we might be made the righteousness of God in him. My dear friends, you will never see the tree of life aright, unless you first look at the cross. It was there that this tree gathered strength to bring forth its after-fruit. It was there, we say, that Jesus Christ, by his glorious merits and his wondrous work achieved upon the cross, obtained power to become the Redeemer of our souls, and the Captain of our salvation.

Come with me, then, by your faith, to the foot of the little mound of Calvary, and let us look up and see this thing that came to pass. Let us turn aside as Moses did when the bush burned, and see this great sight. It is the greatest marvel that ever earth, or hell, or heaven beheld, and we may well spend a few minutes in beholding it.

Our Lord Jesus, the ever-living, the immortal, the eternal, became man, and, being found in fashion as a man, he humbled himself, and died the death of the cross. That death was not on his own account. His humanity had no need to die. He might have lived on, and have seen no death if so he willed. He had committed no offence, no sin, and therefore no punishment could fall upon him.

> "For sins not his own
> He died to atone."

Every pang upon the cross was substitutionary; and

for you, ye sons of men, the Prince of Glory bled, the just for the unjust, that he might bring you to God. There was no smart for himself, for his Father loved him with a love ineffable; and he deserved no blows from his Father's hand, but his smarts were for the sins of his enemies, for your sins and mine, that by his stripes we might be healed, and that through his wounds, reconciliation might be made with God.

Think, then, of the Saviour's death upon the cross. Mark ye well that *it was an accursed death*. There were many ways by which men might die, but there was only one death which God pronounced to be accursed. He did not say—Cursed is he that dies by stoning, or by the sword, or by a millstone being fastened about his neck, or by being eaten of worms, but it was written—" Cursed is every one that hangeth on a tree." By no other death than that one, which God did single out as the death of the accursed, could Jesus Christ die. Admire it, believer, that Jesus Christ should be made a curse for us. Admire, and love; let your faith and your gratitude blend together.

It was a death *of the most ignominious kind*. The Roman law subjected only felons to it, and I believe not even felons, unless they were slaves. A freed Roman must not so die, nor a subject of any of the kingdoms that Rome had conquered, but only the slave who was bought and sold in the market could be put to this death. They counted him worthy to be sold as a slave, and then they put him to a slave's death for you. Besides, they added to the natural scorn of the death *their own ridicule*. Some passed by and wagged their heads. Some stood still and thrust out their tongues.

Others sat down and watched him there, and satisfied their malice and their scorn. He was made the centre of all sorts of ridicule and shame. He was the drunkard's song, and even they that were crucified with him reviled him. And all this he suffered for us. Our sin was shameful, and he was made to be a shame. We had disgraced ourselves and dishonored God, and therefore Jesus was joined with the wicked in his death, and made as vile as they.

Besides, *the death was exceedingly painful*. We must not forget the pangs of the Saviour's body, for I believe when we begin to depreciate the corporeal sufferings, we very soon begin to drag down the spiritual sufferings too. It must be a fearful death by which to die, when the tender hands and feet are pierced, and when the bones are dislocated by the jar of erecting the cross, and when the fever sets in, and the mouth becomes as hot as an oven, and the tongue is swollen in the mouth, and the only moisture given is vinegar mingled with gall. Ah! beloved, the pangs that Jesus knew, none of us can guess. We believe that Hart has well described it when he says that he bore—

"All that incarnate God could bear,
With strength enough and none to spare."

You cannot tell the price of griefs, and groans, and sighs, and heart-breakings, and soul-tearings, and rendings of the spirit, which Jesus had to pay that he might redeem us from our iniquities.

It was a lingering death. However painful a death may be, it is always satisfactory to think that it is soon over. When a man is hanged, after our English custom, or the head is taken from the body, the pain may be great for the instant, but it is soon over and gone. But in crucifixion a man hangs so long, that when Pilate found the Saviour dead, he marvelled that he was dead already. I remember to have heard a missionary say, that he saw a man in Burmah crucified, and that he was alive two days after having been nailed to the cross; and I believe there are authenticated stories of persons who have been taken down from the cross after having hung for forty-eight hours, and after all have had their wounds healed, and have lived for years. It was a lingering death that the Saviour had to die.

Oh! my brethren, if you put these items together, they make up a ghastly total, which ought to press upon our hearts—if we be believers, in the form of grateful affection, or if we be unbelievers, provoking us to shame that we do not love him who loved the sons of men so much.

And *the death of the Lord Jesus Christ for us*, we must also add, *was penal*. He died the death of the condemned. Perhaps most men would feel this to be the worst feature, for if a man shall die by never so painful a death, if it be accidental it misses the sting which must come into it, if it be caused by law, and if especially it be brought by sin, and after sentence has been passed in due form. Now, our Lord Jesus Christ was condemned by the civil and ecclesiastical tribunals of the country to die. And what was more—" It pleased the Father to bruise him; he hath put him to grief." Jesus Christ died without sin of his own, but he died a penal death, because our sins were counted to him. He took upon him our iniquities as though they were his own, and then, being found in the sinner's place, he suffered, as if he had been a sinner, the wrath that was due for sin.

Beloved, I wish it were in my power to set forth Christ crucified—Christ visibly crucified amongst you! Oh! that I could so paint him that the eyes of your heart could see him! I wish that I could make you feel the dolor of his griefs, and sip that bitter cup which he had to drain to the dregs. But, if I cannot do this, it shall suffice me to say that that death is the only hope of sinners. Those wounds of his are the gates to heaven. The smarts and sufferings of Immanuel are the only expiatory sacrifice for human guilt. Oh, ye who would be saved, turn your eyes hither. Look unto him and be saved, all ye ends of the earth. There is life in a look at him; but there is life nowhere else. Despise him, and you perish. Accept him, and you shall never perish, neither shall all the powers of hell devour you. Come, guilty souls! Jesus wants not your tears or your blood; his tears can cleanse you; his blood can purify you. If your heart be not as broken as you would have it, it is his broken heart, not yours, that shall merit heaven for you. If you cannot be what you would, he was for you what God would have him. God is contented with him. Be you contented. Come and trust him! Oh, now may delays be over and difficulties all be solved, and just as you are, without one plea, but that the Saviour bled, come to your heavenly father, and you shall be accepted in the beloved.

Thus, then—Jesus Christ hanging on the cross—is the Tree of Life in its winter.

II. And now, let me show you, as I may be enabled,

THAT SELFSAME TREE OF LIFE WHEN IT HAD BLOSSOMED AND BROUGHT FORTH FRUIT.

There he stands—Jesus—still Jesus—the same, and yet how changed! The same Jesus, but clothed with honor instead of shame, able now to save them to the uttermost that come unto him. My text says of this tree that it bears twelve manner of fruits. I suppose that is intended to signify that a perfect and complete assortment of all supplies for human necessities are to be found in Christ—all sorts of mercies for all sorts of sinners; all kinds of blessings to suit all kinds of necessities. We read of the palm-tree, that every bit of it is useful, from its root to its fruit. So it is with the Lord Jesus Christ. There is nothing in him that we could afford to do without. There is nothing about Jesus that is extraneous or superfluous. You can put him to use in every part, in every office, in every relationship.

A tree of life is for food. Some trees yield rich fruit. Adam in the garden lived only on the fruit of the field. Jesus Christ is the food of his people, and what dainties they have! What satisfying food, what plenteous food, what sweet food, what food precisely suitable to all the wants of their souls Jesus is! As for manna, it was angels' food; but what shall I say of Christ? He is more than that!

"Never did angels taste above,
Redeeming grace and dying love."

Oh! how you are fed! The flesh of God's own Son is the spiritual meat of every heir of heaven. Hungry souls, come to Jesus if you would be fed.

Jesus *gives his people drink* also. There are some tropical trees which, as soon as they are tapped, yield liquids as sweet and rich as milk, and many drink and are refreshed by them. Jesus Christ's heart-blood is the wine of his people. The atonement which he has perfected by his sufferings is the golden cup out of which they drink, and drink again, till their mourning souls are made glad, and their fainting souls are strengthened and refreshed. Jesus gives us the water of life—the wines on the lees well refined, the wine and milk, without money and without price. What a tree of life to yield us both meat and drink!

Jesus is a tree of life *yielding clothing* too. Adam went to the fig-tree for his garments, and the fig-leaves yielded him such covering as they could. But we come to Christ and we find, not fig-leaves, but a robe of righteousness that is matchless for its beauty, comely in its proportions; one which will never wear out, which exactly suits to cover our nakedness from head to foot, and when we put it on makes us fair to look upon, even as Christ himself. Oh, ye who would be rearrayed till ye shall be fit to stand among the courtiers of the skies, come ye to Jesus, and find garments from the Tree of Life!

This tree also yields medicine. "The leaves thereof were for the healing of the nations." Lay a plaster upon my wound, and if it be but the plaster of King Jesus, it will heal it. But one promise from his lips; but one leaf from the tree; but one word from his Spirit; but one drop of his blood, and this is heaven's court-plaster indeed. It is true, there is no balm in Gilead; there is no physician there; and, therefore, the hurt of the daughter of Israel's people was not healed. But there *is* balm in Jesus; there *is* a physician at Calvary, and the hurt of the daughter of God's people shall be healed if she do but fly to Jesus Christ for her healing.

And, what shall I more say? Is there anything else your spirits can want? Oh, children of God, Christ is all? Oh, ye ungodly ones, who have been roaming the wood, there to find the tree that should supply your wants—stop here. This "apple-tree among the trees of the wood" is the tree which your souls require. Stay here, and you shall have all you need. For, listen—this tree *yields a shelter from the storm.* Other trees are dangerous when the tempest howls; but he that shelters beneath the tree of the Lord Jesus shall find that all the thunder-bolts of God shall fly by him, and do him no injury. He cannot be hurt that clings to Jesus. Heaven and earth should sooner pass away than a soul be lost that hides beneath the boughs of this tree. And oh, you who have hidden there to shelter from the wrath of God, let me remind you that in every kind of danger it will also yield you shelter; and if you are not in danger, yet still in the hot days of care you shall find the shade of it to be cool and genial.

"I sat down under the shadow with great delight, and his fruit was sweet unto my taste." Get Christ, and you have got comfort, joy, peace, and liberty; and, when the trouble comes, you shall find shelter and deliverance by coming near to him. He is the tree of life, then, yielding twelve manner of fruits, those fruits being always ripe and always ready, for they ripen every month, all being free to all who desire them, for the leaves are not for the healing of some, but "for the healing of the nations." What a large word! Then there are enough of these leaves for the healing of all the nations that shall ever come. Oh! may God grant that none of you may die from spiritual sickness when these leaves can heal you, and may none of you be filling yourselves with the sour grapes of this world, the poisonous grapes of sin, while the sweet fruits of Christ's love are waiting, which would refresh you and satisfy you.

III. And now, I have to show HOW TO GET AT THE FRUIT OF THIS TREE OF LIFE.

That is the main matter. Little does it boot to tell that there is fruit, unless we can tell how it can be got at. Oh! I wish that some here really wanted to know the way, but I am afraid many care very little about it. Dr. Payson had once been out to tea with one of his people, who had been particularly hospitable to him, and when he was going, the doctor said: —" Well, now, Madam, you have treated me exceedingly well, but how do you treat my Master?" That is a question I should like to put to some of you. How do you treat my Master? Why, you treat him as if he were not Christ, as if you did not want him. But, you do need him. May you find him soon, for when you come to die, you will want him then, and perhaps then you may not find him.

Well, *the way to get the fruit from this tree is by faith.* That is the hand that plucks the golden apple. Canst thou believe? That is the thing. Canst thou believe that Jesus is the Son of God; that he died upon the cross? "Yes," sayest thou, "I believe that." Canst thou believe that in consequence of his sufferings he is able to save? "Ay," sayest thou. Canst thou believe that he will save thee? Wilt thou trust him to save thee? If so, thou art saved. If thy soul comes to

Jesus, and says—"My Lord, I believe in thee, that thou art able to save to the uttermost, and now I throw myself upon thee"—that is faith. When Mr. Andrew Fuller was going to preach before an association, he rode to the meeting on his horse. There had been a good deal of rain, and the rivers were very much swollen. He got to one river which he had to cross. He looked at it, and he was half afraid of the strong current, as he did not know the depth. A farmer, who happened to be standing by, said —"It is all right, Mr. Fuller; you will get through it all right, sir; the horse will keep its feet." Mr. Fuller went in, and the water got up to the girth, and then up to the saddle, and he began to get uncomfortably wet. Mr. Fuller thought he had better turn round, and he was going to do so, when the same farmer shouted—"Go on, Mr. Fuller; go on; I know it is all right;" and Mr. Fuller said, "Then I will go on; I will go by faith." Now, sinner, it is very like that with you. You think that your sins are too deep, that Christ will never be able to carry you over them; but, I say to you—It is all right, sinner; trust Jesus, and he will carry you through hell itself, if it were needful and possible. If you had all the sins of all the men that have ever lived, and they were all yours, if you could trust him, Jesus Christ would carry you through the current of all that sin. It is all right, man! Only trust Christ. The river may be deep, but Christ's love is deeper still. It is all right, man! Do not let the devil make you doubt my Lord and Master. He is a liar from the beginning, and the father of lies, but my Master is faithful and true. Rest on him and it is all right. The waves may roll, the river may seem to be deeper than you thought it to be, and rest assured it is much deeper than you know it to be. But the mighty arm of Jesus—that strong arm that can shake the heavens and the earth, and move the pillars thereof as Samson moved the pillars of Gaza's gates—that strong arm can hold you up, and bear you safely through, if you do but cling to it, and rest in it. Oh soul, rest in Jesus, and you are saved!

Once again. If at the first you do not seem to get this fruit from the tree, shake it by prayer. "Oh!" say you, "I have been praying." Yes, but a tree does not always drop its fruit at the first shake you give it. Shake it again, man; give it another shake! And sometimes when the tree is loaded, and is pretty firm in the earth, you have to shake it to and fro, and at last you plant your feet, and get a hold of it, and shake it with might and main, till you strain every muscle and sinew to get the fruit down. And that is the way to pray. Shake the tree of life until the mercy drops into your lap. Christ loves for men to beg hard. You cannot be too importunate. That which might be disagreeable to your fellow-creatures when you beg of them, will be agreeable to Christ. Oh! get ye to your chambers; get ye to your chambers, ye that have not found Christ! To your bed-sides, to your little closets, and "seek the Lord while he may be found; call ye upon him while he is near!" May the Spirit of God constrain you to pray. May he constrain you to continue in prayer. Jesus must hear you. The gate of heaven is open to the sturdy knocker that will not take a denial. The Lord enable you so to plead, that at last you will say—" Thou hast heard my voice and my supplication; Thou hast inclined thine ear unto me; therefore will I pray unto thee as long as I live."

May God add his blessing to these rambling thoughts, for Jesus' sake. Amen.

A Silly Dove.

"Ephraim also is like a silly dove without heart."—HOSEA vii. 11

THE race of Ephraim is not extinct. Men are to this day very much like what they were in the days of the prophets. The same rebukes are still suitable, as well as the same comforts. As man has altered very little, if at all, in his outward bodily conformation, so has he not varied in the inner constitution; he is much the same to-day as he was in the time of Hosea. In this congregation, in the midst of this City of London, we have too large a company of those who are "like the silly dove without heart."

To proceed at once with the text, I want you to notice four things; first, *a saintly similitude;* secondly, *a secret distinction;* thirdly, *a severe description;* and lastly, *a serious consideration.*

I. Here we have A SAINTLY SIMILITUDE. "Ephraim is like a dove." The people are not compared here to the eagle that soareth aloft and scenteth its prey from afar, nor to the vulture which delights to gorge itself with carrion; they are not likened to any foul and unclean bird which was put aside under the law; but the very figure which is constantly chosen to set forth the beauty of holiness, to describe the believer, and to picture the whole church—nay, that very emblem by which we set forth him who is holiness itself, God the Holy Spirit—that same comparison to a dove is here used to describe those who were without heart. "Ephraim is like a dove"—it is a saintly similitude. Let me remind you that in all congregations there are those who are *like* doves, but not Christ's doves, who never build their nests in the clefts of the rock, in the bosom of the Saviour. They are *like* doves; you can never tell them from genuine believers, and like doves they are perfectly harmless; they do no mischief to others in their lives. Track them, if you will, you will never find them in the ale-house; they sing not the song of the drunkard; no man ever loses anything in business by them. Men may have their pockets picked in the streets, but never by them. Persons may go staggering home under a wound, but that wound never comes from their hand; there is no uncleanness in their heart, and no slander on their tongue; they are amiable, admirable; we might almost hold them up for examples of propriety. Alas! alas! that we have only to look within to find that they are not what they seem.

Moreover, being like doves for harmlessness, they are also like them for loving good company. We find not the dove flying with a host of eagles, but it consorts with its own kind. And oh, how some of you are never happier than when you are either in the Tabernacle or else in some of the classes formed by various members of the congregation! You also find such a pleasant excitement in the prayer-meeting that you are not absent from it except when you are prevented by business. You love being where God's people go; their hymns are sweet to your ears, in their prayers you find some sort of comfort, and in the ministry of the word you take delight. You fly like a cloud and like doves to their windows, and it is a joy to us to see you do it, and yet it may be that, although you know how to congregate like doves, you are " like a silly dove without heart."

Moreover, these persons are still more like the dove, in that they have the same meekness, apparently, as distinguishes the dove. "They hear as my people hear, and sit as my people sit." They are not sceptics; they never object to the exposition of the doctrines to which they listen; they pick no holes in the preacher's coat—they have no particular fault to find either with the style or the matter of his discourse; they decorously frequent the house of God, and behave themselves in a seemly manner when there; nay, more than that, they do seem with meekness to receive the word, though they do not receive it as engrafted into their own hearts; they even receive it with joy when the seed is scattered on them, but having no root in themselves, the good seed comes to nothing. Oh, my dear hearers, it is a great subject for thanksgiving that so many of you are ready and willing to listen to the word with deep and profound respect; but I do beseech you to remember that you may in this be like unto the dove, and yet, after all that, you may be taken in the same net and destroyed with the same destruction as that which fell upon the Ephraimites, who were "like a silly dove without heart."

The dove, you know, is a cleanly feeder, and so we have many who get as far as that. They know the distinction between the precious and the vile; they will not feed on law, they can only live on grace; they have come to know the doctrines of the gospel, and they feed on them—upon pure corn well winnowed. You have only to bring in a little free-will, and straightway they know the chaff from the wheat, and refuse to receive it; they cast it away as refuse metal, which is of no value to them. But, while they have an orthodox head, they have a heterodox heart; while they know the truth and feel it, yet still it is not the right kind of feeling; they have never so received it as to incorporate it into their very being; they have accepted it with the same sort of belief, and in somewhat the same manner, as Simon did in Samaria; but, after awhile, when trouble and persecution shall come, and wax too hot, they will turn aside.

But, I have to add yet further here, that there are some of these persons who are like doves in another respect still more singular. As a dove is molested by all sorts of birds of prey, so these persons do for a time share the lot which befalls the people of God. Why, there are some who for the mere coming to the house of God get nicknamed. They are not saints, but they have to bear the rebuke of saints; and I know some, who have turned out great sinners, that have for a time put up with much scoffing and rebuke for the sake of Christ. When pointed at in the street, it has been part of the manliness of their character to acknowledge that they did frequent such a place of worship. Though their soul has never been stricken by the divine word, yet it has become so sweet in their ear, that they are willing to bear some degree of reproach and scoffing for the sake of it. I should not like to be compelled to say precisely wherein the saint is to be distinguished by outward signs, for really the counterfeits now-a-days are so much like the genuine, that it shall need the wisdom of the infallible God himself to discern between the one and the other. We can have false faith, false repentance, false hope, and false good works. We have all sorts of shammings—paint, varnish, tinsel—and we may so grain that a skilful eye shall scarcely know whether it is the genuine wood or the artists' skill. There are ways of preparing metals, and sometimes the alloy shall seem to have in it for some purposes qualities which the unalloyed metal might lack. O Lord, searcher of hearts, do thou search us, lest we should have applied to us saintly names, and possess a saintly reputation and character, and hold saintly offices, and after all be cast away with the rubbish over the wall, and left to be consumed for ever and ever! But, enough on that point.

II. We have now to call your attention to A SECRET DISTINCTION. "Ephraim is like a dove *without heart.*"

This implies a lack of understanding. The dove knows but little, and experience scarcely teaches it anything. We may almost spread the snare in the sight of that bird, and yet it will fly to it; it is so silly. It does not seem to possess, at least to the outward eye, the wits and senses of some others of the feathered tribe. It has little or no understanding. And oh, how many there are who are like the dove externally, and have no real knowledge of the truth! They rest in the letter, and think that is enough. I solemnly believe that there are thousands that have not the shadow of an idea of the meaning of the words which they hear every Sabbath-day in a form of prayer. They go through those prayers; that they would do if the words were put in any other way. Doubtless they would get as much good out of them, if they were thrown together in wild disorder, as they do out of the beautiful and magnificent array in which they are marshalled. Many who come and hear the most simple prayers go away and say, "It is a riddle to me; I cannot understand how people will sit and listen to that." Either they condemn them as trite or else as fanatical. They cannot understand them. You may fetch a clodhopper, and set before him the masterpiece of an eminent old painter, and tell him, "That picture is worth sixty thousand pounds." He looks, opens his mouth, stares again, and says he can't make anything of it; he can't see where the money could go. He'd sooner have carts, and horses, and pigs, and cows, and sheep. He sees nothing in that. Well, now, to some extent, we might almost sympathize with him; but the high art critics despise the man at once for having no soul above his clod. And, it is just the same in spiritual things. Exhibit the glories of the person of Christ, and the matchless wisdom of the plan of salvation; that man can see nothing in it; "It is, no doubt, a very good and very proper thing," he will attend to it, and so on; and then he goes to church, and thinks he is pious, sits in his seat, and goes through the routine, and then supposes he is reconciled to God. Oh! how many such silly doves we have fluttering in and out of our places of worship. As a quaint old preacher said, there were scarce seats for the saints on account of the number of simpletons that came to listen.

But, again, they were silly doves without heart, because, lacking an understanding heart, they also lacked a decided heart. Sometimes, however, the dove would be slandered if we should use her as a metaphor in this respect. Have you not seen the dove, when, from afar, with her quick eye, she has seen her cot, fly straight away, over miles of sea and land, straight to her beloved home? There she could not be used as a metaphor of the ungodly, but of a child of Jesus, who thus flies to him over the wild waves of sin. But, perhaps, you have seen the dove as first she rises in the air, and then flies round and round. She deliberates in order to find out which is the right direction, and, when she has made up her mind, away she flies straight as an arrow to the goal. But, while she is fluttering about, she is an apt emblem of some men. They are undecided whether for God or Baal. They halt, to use Elijah's figure, between two opinions. "How long halt ye between two opinions? If God be God serve him, but if Baal, then follow him." On Sundays they go to church, but on Mondays they put it off; the weather is too rough, or something else prevents them going to the prayer-meeting. On Sunday they say—

"My willing soul would stay
In such a frame as this,
And sit and sing herself away,
To everlasting bliss."

But, on Monday or Tuesday the sound of the wheels in the street, and the noise of them that buy and sell, put the music of Jerusalem out of their ears, and they would fain go back to the world again. Ah, they are silly doves, without understanding and without decision. Nay, there are some who may be said to have a sort of decision for a time; but they are like the dove, in that they are without resolution. The dove seeks to fly in one direction; somebody claps his hands and she changes in a moment; or else he sprinkles a handful of barley on the ground, and, though she was flying yonder, she is over here again. How many persons there are of that kind, setting their faces to Zion, intending to join the church; perhaps they have seen the elders and the pastor, and been accepted; but, after a little time, they say, " Well, they did not know all about it; there are more frightful things than they dreamt of in it!" Like Pliable, they would go to heaven, but they get into the Slough of Despond, and there is queer stuff there that gets into the ears and mouth, and so they get out on the side nearest home, and tell Christian he may have the brave country all to himself, for they don't like the miry places on the way. Or, it may be, that some old companion comes up from the country, and he will treat them to some place of amusement; or, perhaps, it may be stronger than that. Or there is the gain to be got in some branch of business that is not quite so honest as it might be; but does not the money count as well? Isn't it as good to spend? Will not other men think it worth twenty shillings to the pound, however it may have been gained? These people, who seemed so true and warm-hearted, are like the silly dove without resolution, and fly away again to their old haunts and become just what they used to be.

So likewise there are many, like a dove, without bold hearts. They never turn upon a persecutor. They never stood in the gap with Mr. Valiant-for-Truth, holding the sword in their hand. They cannot open their mouth to speak for Jesus, but they run away when they ought to stand out like a lion against their foes; they never give a reason for the hope that is in them. We have plenty of Baptist churches educating cowards by the score. They never come out before the whole church—that would be too trying for their nerves. They are never expected to come out boldly on the Lord's side. Too often baptism is administered somewhere in a corner, when as few as possible are present; and, in that way, where we ought to have lion-like men, we breed those who hide their principles, and are ready to amalgamate with any sect of people so long as they can but bear the name of Christians. I would to God, dear friends, we had bolder men for our Lord and Master. Be as full of love as you can, but take care that you mix iron with your constitution. Silly are the doves that have no bold heart for God. The day will come when only the bold heart shall win, and the faint heart shall be shut out as the fearful and unbelieving, who are to have their portion in the lake that burneth with fire and brimstone.

Too many, also, there are like a silly dove, in that they have a powerless heart. If you visit a great manufactory where there is a large engine, you will notice that the amount of power used in the factory is proportionate to the capacity of the steam engine. If that should work but feebly, then the wheels cannot revolve beyond a proportionate rate, and every part soon discovers that there is some lack of motive force. Now, man's heart is the great steam-engine of his whole being; and if he has a heart that palpitates with swift strokes it will set his whole nature in motion, and that man will be mighty for his Lord and Master; but if he has a little, insignificant heart that never did glow, and never did burn, and never did know anything about the warmth, and life, and heat, and power, and benediction of God's love, then he will fritter away his time, knowing the right and doing the wrong, loving in some sort the thing that is beautiful, but still following that which is deformed; giving his name to God, and giving what little strength he has to the other side. Brethren, I would to God there were not so many in all our communities that have but a pigeon's heart, or a dove's heart, or no heart at all. The root of the matter lies here: these Ephraimites have not renewed hearts, and so they fail. Verily, verily, it is true to this hour as in Jesu's day, "Except a man be born again he cannot see the kingdom of God." Men do strive to see it in their own way. But, until the effectual grace of God comes down to turn their hearts from the great and extraordinary confidence which their proud flesh has in their own works, they never will see, they never can see, the kingdom of God. How many like Ephraim, then, have the heart altogether wrong because it is not renewed; therefore it has none of those qualifications which tend to make the man what he should be.

III. With great brevity, we notice, in the third place,

A SEVERE DESCRIPTION. "Ephraim is like a *silly* dove." It is a fine word, that word "silly." Hardly do I know another that is so eminently descriptive. There may be some sort of dignity in being a fool, but to be silly—to attract no attention except ridicule—is so utterly bad, that I do not know how a more sarcastic epithet could be applied. "Ephraim is like a silly dove without heart." And why silly? Why, it is silly, of course, to profess to be a dove at all, unless a dove at heart; silly of you to enslave yourselves with the customs of a country of which you are not a citizen—to bind yourselves with the rules of a family of which you are not a member. We find men, when they go to another country, if there is a conscription there, only too willing to plead their own nationality, in order to escape it; and yet we have persons who will serve in the Christian conscription, who give as God's people give, and outwardly do what God's people do, and yet they are not of the nation, but are aliens from the commonwealth of Israel. Is not this silly—to take the irksome toil, and not to get the joy and the benefit of it? You are silly to go and work in the vineyard, though you have never eaten of the clusters, and never can unless your heart be set right in the sight of God. Isn't it silly, then, to profess to be a dove at all, and yet not to be a dove? Isn't it silly, again, to think you can pass muster when your heart is wrong—to fancy that if you fly with the crowd you shall enter heaven without being seen? Dost thou think to deceive Omniscience? Dost thou think Infallible wisdom will not discern thee? Dost thou think to enter heaven while thy soul is estranged from

God? Then, indeed, thou art worse than a fool; thou art "silly" to think such a thing. How canst thou thus hope to deceive thy God? What more silly than to play fast and loose in this way? Silly to sing the song of Zion; and then the song of lasciviousness. There is something dignified even in the devil himself; there is something awful about the grandeur of his wickedness, because he is consistent in it; but, there is nothing of that in you, because you are here and there, everywhere and nowhere. You are this and that—everything by turns and nothing long. And don't you see what you do? Some of you are so silly as to hasten your own condemnation. You know that to be without God and without Christ will ruin you, and yet you do that which keeps you from going to Christ; you hug the sins that prevent your laying hold on him, and still dandle upon your knee the lusts which you know will shut the gates of heaven against you. Like Ephraim you are silly enough to trust in that which will be your ruin. Some of you rest upon good works, or hope to be saved by good feelings. You go to Egypt and to Assyria. The two powers which had oppressed Ephraim were still the powers in which he trusted. You are silly again, because when there is so much danger you do not fly to the place of shelter. O silly dove, when the hawk is abroad not to seek the clefts of the rock to hide itself in its dove-cot! And how silly are some of you? Day after day, year after year, Satan is hawking after you; the great fowler is seeking your destruction; but the wounds of Christ are open to you, and the invitation of the gospel is freely given to you, and yet, so silly are you, that though you know better, you prefer the pleasures of the day to the joys of eternity. Yet I know not that you do *prefer them*, only somehow or other you are too silly to take the preference, and you go on like a child that is playing on the hole of the cockatrice, making mirth over your damnation, too artless, too silly to make up your minds either for heaven or hell. I know there are some such in this house. Would God that the arrow would find out the right persons; but too often these doves are so silly in another respect that they will not let the appeals come home to them. They say, "It can't be for me, for I go to Mr. A's or Mrs. B's class; it can't be for me, for I go to the prayer-meeting; I contribute to the College, and every good work;" yet all the while it means just you who act upon your own whims, but not for God, who give God anything but your heart, who are ready to make a sacrifice of all, except that you refuse that which he asks of you—"My son, give me thine heart." It was considered to be a sign of great calamity when the Roman augur slew a bullock and found no heart, and it is the worst of all calamities when a man has no heart to give to God. "This people draweth nigh to me with their lips, but their heart is far from me," is one of the complaints against Israel of old, and one of the sins which made the prophets weep, and Jerusalem to be ploughed like a field.

IV. I close with just a word upon the fourth point, and that is, A SERIOUS CONSIDERATION. There are one or two things I would say solemnly, softly, and hopefully. O that they may stick upon the memory and the conscience of many.

Those of you, my hearers, who have been long sitting in this tabernacle, some of you ever since it was built, and before then in other places under our ministry for many years past, and yet are just the same as you used to be, ought to recollect how sadly we look on those who are not saved. It is no rare thing to find the attendant of the sanctuary an unbeliever. It is a common thing to find the child of converted parents, the lad educated at the Sabbath-school, the man who has always had a seat in God's house, still having no hope and without God in the world. Think of that! Be not deceived; the gospel will harden such people as you are. Speaking after the manner of men (for with God all things are possible, and a sovereign God doeth as he wills), it does seem less and less probable that you ever should be called by grace after you have sat and listened to the Word so long. The voice that did startle now soothes you; the manner that once attracted the eye, and sometimes seemed to touch the heart, fails to do either; and the very truth that once went over your heads like a crash of thunder has so little force in it now, that you sleep under the sound thereof. Think of that, you that are like a silly dove without heart. Remember, too, that some of the vilest sinners that have ever lived have been manufactured out of this raw material. Some of the grossest men were once credulous and apparently meek-hearted hearers of the Word, but they sat under the preaching of the gospel till they grew ripe enough to deny God and curse him. The unsanctified hearing of the gospel has sometimes produced more gigantic specimens of sin than the deaf ear of the adder. Beware, my hearer! I know you will say with Hazael, "Am I a dog that I should do this thing?" Yes, there is dog and devil enough in you, unless you have been changed by grace, to do that thing and twenty other things that you have never dreamt of yet. Think what a multitude of souls in hell there are like you—silly doves without heart. Many of the population of that place of wailing once heard the gospel, heard it with gladness, and received it for a time. But they had no root, and so the impression withered away. They never had been called effectually by grace, and never had been renewed, although they had all the outward semblances of holiness. They have gone! You might hear their howls if ye had ears. Hark! Even now, your soul may listen to their groans and moans, the lesson of all which would be, "Make your calling and election sure, and be not satisfied with the name to live while you are dead." May the Spirit of the living God stir you up to this; for, if not, I have one more consideration—*Remember how soon you may be in hell yourself.* And they who go there, if they have been such as you are, go there with a vengeance. To go from under the shadow of the pulpit is terrible. To go from the sacramental cup in the church to drink the cup of devils; from the song of saints to the weeping, and wailing, and gnashing of teeth of lost souls; from all the hallowed joys of God's Sabbath, of God's house, and of his Word, down to the unutterably infamy of spirits that have no love to God, but curse him day and night—my hearers, that may be your lot within an hour, a week, a year. It matters not what the period may be, for, if it ever be your lot, the time past shall seem to have been but the twinkling of an eye for its joy, though it may appear to you to have been ages for the awful responsibility which the day of mercy will have entailed upon you. " Repent and be baptized every one of you." As Peter said so say I. If we have not as yet received Christ, lay hold on eternal life, and oh that the Spirit of the living God, while I *generally* preach the Word, may *particularly* apply it, finding out his own chosen and gathering them out of the ruins of the Fall, that they may be jewels in the crown of the Redeemer. The Lord make us doves, but God forbid that we should be " silly doves without heart."

Our Banner.

"Thou hast given a banner to them that fear thee, that it may be displayed because of the truth."—PSALM lx. 4.

MOST writers upon this Psalm, after having referred the banner to the kingdom of David, say that there is here a reference to the Messiah. We believe there is. Nor is that reference an obscure allusion. In the Lord Jesus we find the clue to the history and the solution to the prophecy. He is the banner—he is the ensign that is lifted up before the people. He is the Jehovah Nissi, "the Lord my banner," whom it is our joy to follow, and around whom it is our delight to rally. We shall not stay to prove this, though we might readily do so. The banner here intended is no other than the Lord Jesus Christ in the majesty of his person—in the efficacy of his merit—in the completeness of his righteousness—in the sureness of his triumph—in the glory of his advent. If you read it, with an eye to him, you have the meaning at once: "Thou hast given Christ as a banner to them that fear thee, to be displayed because of the truth." Now let us consider *our Lord Jesus Christ*—first, *as he is compared to a banner;* secondly, *by whom he is given;* thirdly, *to whom he is given;* and fourthly, *for what purpose.*

I. The banner was far more useful, I suppose, in ancient than it is in modern warfare. Times have changed, and we are changed by them. Yet we speak with reverence still of the old flag. There is still some meaning when we say—"The flag that's braved a thousand years the battle and the breeze." The soldier still loves the flag of his country, and the sailor still looks with patriotic pride to the flag that so long floated at England's mast head. Our metaphor, however, rather points to ancient than present usage.

We should notice, first of all, that the banner was lifted up and displayed *as the point of union.* When a leader was about to gather troops for a war he hoisted his banner, and then every man rallied to the standard. The coming to the standard, the rallying round the banner, was the joining with the Prince, the espousing his cause. In the day of battle, when there was ever a difficulty and a likelihood that the host would be put to flight, the valiant men all fought around the banner. Its defence was of the first and chief consequence. They might leave the baggage for awhile, they might forsake the smaller flags of the divisions, but the great banner, the blood-red banner that with prayer had been consecrated—they must all gather round it and there shed their best blood. Christ, my brethren, is the point of union for all the soldiers of the cross. I know of no other place where all Christians can meet. We cannot all meet—I am sorry that we cannot—at the baptismal stream. There are some who will not be baptized. They persist still in the sin of putting drops

of water for the ordained flood, and bringing infants
where faith is required. We cannot all meet even around
the table of the Eucharist; there are some who put
aside their brethren, because they do not see eye to eye
with them; and even the table of the Lord's Supper
has become sometimes a field of battle. But, we can
meet in the person of Christ; all true hearts can meet
in the work of Christ. This is a gospel that we all love,
if we be Christians, and far hence be those who are not.
Hither to thy cross, O Jesus, do we come. The church-
man, laden with his many forms and vestments; the
Presbyterian, with his stern covenant and his love of
those who stained the heather with their blood; the
Independent, with the passion for free liberty and the
separateness of the churches; the Methodist, with his
various intricate forms of church Government, sometimes forms of bondage, but still forms of power; the
Baptist, remembering the ancient pedigree and the days
in which his fathers were hounded even by Christians
themselves, and counted not worthy of that name—they
come, they come! Multitudes of opinion divide them;
they see not eye to eye; here and there they will have
a skirmish for the old landmarks; and rightly so, for
we ought to be jealous, as Josiah was, to do that which
is right in the sight of the Lord, and neither decline
to the right hand nor to the left. But, to the cross!
To the cross! To the cross! and then, all weapons
of internecine war being cast aside, we are brethren,
fellow-comrades in blessed evangelical alliance; we are
prepared to suffer and to do for his dear sake. Forward then, Christians, to the point of union! Much
as I value thorough reformation in times of peace, little

care for I aught beside the cross in the day we defend our coasts, or when the hosts go forth to battle. Is our crusade against the powers of darkness? With the salvation of sinners for my one undivided aim, little care I for anything but the lifting up of my Master's Gospel, and the proclamation of the Word of mercy through his flowing blood.

Again, the banner in time of war, was the great guide-star; it was the direction to the soldier. You will remember what special care they took in the day of battle that in case the standard-bearer should fall there might still be some means of guiding the warriors.

"And if my standard-bearer fall, as fall full well he may,
For never saw I promise yet of such a deadly fray,
Press where ye see my snow-white plume amid the ranks of war,
And be your oriflamme to-day the helmet of Navarre."

So to this day the cross is the great guide of the Christian in the day of battle. There is no fear that it shall ever fall; we need not be alarmed that Jesus Christ, the same yesterday, to-day, and for ever, shall ever fail. Fix your eye upon him, Christian—"looking unto Jesus"—and if you would know which way to fight, fight in his footsteps, imitate his every action, be your life his life, be your death his death. Let it be life by virtue of the death; never need you stop to ask directions; the life of Christ is the Christian's charge. You need not turn to your fellow-believer, and say, "Comrade, what are we to do just now? The smoke of battle gathers and the cries are various; which way shall I go?" Looking unto Jesus, the Author and Finisher of your faith, who, for the joy that was set before him, endured the cross, despising the shame, and is set down at the right hand of the throne of God, press forward, saying, "God hath given to me a banner because of the truth." In these two respects, as the central point for rallying, and as the direction to the warrior, Christ is our banner.

And the banner, let it be remembered, is always *the object of chief attack*. The moment the adversary sees it, his object is to strike there. If it be not the most vulnerable point, it shall be at least the point where the adversary's power is most felt. Did they not of old aim their shots at the flagstaff to cut down the banner? Whenever the old Knights of the Red Cross fought the Saracens they always endeavored to make their steel ring upon the helmet of men whose hand held the crescent, the standard of Mohammed; ever the fight was bloodiest around the standard. Sometimes, when the battle was over, if you walked the field you would see it strewn with legs and arms and mangled bodies everywhere. In one place there would be a heap where they were piled one upon another, a great mountain of flesh and armor, broken bones and smashed skulls, and you would ask, "What is this? How came they here? How trampled they so one upon another, and fought in pools of human blood?" The answer would be, " 'Twas there the standard-bearer stood, and first the adversary made a dash and stole the banner, and then fifty knights vowed to redeem it, and they dashed against their foes and took it by storm, and then again hand to hand they fought with the banner between them, first in one hand and then in another, changing ownership each hour. Well, dear friends, Christ Jesus has always been the object of attack. You will remember when justice came forth against the elect it made five rents in the great banner, and those five rents all glorious are in that banner still. Since that day many a shot has sought to riddle, but not one has been able to touch it. Borne aloft first by one hand and then by another, the mighty God of Jacob being the strength of the standard bearers, that flag has bidden defiance to the leaguered hosts of the flesh and the devil; but never has it been trailed in the mire, and never once carried in jeering triumph by the adversary. Blessed are the rents in the banner! for they are the symbol of our victory. Those five wounds in the person of the Saviour are the gates of heaven to us. But, thank God, there are no more wounds to be endured. The person of our Lord is safe. His gospel, too, is an unwounded gospel, and his mystical body is uninjured. "Not a bone of him shall be broken." Yes; the gospel is unharmed after all the strife of ages. The infidel threatens to rend the gospel to pieces, but it is as glorious as ever; modern scepticism sought to pull it thread from thread, but has not been able so much as to rend a fragment of it. Every now and then fresh adversaries have found out some new methods of induction or declamation, essaying to prove the gospel to be a lie, and Christ an impostor. Have they succeeded? Nay, verily, they all have to fly the field. The good old banner of the Lord Omnipotent, even Christ Jesus, still stands erect above them all. We have had, therefore, three things—the rallying point, the guide-star, the object of attack.

And why should the banner be the object of attack but for this very reason, that it is *the symbol of defiance.*

As soon as ever the banner is lifted up, it is, as it were, flapped in the face of the foe. It seems to say to him, " Do your worst—come on ! We are not afraid of you —we defy you ? " So, when Christ is preached, there is a defiance given to the enemies of the Lord. Every time a sermon is preached in the power of the Spirit, it is as though the shrill clarion woke up the fiends of hell, for every sermon seems to say to them, " Christ is come forth again to deliver his lawful captives out of your power; the King of kings has come to take away your dominions, to wrest from you your stolen treasures, and to proclaim himself your Master." Oh, there is a stern joy that the minister sometimes feels when he thinks of himself as the antagonist of the powers of hell. Martin Luther seems always to have felt it when he said, " Come, let us sing the forty-sixth Psalm, and let the devil do his worst ? " Why, that was lifting up his standard—the standard of the cross. If you want to defy the devil, don't go about preaching philosophy ; don't sit down and write out fine sermons, with long sentences, three-quarters of a mile in extent; don't try and cull fine, smooth phrases that will sound sweetly in people's ears. The devil doesn't care a bit for this; but talk about Christ, preach about the sufferings of a Saviour, tell sinners that there is life in a look at him, and straightway the devil taketh great umbrage. Why, look at many of the ministers in London ! They preach in their pulpits from the first of January to the last of December, and nobody finds fault with them, because they will prophesy such smooth things. But let a man preach Christ, let him declaim about the power of Jesus to save, and press home gospel truth with simplicity and boldness, straightway the fiends of darkness will be against you; and, if they cannot bite, they will show that they can howl and bark. There is a defiance, I say, it is God's defiance; his gauntlet thrown down to the confederated powers of darkness, a gauntlet which they dare not take up, for they know what tremendous power for good there is in the uplifting of the cross of Christ. Wave, then, your banner, O ye soldiers of the cross; each in your place and rank keep watch and ward, but wave your banner still; for though the adversary shall be wroth, it is because he knoweth that his time is short when once the cross of Christ is lifted up.

We have not quite exhausted the metaphor yet. The banner was ever a source of consolation to the wounded. There he lies, the good knight; right well has he fought without fear and without reproach; but a chance arrow pierced the joints of his harness, and his life is oozing out from the ghastly wound. There is no one there to unbuckle his helmet or give him a draught of cooling water; his frame is locked up in that hard case of steel, and though he feels the smart he cannot gain the remedy, He hears the cries, the mingled cries, the hoarse shouts of men that rush in fury against their fellows: and he opens his eyes—as yet he has not fainted with his bleeding. Where, think you, does he look? He turns himself round. What is he looking for? For friend? For comrade? No. Should they come to him he would say, "Just lift me up, and let me sit against that tree awhile, and bleed here; but go you to the fight." Where, where is that restless eye searching, and what is the object for which it is looking? Yes, he has it; and the face of the dying man is brightened. He sees the banner still waving, and with his last breath he cries, "On! on! on!" and falls asleep content, because the banner is safe. It has not been cast down. Though he has fallen, yet the banner is secure. Even so every true soldier of the cross rejoices in its triumph. We fall, but Christ does not. We die, but the cause prospers. As I have told you before, when my heart was most sad—sad as it never was before nor since—that sweet text, "Him hath God the Father exalted, and given him a name that is above every name," quite cheered my soul, and set me again in peace and comfort. Is Jesus safe? Then it never matters what becomes of me. Is the banner right? Doth it wave on high? Then the fight is ours still; the adversary hath not won the day. He hath felled one and another, but he himself shall be broken in pieces, for the banner still glares in the sun.

And, lastly, the banner is *the emblem of victory*. When the fight is done, and the soldier cometh home, what bringeth he? His blood-stained flag. And what is borne highest in the procession as it winds through the streets? It is the flag. They hang it in the minster; high up there in the roof, and where the incense smoketh, and where the song of praise ascendeth, there hangs the banner, honored and esteemed, borne in conflict and in danger. Now, our Lord Jesus Christ shall be our banner in the last day, when all our foes shall be under our feet. A little while, and he that will come shall come, and will not tarry. A little while and we shall see Jehovah's banner furled.

"Sheathed his sword; he speaks! 'tis done,
And the kingdoms of this world are the kingdoms of his Son."

And then Jesus, high above us all, shall be exalted, and through the streets of the holy city the acclamations shall ring, " Hosanna, Hosanna, blessed is he that cometh in the name of the Lord."

II. Let us turn to our second point for a moment. It is this: Who gave us the banner? BY WHOM GIVEN? Soldiers often esteem the colors for the sake of the person who first bestowed them. You and I ought to esteem the gospel of our precious Christ for the sake of God who gave him to us. " *Thou* hast given a banner." God gave us the banner in old eternity. Christ was given by the eternal Father, from everlasting, or ever the earth was, to his elect people, to be the Messiah of God, the Saviour of the world. He was given in the manger, when the word was made flesh, and dwelt among us. He was given upon the cross, when the Father bestowed every drop of the Son's blood, and every nerve of his body, and every power of his soul, to bleed and die, the just for the unjust, to bring us to God. "*Thou* hast given us a banner." That banner was given to each one of us in the day of our conversion. Christ became from that time forth, our glory and our boast. And he is given to some of us, especially, when we are called to the ministry, or when the Holy Spirit's guidance puts us upon an extraordinary work for Christ. Then is the banner in a direct and especial manner committed to our care. I know there are some here who have had this banner given them to carry it in the midst of the Sunday-school. Some of you have it. A dear sister here has it. A beloved brother has to bear it in the midst of many of this congregation. The young men of our College, of our evening classes, and many others of you have that banner, that you may bear it in the streets, that you may lift up the name of Jesus in the causeways, and in the places of assembly. And, in a certain measure, shall all of you have that banner given to you, that in your sphere of duty you may talk of Jesus, and lift up his dear name.

Now, inasmuch as God himself gives the banner, with what reverence should we look upon it, with what ardor should we cluster round it, with what zeal should we defend it, with what enthusiasm should we follow it, with what faith and confidence should we rush even into death itself for its defence!

III. Ask again, TO WHOM IS THIS BANNER GIVEN? The text says " Thou hast given a banner *to them that fear thee.*" Not to all men. God has a chosen people. These chosen people are known in due time by their outward character. That outward grace-wrought character is this, they fear God. Now, they that fear God are the only persons that ought to carry the banner. Shall the banner be put in the drunkard's hands? Shall the great truth of Christ be left to those who live in sin? Oh, it is a wretched thing when men come into the pulpit to preach who have never known and felt the power of the Gospel themselves. Time was, but times are changed somewhat, when in multitudes of our parish pulpits men whose characters were unhallowed preached to others what they never practised themselves. To such the banner ought not to be given. Men must fear God, or else they are not worthy to bear it. Moreover, none but these can bear it. What they bear is not the banner; it is but an imitation of it. It is not Christ they preach ; it is a diluted thing that is not the gospel of Jesus. They cannot proclaim it to others till they know it themselves. It is given to them that fear God, because they will have courage to bear it. Fear is often the mother of courage. To fear God makes a man brave. To fear man is cowardly, I grant ; but to fear God with humble awe and holy reverence is such a noble passion that I would we were more and more full thereof, blending, as it were, the fear of Isaac with the faith of Abraham. To fear God will make the weakest of us play the man, and the most craven of us become heroes for the Lord our God. Now, inasmuch as this banner is given to those that fear God, if you fear God it is given to you. I do not know in what capacity you are to bear it, but I do know there is somewhere or other where you have to carry it. Mother, let the banner wave in your household. Merchant, let your banner be fixed upon your house of business. Let it be unfurled and fly at your masthead, O sailor. Bear your banner, O soldier, in your regiment. Yours is a stern duty, for alas, the Christian soldier hath a path of trial that few men have trodden. God make you faithful, and may you be honored as the good soldiers of Jesus Christ. Some of you are poor, and work hard in the midst of many artisans who fear not God. Take your banner with you. Never be ashamed of your colors. You cannot be long in a workshop before your companions will pull their colors out. They will soon begin talking to you about their sinful pleasures, their amusements, perhaps their infidel principles. Take your banner out likewise. Tell them that it is a game two can play at; never allow a man to show his banner without you showing yours. Don't do it ostentatiously; do it humbly, but do it earnestly and sincerely. Remember your banner is one that you never need be ashamed of; the best of men have fought under it; nay, he who was God as well as man hath his own name written on the escutcheon. Surely, then, you need not be ashamed to wave it anywhere and everywhere. You can think bravely; now be great in act as you have been in thought!

"Presence of mind and courage in distress
Are more than armies to procure success."

IV. And, indeed, this was our last question—WHAT WAS THIS BANNER GIVEN TO US FOR? Our text is very explicit. It was given to us to be "*displayed because of the truth.*" It was to be displayed. In order to display a banner, you must take it out of its case. Members of this congregation, brethren in the church, I pray you study the Scriptures much. I would not have men attempt to preach unless they have some power. To go forth without some study would be like a man attempting to do execution with a gun that had much powder in it and no shot. Do unfurl the banner; to this end husband well your time. Young men, save your spare hours to study the Bible. Steal them from your sleep if you cannot get them anyhow else. Sunday-school teachers; be diligent in your preparations for your classes. Get your banner out of the case. It is of little service lifting it up in the midst of the ranks without its being unfurled. See that ye know the holy art of unfurling it. Practise it; study it; be well acquainted with him who is the wisdom of God and the power of God. And after the flag is unfurled, it needs to be lifted up. So, in order to display Christ, you must lift him up. Lift him up with a clear voice as one that has something to say that he would have men hear. Speak of him boldly as one who is not ashamed of his message. Speak affectionately, speak passionately, speak with your whole soul, let your whole heart be in every word you say, for this it is to lift up the banner. But besides lifting up the banner you must carry it, for it is the business of the standard-bearer not merely to hold it in one place, but to bear it here and there if the plan of battle shall change. So bear Christ to the poor lodging-houses, to the work-houses, to the prisons, if you can get admittance, to the back streets, to the dark slums, to the cellars, to the solitary attic, to the crowded rooms, to the highways and the by-ways; and you especially who are private Christians, and not preachers, bear it from house to house. We had a complaint the other day that some of you had been going from house to house to try and talk to others about their souls; you had entrenched upon the parochial bounds of the authorized gamekeeper. I pray you entrench again. What is my parish? The whole world is my parish; let the whole world be your parish likewise. What does it matter to us if the world be parcelled out among men who probably do little or nothing. Let us do all we can. No man hath any right to say to me, "Visit in such and such a district, not here—this is my ground." Who gave it to you? Who gave him lordship of the world or any portion of it? "The earth is the Lord's, and the fulness thereof." The earth is your field, and no matter upon whose district, territory, or parish. Let me encourage you that love the Saviour. You have the pure gospel; go and spread it. Let nothing confine you, or limit your labors, except your strength and your time. Still, after all, if we carry the gospel, and lift up the banner, it will never be displayed even then, unless there is wind to blow it. A banner would only hang like a dead flag upon the staff if there were no wind. Now, we cannot produce the wind to expand the banner, but we can invoke heavenly aid. Prayer becomes a prophecy when ye say, "Awake, O heavenly wind, and blow, and let this banner be displayed." The Holy Spirit is that gracious wind who shall make the truth apparent in the hearts of those who hear it. Display the banner, talk of Christ, live Christ, proclaim Christ everywhere. He is given to you for this very purpose. Therefore, let not your light be hid or put under a bushel. "Ye are the light of the world. Let your light shine before men." Let the old flag be held up by fresh hands. Go ye forth in new times, with new resolves, and may ye have constant renewings as new opportunities open before you.

Oh, but are there not some of you who could not bear this banner? Let me invite such to come and take shelter under it. My Master's banner, wherever it goes, gives liberty. Under the banner of Old England there never breathes a slave. They tread our country, they breathe our air, and their shackles fall. Beneath the banner of Christ no slave can live. Do but look up to Jesus, relying upon his suffering in your stead, and bearing your sins in your place and room, and forthwith you shall have acceptance in the Beloved, and the peace of God which passeth all understanding shall keep your heart and mind through Jesus Christ. So may God enlist you beneath his banner to his glory. Amen.

Our Champion.

"And Samson lay till midnight, and arose at midnight, and took the doors of the gate of the city, and the two posts, and went away with them, bar and all, and put them upon his shoulders, and carried them up to the top of an hill that is before Hebron."—JUDGES xvi. 3.

POOR Samson! We cannot say much about him by way of an example to believers. We must hold him up in two lights—as a beacon and as a prodigy. He is a beacon to us all, for he shows us that no strength of body can suffice to deliver from weakness of mind. Here was a man whom no fellow-man could overcome, but he lost his eyes through a woman—a man mighty enough to rend a lion like a kid, yet, in due time, though himself stronger than a lion, he is bound with chains. When I think of the infatuation of which Samson was the subject, and remember how we are men of like passions with him, I can only, for myself and for you, put up the prayer, "Lord, hold thou me up, and I shall be safe." And Samson is also a prodigy. He is more a wonder as a believer than he is even as a man. It is marvellous that a man could smite thousands of Philistines with no better weapon than the jaw-bone of a newly killed ass, but it is more marvellous still that

Samson should be a saint, ranked among those illustrious ones saved by faith, though such a sinner. St. Paul has put him among the worthies in the eleventh chapter of the Hebrews. Paul wrote by inspiration. Therefore, there can be no mistake about it—Samson was saved. Indeed, when I see his child-like faith, the way in which he dashed against the Philistines, hip and thigh, and smote them with a great slaughter—the way in which he cast aside all reckonings and probabilities, and in simple confidence in his God cast himself about to do the most tremendous feats of valor—when I see this, I cannot but wonder and admire. The Old Testament biographies were never written for our imitation, but they were written for our instruction. Upon this one matter, what a volume of force there is in such lessons! "See," says God, "what faith can do. Here is a man, full of infirmities, a sorry fool; yet, through his child-like faith he lives. The just shall live by faith. He has many sad flaws and spots, but his heart is right towards God; he does trust in his Lord, and he does give himself up as a consecrated man to his Lord's service, and, therefore, he shall be saved." I look upon Samson's case as a great wonder, put in Scripture for the encouragement of great sinners. If such a man as Samson, nevertheless, prevails by faith to enter the kingdom of heaven, so shall you and I. Though our characters may have been disfigured by many vices, and hitherto we may have committed a multitude of sins, if we can trust Christ to save us he will purge us with hyssop, and we shall be clean; he will wash us, and we shall be whiter than snow; and in our death we shall fall asleep in the arms of sovereign mercy to wake up in the likeness of Christ.

But, I am going to leave Samson alone, except as he may furnish us with a picture of our Lord Jesus Christ. Samson, like many other Old Testament heroes, was a type of our Lord. He is specially so in this case. I shall invite you to look at Christ rather than Samson. First, *come and behold our champion at his work;* then, *let us go and survey the work when he has accomplished it;* and, thirdly, *let us inquire what use we can make of the work which he has performed.*

I. Come with me, then, brethren, AND LOOK AT OUR MIGHTY CHAMPION AT HIS WORK. You remember when our Samson, our Lord Jesus, came down to the Gaza of this world, 'twas love that brought him; love to a most unworthy object, for he loved the sinful church which had gone astray from him many and many times; yet came he from heaven, and left the ease and delights of his Father's palace to put himself among the Philistines, the sons of sin and Satan here below. It was rumored among men that the Lord of glory was in the world, and straightway they took counsel together how they would slay him. Herod makes a clean sweep of all the children of two years old and under, that he may be sure to slay the new-born Prince. Afterward scribes and priests and lawyers hunt and hound him. Satan tempts him in the wilderness, and provokes him when in public. Death also pursues him, for he has marked him as his prey. At last the time comes when the triple host of the Saviour's foes has fairly environed him and shut him in. They have dragged him before Pilate; they have scourged him on the pavement; they drag him while his back drips on the stones of Jerusalem's streets; they pierce his hands and his feet; they lift him up, a spectacle of scorn and suffering; and now, while dying in pangs extreme, and especially when he closes his eyes, and cries out, " It is finished," sin, Satan, and death all feel that they have the Champion safe. There he lies silently in the tomb. He who is to bruise the serpent's head is himself bruised. O thou who art the world's great Deliverer, there thou liest, as dead as any stone! Surely thy foes have led thee captive, O thou mighty Samson! He sleeps; but think not that he is unconscious of what is going on. He knows everything. He sleeps till the proper moment comes, and then our Samson awakes; and what now? He is in the tomb, and his foes have set a guard and a seal that they make keep him there. Will any help him now to escape out of their charge? Is there any man that will give his aid now? No, there is none! If the Champion escapes it must be by his own single-handed valor. Will he make a clear way for himself, and come up from the midst of his foes? You know he will, my brethren, for the moment the third day is come he touches the stone, and it is rolled away. He has defeated death; he has pulled up his posts and bar, and taken away his gates. As for sin he treads that beneath his feet: he has utterly o'erthrown it, and Satan lies broken beneath the heel that once was bruised. He has broken the dragon's head, and cut his power in pieces. Solitary and alone, his own arm brings salvation, and his righteousness sustains him. Methinks I see him now as he goes up that hill which is before Hebron—the hill of God. He bears upon his shoulders the o'erthrown gates, the tokens of his victory over death and hell. Posts and gates and bar and all, he bears them up to heaven. In sacred triumph he drags our enemies behind him. Sing to him! Angels, praise him in your hymns! Exalt him, cherubim and seraphim! Our mightier Samson hath gotten to himself the victory, and cleared the road to heaven and eternal life for all his people! Ye know the story. I have told it ill, but it is the most magnificent of all stories that e'er were told. "Arms, and the man, I sing," said one of old; but the cross and of him I sing. 'Tis mine to tell of him who espoused the cause of his people, and, though for awhile captive and bound, broke the green withs, and having gained the victory for himself, liberated others also, then goes at the head of his people along the way which he has opened—a way which leadeth to the right hand of God.

II. Let us go now, dear brethren, and calmly consider the work itself.

We will stand at the gates of this Gaza, and see what the Champion has done. Those are ponderous hinges, and they must have held up huge doors. We will look at these doors, and posts, and this bar. Why, it is a mass of iron that scarce ten men could lift, and it might take fifty more to carry those huge doors. They scarce were moved even on their hinges without the efforts of some dozen men; and yet this one man carried them all, and I read not that his shoulders were bent or that he grew weary. Seven miles at least Samson carried that tremendous load, up hill all the way, too! Still he bore it all without staggering, nor do I find that he was faint as he was aforetime at Ramath-lchi.

I will not linger upon Samson's exploits. Rather would I draw your thoughts to the Captain of our salvation. See what Christ has carried away. I said that he had three enemies. These three beset him, and he has achieved a threefold victory.

There was death. My dear friends, Christ, in being first overcome by death, made himself a conqueror over death, and hath given us also the victory; for concerning death we may truly say, Christ has not only opened the gates, but he has taken them away; and not the gates only, but the very posts, and the bar, and all. Christ hath abolished death, and brought life and immortality to light. He hath abolished it in this sense—that, in the first place, the cause of death is gone. Believers die, but they do not die for their sins. "Christ died for our sins according to the Scriptures." We die, but it is not any longer as a punishment to us. It is the fruit of sin, but it is not the curse of sin that makes the believer die. To other men death is a curse; to the believer I may almost put it among his covenant blessings, for to sleep in Jesus Christ is one of the greatest mercies that the Lord can give to his believing people. The curse of death, then, being taken away, we may say that the posts are pulled up. Christ has taken away the after results of death, the soul's exposure to the second death. Unless Christ had redeemed us, death, indeed, would have been terrible; for it would have been the shore of the great lake of fire. When the wicked die they are judged to punishment. If they rise, it is but to receive in their bodies and in their souls the due reward of their sins. The sting of death is the second death—the afterwards.

To die—to sleep—ay, that were nothing; but to dream in that sleep! "Ay, there's the rub!" said the world's poet; and there men will find the rub is; "for in that sleep of death what dreams shall come!"—nay, not what "dreams," but what substantial pains, what everlasting sorrows, what dread miseries! These are not for Christians. There is no hell for you, believer. Christ has taken away posts, and bar, and all. Death is not to you any longer the gate of torment, but the gate of paradise. Moreover, Christ has not only taken away the curse, and the after results of death, but from many of us he has taken away the fear of death. He came on purpose to deliver "those, who through fear of death, were all their life-time subject to bondage." There are not a few here who could conscientiously say that they do not dread death; nay, but rather look forward to it with joyful expectation. We have become so accustomed to think of our last hours that we die daily, and when the last hour shall arrive, we can only say, "Our marriage day has come."

"Welcome sweet hour of full discharge
That sets my willing soul at large."

We shall hail the summons to mount beyond this land of woes, and sighs, and tears to be present with our God. The fear of death having been taken away, we may truly say that Christ has taken away posts, and bar, and all. Besides, beloved, there is a sense in which it may be said that Christians never die at all. "He that liveth and believeth in me, though he were dead, yet shall he live." "He that liveth and believeth in me shall never die." They do not die; they do but "sleep in Jesus, and are blessed." But the main sense in which Christ has pulled up the posts of the gates of death is that he has brought in a glorious resurrection. Grave, thou canst not hold thy prisoners; they must rise! O death, thy troops of worms may seem to devastate that fair land of human flesh and blood; but that body shall rise again with more blooming beauty than that with which it fell asleep. It shall upstart from its bed of dust, and silent clay, to dwell in realms of everlasting day. Conceive the picture if you can! If you have imagination, let the scene now present itself before your eyes. Christ the Samson sleeping in the dominions of death; death boasting and glorifying itself that now it has conquered the Prince of Life; Christ waking, striding to that gate, dashing it aside, taking it upon his shoulders, carrying it away, and saying as he mounts to heaven, "O death, where is thy sting? O grave, where is thy victory?"

Another host which Christ had to defeat was the army of sin. Christ had come among sinners, and sins beset him round. Your sins and my sins beleaguered the Saviour till he became their captive. In him was no sin, and yet sins compassed him about like bees. Sin was imputed to him; the sins of all his people stood in his way to keep him out of heaven as well as them. When Christ was on the cross, my brethren, he was looked upon by God as a sinner, though he never had been a sinner; and when in the grave, he could not rise until he was justified. Christ must be justified as well as his people. He was justified not as we are, but by his own act. We are not justified by acts of our own as he was. All the sin of the elect was laid upon Christ; he suffered its full penalty, and so was justified. The token of his justification lay in his resurrection. Christ was justified by rising from the dead, and in him all his people were justified too. I may say, therefore, that all our sins stood in the way of Christ's resurrection ; they were the great iron gate, and they were the bar of brass, that shut him out from heaven. Doubtless, we might have thought that Christ would be a prisoner for ever under the troops of sin, but, oh, see him, my brethren. See how the mighty Conqueror, as he bears our sins " in his own body on the tree," stands with unbroken bones beneath the enormous load, bearing

> " All that incarnate God could bear,
> With strength enough but none to spare."

See how he takes those sins upon his shoulders, and carries them right up from his tomb, and hurls them away into the deep abyss of forgetfulness, where, if they be sought for, they shall not be found any more forever.

As for the sins of God's people, they are not partly taken away, but they are as clean removed as ever the gates of Gaza were—posts, gates, bars, and all ; that is to say, every sin of God's people is forgiven.

> " There's pardon for transgressions past,
> It matters not how black their cast ;
> And, oh, my soul, with wonder view,
> For sins to come there's pardon too '

Every sin that all the elect did commit, are committing, or shall commit, was taken away by Christ, taken upon the shoulders of the atonement and carried away. There is no sin in God's book against his people ; he seeth no sin in Jacob, neither iniquity in Israel ; they are justified in Christ for ever. Moreover, as the guilt of sin was taken away, the punishment of sin was consequently taken away too. For the Christian there is no stroke from God's angry hand; nay, not so much as a single frown of punitive justice. The believer may be chastised by a Father's hand; but God, the Judge of all, has nothing to say to the Christian, except, "I have absolved thee: thou art acquitted." For the Christian there is no hell, no penal death, much less any second death. He is completely freed from all the punishment as well as the guilt of sin, and the power of sin is removed too. It may stand in our way to keep us in perpetual warfare; but, oh, my brethren, sin is a conquered foe to us. There is no sin which a Christian cannot overcome if he will only rely upon his God to do it. They overcame through the blood of the Lamb, who wear the white robe of heaven, and you and I may do the same. There is no lust too mighty, no besetting sin too strongly entrenched. We can drive these Canaanites out. Though they have cities walled to heaven, we can pull their cities down, and overcome them through the power of Christ. Do believe it, Christian, that thy sin is virtually a dead thing. It may kick and struggle. There is force in it for that, but it is a dead thing. God has written condemnation across its brow. Christ has crucified it, "nailing it to his cross." Do you go now and bury it for ever, and the Lord help you to live to his praise. Oh, blessed be his name! Sin, with the guilt, the power, the shame, the fear, the terror of it, all is gone. Christ has taken posts, and bar, and all up to the top of the hill.

Then there was a third enemy, and he also has been destroyed—that was Satan. Our Saviour's sufferings were not only an atonement for sin, but they were a conflict with Satan, and a conquest over him, and Satan is a defeated foe. The gates of hell cannot prevail against the church; but, what is more, Christ has prevailed against the gates of hell. As for Satan the posts, and bar, and all have been plucked up from his citadel in this sense—that Satan has now no reigning power over believers. He may bark at us like a dog, and he may go about like a roaring lion, but to rend and to devour are not in his power. There is a chain about the devil's neck, and God lets him go as far as he likes, but no further. He could not tempt Job without first asking leave, and he cannot tempt you without first getting permission. There is a permit needed before the devil dares so much as look on a believer, and God gives him permission; and so, being under divine authority and permission, he will not be allowed to tempt us above what we are able to bear. Moreover, the exceeding terror of Satan is also taken away. A man has met Apollyon foot to foot, and overcome him. That man in death triumphed over Satan. So may you and I. The *prestige* of the old enemy is gone. The dragon's head has been broken, and you and I need not fear to fight with a broken-headed adversary. When I read John Bunyan's description of Christian's fight with Apollyon, I am struck with the beauty and truth of the description, but I cannot help thinking—" Oh! if Christian had known how thoroughly Apollyon had been thrashed in days gone by, by his Master, he would have thrown that in his face, and made short work of him." Never encounter Satan without recollecting that great victory that Christ achieved on the tree. Do not be afraid, Christian, of Satan's devices or threatenings. Be on your watch-tower against him. Strive against him, but fear him not. Resist him, being bold in the faith, for it is not in his power to keep the feeblest saint out of heaven, for all the gates which he has put up to impede our march have been taken away, posts, and bar, and all, and our God the Lord has gotten to himself the victory over the hosts of hell.

III. We will now see HOW WE CAN USE THIS VICTORY. Surely there is some comfort here—comfort for you, dear friend, over yonder. You have a desire to be saved; God has impressed you with a deep sense of sin; the very strongest wish of your soul is that you might have peace with God. But you think there are so many difficulties in the way—Satan, your sins, and I know not what. Beloved, let me tell thee, in God's name, there is no difficulty whatever in the way except in thine own heart, for Christ has taken away the gates of Gaza—gates, posts, bar, and all. Mary Magdalene said to the other Mary, when they went to the sepulchre, "Who shall roll us away the stone?" That is what you are saying; and when they came to the place the stone was rolled away. That is your case, poor troubled conscience; the stone is rolled away. What? you cannot believe it? There is God's testimony for it— "Though your sins be as scarlet, they shall be as white as snow; though they be red like crimson, they shall be as wool." You want an atonement for your sins, do you? "It is finished." You want some one to speak for you. "He is able to save unto the uttermost, seeing he ever liveth to make intercession for us." Canst thou believe in the mercy of God in Christ, and rest thy poor guilty soul upon the merit of his doing and the virtue of his dying? If thou canst, God is reconciled to thee. There may have been great mountains between thee and God. They are all gone. There may have been the Red Sea of thy sins rolling between thee and thy Father. That Red Sea is dried up. I tell thee, soul, if thou believest in Christ Jesus, not only is there way of access between thy soul and God, but there is a a clear way. You remember, when Christ died, the veil of the temple was rent in twain. There was not a little slit for sinners to creep through, but it was rent in twain from the top to the bottom, so that big sinners might come, just in the same way as when Samson pulled up gates, posts, bar, and all, there was a clear way out into the country for all who were locked up in the town. Prisoner, the prison doors are open. Captive, loose the bonds on thy neck; be free! I sound the trump of jubilee. Bond-slaves, Christ hath redeemed you. Ye who have sold—

"Your heritage for naught,
Shall have it back unbought,
The gift of Jesus' love."

The Lord hath anointed his Son Jesus " to preach liberty to the captives, and the opening of the prison doors to them that are bound." Trust thou him. Oh, may his mercy lead thee now to trust him, for there is really nothing to prevent thy salvation if thou restest in him. Between thy soul and God, I tell thee, there is no dividing wall. "He is our peace." "He hath made us both one, and reconciled us to God by his blood." May those few words be kept and treasured up by such as need them. Some of you want them. May the Spirit of God put them into your hearts, and lay them up there, that you may find comfort in Christ!

But is there not something more here? Is there not here some ground of exhortation to Christians? Brethren, have not some of you been tolerating some sin—some besetting sin, which you think you cannot overcome? You would be more holy, but this thought makes your arm nerveless against your own sin—you are not able to overcome it. So you think that Christ has left the posts, do you? I tell you, no; "he that is born of God sinneth not." He that is born of God is perfect, and he sinneth not with allowance; he sinneth not with constancy; and it is his power, with the Holy Spirit's aid, to overcome his sin; and it is his duty as well as his privilege to go to war against the stoutest of his corruptions till he shall tread them under foot.

Now, will you believe it, brethren, that in the blood of Christ, and in the water that flowed with it from his side, there is a sovereign virtue to kill your sins? There is nothing standing between you and the pardon of your sins but your unbelief, and if you will shake that off, you shall march through the gate triumphant.

Once more, and I have done. Is not this an incentive for us who profess to be servants of Christ to go out and fight with the world, and overcome it for Christ? Brethren, where Jesus leads us it needs not much courage to follow. "The earth is the Lord's, and the fulness thereof." Let us go and take it for him! Nations that "sit in darkness shall see a great light." Satan may have locked up the world with bigotry, with idolatry, and with superstition, as with posts and bars, but the kingdom is the Lord's; and if we will but rouse ourselves to preach the Word we shall find that the Breaker has gone up before us, and broken and torn away the gates, and we have nothing to do but to enter with an easy victory. God help us to do so!

And now, as we come to the Lord's table, let us have this vision before us of our glorious Samson achieving his mighty victory; and, while we weep for sin, let us praise his superlative power and love that has done such marvels for us. The Lord give us to enjoy his presence at this table, and he shall have the praise! Amen.

The Fainting Hero.

"He was sore athirst, and called on the Lord, and said, Thou hast given this great deliverance into the hand of thy servant: and now shall I die for thirst, and fall into the hand of the uncircumcised?—JUDGES xv. 18.

YOU will remember the occasion on which these words were spoken. Samson had been brought down from the top of the rock, bound with cords by his own brethren, and given up as a captive into the hands of the Philistines. But, no sooner did he reach the Philistines than the supernatural force of God's Spirit came upon him, and he snapped the cords as though they had been but tow; and seeing the jaw-bone of a newly slaughtered ass lying near to hand, he grasped that strange weapon, and fell with all his might upon the hosts of the Philistines; and though, no doubt, they took to speedy flight, yet the one man, smiting them hip and thigh, left no less than a thousand persons dead upon the ground; and as he piled up the heaps of the slain, he looked with grim satisfaction upon the slaughter which he had wrought, crying—"Heaps upon heaps; heaps upon heaps; with the jaw-bone of an ass have I slain a thousand men!" There was, perhaps, a little of vaunting and vain-glorying in his conduct; but, in a moment, a sudden faintness gathered over him. He had been exerting himself most marvellously, straining every nerve and muscle, and now, being sore athirst, he looked round him for a stream of water, but there was none; and he felt as if for lack of water he must die, and then the Philistines would rejoice over him. With that simple-minded faith which was so characteristic of Samson, who was nothing but a big child, he turned his eye to his heavenly Father, and cried—"O Jehovah, thou hast given me this great deliverance, and now shall I die for thirst? After all that thou hast done for me, shall the uncircumcised rejoice over me because I die for want of a drink of water?" Such confidence had he that God would interpose on his behalf.

Now, my drift is the comforting of God's saints, especially in coming to the table of their Lord. I have thought there may be many of you who are feeling in an unhappy and a distressed frame of mind, and that by referring you to what God has already done for you I might lead you to set a lighter estimate upon your present trouble, and enable you to argue that he who has wrought great deliverances for you in the past will not suffer you to lack in the future.

I. YOU HAVE ALREADY, MY BROTHERS AND SISTERS, EXPERIENCED GREAT DELIVERANCES.

Happy is it for you that you have not had the slaying of a thousand men, but there are "heaps upon heaps" of another sort upon which you may look with quite as much satisfaction as Samson, and perhaps with less mingled emotions than his, when he gazed on the slaughtered Philistines. See there, beloved, the great heaps *of your sins*, all of them giants, and any one of them sufficient to drag you down to the lowest hell. But, they are all slain; there is not a single sin that speaks a word against you. "Who shall lay anything to the charge of God's elect?" Another arm than yours has done it, but the victory is quite as complete. Christ returns with dyed garments from Bozrah; he has trodden the wine-press of God's wrath, and I may almost say that the blood which stains his apparel is the blood of your sins, which he has utterly destroyed for ever. Look at their number. Take so many years, and make each year a heap. Divide them, if you will, into groups and classes; put them under the heads of the ten commands, and there they lie, in ten great heaps, but every one of them destroyed.

Think, too, of *the heaps of your doubts and fears.* Do you not remember when you thought God would never have mercy upon you? Let me remind you of the low dungeon where there was no water, when the iron entered into your soul. Some of us can never forget the time when we were under conviction. Moses tied us up to the halberts, and took the ten-thonged whip of the law, and laid it upon our backs most terribly, and then seemed to wash us with brine as conscience reminded us of all the aggravations which had attended our sins. But, though we feared we should have been in hell, though we thought that surely the pit would shut its mouth upon us; yet, here we are living to praise God, as we do this day, and all our fears are gone. We rejoice in Christ Jesus. God "hath not dealt with us according to our sins, nor rewarded us after our iniquities." "Heaps upon heaps" of fears have we had; bigger heaps than our sins, but there they lie—troops of doubters. There are their bones and their skulls, as Bunyan pictured them outside the town of Mansoul; but they are all dead, God having wrought for us a deliverance from them.

Another set of foes that God has slain includes *our temptations*. Some of us have been tempted from every quarter of the world, from every corner of the compass. Sometimes it has been pride; at another time despair. Sometimes it has been too much of the world, and at others it has been too little. Sometimes we have been too strong and puffed up; at other times we have been too weak and cast down. There has sometimes been a lack of faith, and at others our fervency may have been inflamed by the flesh. The best of men are shot at with the devil's worst darts. You have been tempted by Satan; you have been tempted by the world; your nearest and dearest friends have, perhaps, been your worst tempters, for, "a man's foes shall be they of his own household." There has not been a bush behind which an enemy has not lurked, no inch of the road to Canaan which has not been overgrown with thorns.

"Trials of every shape and name
Await the followers of the Lamb,
Who leave the world's deceitful shore,
And leave it to return no more."

But, look back upon them. Your temptations, where are they? Your soul has escaped like a bird out of the snare of the fowler, and this night you can say, "They compassed me about like bees; yea, like bees they compassed me about; but in the name of God have I destroyed them; I have passed safely where others have been ruined; I have walked along the walls of salvation when others have been lying at the foot thereof, dashed in pieces by their presumption and their self-confidence; 'heaps upon heaps' of my temptations have been slain, and thou, O God, hast wrought for me a great deliverance!"

So, let me say, in the next place, *has it been with most* of your sorrows. You, sons and daughters of tribulation, have sometimes sat down and said, "All these things are against me!" You have lost children, friends have died, business has departed, wealth has melted, almost every comfort has had a blight upon it. Like Job's messengers, evil tidings have followed one another, and you have been brought very low. But, beloved in Christ Jesus, you have been delivered. "Many are the afflictions of the righteous, but the Lord delivereth him out of them all." It has been so in your case. Whatever form the affliction has taken, mercy has taken a form to meet it. When the arrow flew, God was your shield; when the darkness gathered, he was your sun; when you had to fight, he was your sword; when you needed to be supported, he was your rod and your staff.

> "Thus far we've proved that promise good
> Which Jesus ratified with blood;
> Still is he gracious, wise, and just,
> And still in him let Israel trust."

I will let no man in this congregation take a place before me in obligation to the Most High. Brethren, we are all debtors, and I count myself most of all a debtor. I boast that I have nothing to boast of. I would desire to lie the lowest, and to take the meanest place, for I owe most of all to the grace of God. When I look back to my parentage, when I see whence the Lord has brought me, and what he has done for me and by me, I can only say, "Thou hast given to thy servant this great deliverance!" And, I suppose, if all the people of God could meet here one by one, they would each claim that there is something peculiar in their every case; each one would say, "There is something in the deliverance God has wrought for me that demands of me a special song;" therefore, let the whole of us together, who have "known and tasted that the Lord is gracious," look back upon the past with thankfulness and praise to the Lord.

II. YET FRESH TROUBLES WILL ASSAIL YOU, AND EXCITE YOUR ALARM. Thus Samson was thirsty. This was a new kind of want to him. He was so thirsty that he was near to die. The difficulty was totally different from any that Samson had met before. Shake those Samsonian locks in which thy strength lieth, but they cannot distil a single drop of dew to moisten thy mouth! The strong man is as much amenable to thirst as the weak, and that arm which could slay a thousand Philistines, cannot open a fountain in the earth, draw down a shower from the skies, or yield to thirst a single draught of water. He is in a new plight. Of course it seems to you to be a far simpler matter than he had known before, and so it was. Merely to get thirst assuaged is not anything like so great a thing as to be delivered from a thousand Philistines. But I dare say when the thirst was upon him, and oppressed him, Samson felt that little present difficulty more weighty and severe than the great past difficulty out of which he had so specially been delivered. Now I think, beloved, there may be some of you who have been forgiven, saved, delivered, and yet you do not feel happy to-night. " God has done great things for you, whereof you are glad," yet you cannot rejoice; the song of your thanksgiving is hushed. A little inconvenience in getting into your pews; a hasty word spoken by somebody outside the gate; the thought of a child at home, something which is very little and insignificant compared with all that God has wrought for you, will sometimes take away the present joy and comfort of the great, the unspeakably great boons which you have received. You may know your standing in Christ, and yet some little trouble keeps buzzing about your ears, and may be distracting you even now. Let me say two or three words to you. It is very usual for God's people, when they have had some great deliverance, to have some little trouble that is too much for them. Samson slays a thousand Philistines, and piles them up in heaps, and then he must needs die for want of a little water! Look at Jacob; he wrestles with God at Peniel, and overcomes omnipotence itself, and yet he goes " halting on his thigh !" Strange, is it not, that there must be a touching of the sinew whenever you and I win the day? It seems as if God must teach us our littleness, or nothingness, in order to keep us within bounds. Samson seems to have crowed right loudly when he said, " Have I slain a thousand men?" Ah! Samson, it is time thy throat became hoarse when thou canst boast so loudly. The mighty man has to go down on his knees and cry, " O God, this thirst will overcome thy hero; send me, I pray thee, a draught of water." God has ways of touching his people, so that their energy soon vanishes. "I said my mountain standeth firm, I shall not be moved; thou didst hide thy face, and I was troubled." Now, dear child of God, if this is your case, I say it is not an unusual one. There is a reaction which generally follows any strong excitement. No doubt the excitement of having slain the Philistines would naturally be followed by depression of spirits in Samson. When David had mounted the throne of Israel there came the reaction, and he said, "I am this day weak, though anointed king." You must expect to feel weakest just when you are enjoying your greatest triumph.

I have already said that the use of all this is to make a man feel his weakness. I hope it makes you feel yours. What fools we are, brethren, and yet if some one else were to call us fools we should not like it, though I do not doubt but that we are very well named, whoever may give us the title, for the whole of heaven cannot make us rejoice if we have one pain in our head; and all the harps of angels, and our knowledge of our interest in "the glory that is to be revealed," cannot make us happy if some little thing happens to go contrary to our minds. Somebody trod on the corns of your pride as you were coming in here, and if an angel had preached to you you would not have enjoyed it, because of your mind being discomposed. Oh! simpletons that we are! The table is daintily spread; the manna of heaven lies close to our hand, but, because there is a little rent in the garment, or a small thorn in the finger, we sit down and cry as though the worst of ills had happened to us! Heaven is thine own, and yet thou criest because thy little room is scantily furnished! God is thy Father, and Christ thy brother, and yet thou weepest because a babe has been taken from thee to the skies! Thy sins are all forgiven, and yet thou mournest because thy clothes are mean. Thou art a child of God, an heir of heaven, and yet thou sorrowest as though thou wouldst break thy heart because a fool hath called thee ill names! Strange is it! foolish; but such is man—strangely foolish, and only wise as God shall make him so.

III. If, my brethren, you are now feeling any present trouble pressing so sorely that it takes away from you all power to rejoice in your deliverance, I want you to remember that YOU ARE STILL SECURE. God will as certainly bring you out of this present little trouble as he has brought you out of all the great troubles in the past.

He will do this for two reasons, both of which are found in the text. The first is, because *if he does not do it your enemy will rejoice over you.* "What," saith Samson, "shall I fall by the hand of the uncircumcised? Faint, weary, thirsty, shall I become their victim—I who was once their terror, and made the damsels of Gath and of Askelon to weep instead of to dance? Shall *I* be slain?" And what say you? But hush your gloomy forebodings. If you perish, the honor of Christ will be tarnished, and the laughter of hell will be excited. Bought with Jesu's blood, and yet in hell! —what merriment there would be in the pit? Justified by the righteousness of Christ, and yet lost—what a theme of scorn for fiends! Sanctified by the Spirit of God, and yet damned—oh! what yells of triumph would go up from the abode of Apollyon and his angels!

What! a child of God forsaken of his Father! A jewel plucked from Jesu's crown! A member rent from Jesu's body! Never, never, never! God will never permit the power of darkness to triumph over the power of light. His great name he ever hath in respect, and the ruin of the meanest believer would be the cause of dishonor and disrespect to God, therefore you are safe! Oh! it is such a blessed thing when you can run behind your God for shelter. Some youngster out in the street has been offending his fellow, and is likely to receive a blow; but here comes his father, and he runs behind his father's skirt and feels that there is no fear for him now. So let us shelter ourselves behind our God. Better than brazen wall, or castle, or high tower, shall Jehovah be to us, and we may then look at all our enemies, and say, as Isaiah did to Sennacherib, " The virgin daughter of Zion hath despised thee, and shaken her head at thee!" The uncircumcised shall not rejoice; the daughters of Philistia shall not triumph. We are our God's, and he will keep his own until the day when he shall display them as his jewels.

That is one reason for confidence, but another reason is to be found in the fact that *God has already delivered you.* I asked you just now to walk over the battle-field of your life, and observe the heaps upon heaps of slaughtered sins, and fears, and cares, and troubles. Do you think he would have done all that he has done for you if he had intended to leave you? The God who has so graciously delivered you hitherto has not changed; he is still the same that he ever was. I have no doubt about the sun rising to-morrow morning; he always has done so since I have been able to see him. Why should I doubt my God, for he is more certain than the sun? The Nile ceases not to make Egypt laugh with plenty; men trust it, and why should not I trust my God, who is a river full of water, overflowing with lovingkindness. If we never doubt God till we have cause to do so, distrust will be banished from our hearts for ever. Of men we speak as we find; let us do the same with God. Was he ever a wilderness to you? When did he forsake you? When did your cries return without an answer? What, has he ever said, "I have blotted you out of my book, and I will remember you no more!" You have doubted him, wickedly and wantonly, but never have you had any cause for suspicion or mistrust. Now, since he is "the same yesterday, and to-day, and for ever," the God who delivered you out of the jaw of the lion and out of the paw of the bear, will yet deliver you out of your present difficulty.

Bethink you, dear friend, if he does not do so *he will lose all that he has done*. When I see a potter making a vessel, if he is using some delicate clay upon which he has spent much preliminary labor to bring it to its proper fineness; and if I see him again, and again, and again moulding the vessel—if I see, moreover, that the pattern is coming out—if I know that he has put it in the oven, and that the colors are beginning to display themselves—I bethink me were it common delf ware I could understand his breaking up what he had done, because it would be but worth little; but since it is a piece of rich and rare porcelain upon which months of labor had been spared, I could not understand his saying, "I will not go on with it;" because he would lose so much that he has already spent. Look at some of those rich vessels by Bernard de Palissy, which are worth their weight in gold, and you can hardly imagine Bernard stopping when he had almost finished, and saying, "I have been six months over this, but I shall never take the pains to complete it."

Now, God has spent the blood of his own dear Son to save you; he has spent the power of the Holy Spirit to make you what he would have you be, and he will never stay his mighty hand till his work is done. "Hath he said, and shall he not do it? Hath he begun, and shall he not complete?" God will have no unfinished works. When Jehovah's banner is furled, and his sword is sheathed, then shall he cry—

" 'Tis done,
For the kingdoms of this world
Are the kingdoms of my Son."

In that day every vessel that he prepared for glory shall stand in that glory, having been made perfectly meet for it. Do not, then, despair, because of your present trouble.

Doubtless some of you are saying that I am speaking as one who does not know the occasion or the bitterness of your peculiar distress. My dear friends, I do not care to know it. Enough for me to know that if God has wrought for his servants so great a deliverance as he has done, the present difficulty is only like Samson's thirst, and I am sure he will not let you die of faintness, nor suffer the daughter of the uncircumcised to triumph over you. "Ah!" says one, "it is all very well talking, but mine is a very, very, very peculiar case." Well, then, dear brother, there is a special reason why God should deliver you, because, if Satan could overcome in that peculiar case, he would then say that he could have overcome all the saints if he could have got them into the same corner, and he would loudly boast, just as though the whole had perished. But I do not think that your case is so very peculiar; it is only the way in which you look at it. The road of sorrow has been well trodden; it is the regular sheep-track to heaven, and all the flock of God have had to pass along it. So, I pray you, cheer up your heart with Samson's words, and rest assured that God will deliver you soon.

And now, while I have been talking thus, the thought has sprung up in my breast that many people listen to me who are not Christians. My friends, my great wonder is, what some of you do without God. I can hardly understand how the rich man can have any comfort without God, for he must suffer from bereavement and bodily pain as well as the poor. Those silly butterflies of fashion, who spend all their time in flitting about from flower to flower, are so heartless and thoughtless that I cannot comprehend how they can do without God. With empty heads and silly hearts men and women can make gods of anything; their own pretty persons can be quite sufficient object for their idiotic worship. But a man that stands right straight up, a sensible thinking man—a working man if you will—I do not mind whether he works with the dry heat of his brain or with the damp sweat of his face—I cannot understand how a man like this, with organs of thought and a reasoning soul, can go on without God. There must be pinches with some of you when you want a God. I had been in a madhouse a dozen times if it had not been for my God. My feet had altogether gone into the chambers of despair, and I had ended this life, if it had not been for the faithful promises of the God that keeps and preserves his people. My life has not been a miserable, but a happy one ; and yet I tell you that there have been times in it when I could not have done without my God. I do not understand what some of you, who are always at the pinch, do without God. There are many such here. You are poor ; you are not often without sickness; you were born inheritors of maladies that make your life wretched ; your children are sickly about you ; it is as much as you can do by Saturday night to make ends meet ; you are frequently in debt; you are constantly in trouble. Oh! I cannot tell what you do without God. Why, you have nothing here, and no hope of anything hereafter! Poor souls, I could weep for you to think that you are without God!

I went some time ago into the house of our brother Stephenson; a good soldier of the cross was he: he fell asleep in Jesus; and when I saw his weeping sons and daughters, I felt, "I have easy work here." I said to them, "Why, what a mercy it is that your father is gone, for he has lingered long in pain, and you know how ready he was to enter into rest." That was very different from what sometimes happens. Only a little while ago a sister came to me weeping as if she would break her heart. "Ah, sir," said she, "my brother is dead, and he died without hope." It was a sad case, but then she had a God to repair to even under that sharp trial. But, when death comes into *your* house, you have no God! I knelt down and prayed with those poor weeping girls this morning, and, though their father was but just dead, I marked that the voice of prayer had evidently a soothing charm about it, and though they wept, yet it seemed to soothe and pacify them. But some of you do not pray, and, therefore, this comfort cannot be yours.

And you will come to die soon. When the death-thirst is in your throat, what do you think you will do without God? To die in God's presence, is simply to let life blossom into something better than life; but to die without God must be horrible! You will not want your boon companions then. Strong drink will not pacify you then. Music will have no charms for you then. The love of a tender and gentle wife can yield you but sorry comfort then. You may lay your money bags at your side, but they will not calm your palpitating heart then. You will hear the boomings of the waves of the great sea of eternity; you will feel your feet slipping into the dreadful quicksand; you will clutch about you for help, but there will be none! Instead thereof, invisible hands shall begin to pull you down. And down through the dark sea you must descend to those darker depths where dread despair will be your everlasting heritage!

But there is hope yet. Whosoever believeth in the Lord Jesus Christ shall be saved. Turn thine eye to Christ, poor sinner, as he hangs there suffering in man's stead, taking human guilt on himself, and being punished for it as though it were his own. Trust him, sinner, and resting in Jesus, thou shalt be saved!

Women's Rights.—A Parable.

"And Moses brought their cause before the Lord."—Num. xxvii. 5.

BY the help of God the Holy Spirit, I want to use this incident, which forms a kind of episode in the rehearsal of the history of Israel's forty years' wanderings in the wilderness, for a twofold purpose. First, let me indicate its general teaching, and, secondly, let me take it as a ground of appeal to certain special classes.

In respect to ITS GENERAL TEACHING.

I would ask your attention, and exhibit for your imitation, *the faith* which these five young women, the daughters of Zelophehad, *possessed with regard to the promised inheritance.* You must remember that the children of Israel were still in the wilderness. They had not seen the promised land, but God had made a covenant with them that they should possess it. He had declared that he would bring them into a land which flowed with milk and honey, and there plant them; and that that land should belong to them and to their descendants by a covenant of salt for ever. Now, these women believed in this heritage. They were not like Esau, who thought so little of the inheritance that he sold it to his brother Jacob for a mess of pottage; but they believed it to be really worth having; they regarded it, though they had never beheld it, as being something exceedingly substantial, and, so looking upon it, they were afraid lest they should be left out when the land was divided; and, though they had never seen it, yet, being persuaded that it was somewhere, and that the children of Israel would have it in due time, their anxiety was lest they, having no brothers, should be forgotten in the distribution, and so should lose their rights. They were anxious about an inheritance which they had never seen with their eyes. Now, herein I hold them up to the imitation of this present assembly. There *is* an inheritance far better than the land of Canaan. Oh, that we all believed in it, and longed for it! It is an inheritance, however, which eye hath not seen, and the sound whereof ear hath not heard. It is a city whose streets are gold, but none of us have ever trodden them. Never hath traveller to that country come back to tell us of its glories. There the music never ceases; no discord ever mingles in it: it is sublime; but no member of the heavenly choir has ever come to write out for us the celestial score, or to

> "Teach us some melodious sonnet
> Sung by flaming tongues above."

It is not a matter of sight; it must be to each one of us a matter of faith. By faith we know that there is another and a better land. By faith we understand that our disembodied souls shall mount to be with Christ, and that, after awhile, our bodies also shall rise to join our spirits, that body and soul may together be glorified for ever in the presence of our gracious Redeemer. We have never seen this land however; but there be some of us who as firmly believe in it as if we had seen it, and are as certain of it and as persuaded, as though these ears of ours had listened to its songs of joy, and these feet of ours had trodden its streets of gold.

There was this feature, too, about the faith of these five women—they knew that the inheritance *was only to be won by encountering great difficulties.* The spies who came back from the land had said that the men who dwelt in it were giants. They said, "We were in their sight at grasshoppers; yea, we were in our own sight as grasshoppers when we looked upon them." There were many in the camp of Israel, I have no doubt, who said, "Well, I would sell my share cheaply enough; for though the land be there, we never can win it; they have cities walled up to heaven, and they have chariots of iron; we can never win the place." But these women believed that though they could not fight, God could; and though they had never put their fingers to a more terrible instrument than a needle, yet did they believe that the same right arm which got to itself the victory when they went with Miriam, dancing to the timbrel's jubilant sound, would get the victory again, and bring his people in, and drive out the Canaanites, even though they had walled cities and chariots of iron. So these women had strong faith. I would to God that you had the same, all of you, dear friends; but I know that some of you who do believe that there is a land which floweth with milk and honey are half afraid that you shall never reach it. They are vexed with many doubts because of their own weakness, which, indeed, should not make them doubt, but should make them despair utterly if the getting of the goodly land depended upon their own fighting for it and winning it. But, inasmuch as "the *gift* of God is eternal life," and God himself will give it to us, and inasmuch as Jesus has gone up on high to prepare a place for us, and has promised that he will come again and receive us unto himself, that where he is there we may be also, I would to God that our doubts and fears were banished, and that we said within ourselves, "We are able to go up and attack the land, for the Lord, even the Lord of hosts, is with us; Jehovah-nissi is our banner; the Lord our righteousness is our helper, and we shall surely enter into the place of the beloved, and shall join the general assembly and church of the first-born whose names are written in heaven."

I commend the faith of those women to you because, believing in the land, and believing that it would be won, *they were not to be put about by the ill report of some who said that it was not a good land.* There were ten out of the twelve who spied out the land, who said, " It is a land that eateth up the inhabitants thereof." They brought back an evil report. But, whoever may have been perverted by these falsehoods, these five women were not. Others said, " Why, the land is full of pestilence and full of hornets, and those who live in it now are dying," forgetting that God was making them to die in order to bring in the children of Israel in their stead; and so they said, " who cares to have a portion there? Give us the leeks and the garlic, and the onions of Egypt, and let us sit again by the flesh-pots that we had at Rameses; but as for going on to this Canaan, we will never do it." But these five women, who knew that if there were troubles in the household *they* would be sure to have their share of them, that if the bread ran short they would be the most likely to feel the straitness of it, and that if it were a land of sickness *they* would have to be the nurses, yet coveted to have their share in it, for they did not believe the ill report. They said : " No ; God hath said it is a good land ; a land of hills and valleys, a land of brooks and rivers, a land of oil-olives, a land out of whose bowels they might dig iron, and brass, and gold, and silver ; and we will not believe what these spies say ; it is a good land, and we will go in and ask for our share in it." So I commend their faith in this respect. I know some of you are occasionally met by sneering sceptics, and they say, " There is no such land ; we have never seen it ; are you such fools as to believe it ; are you going on a pilgrimage over hedge and ditch, helter-skelter, after a country that you know nothing of? Are you going to be led by the nose ? Trust that old-fashioned book ; and take his word, and nothing but his word, and believe it ?" Oh, I hope there are many of us—would that all of us were in that vein of thought—who can say, " It is even so." Stand back Mr. Atheist, and stop us not, for we are well persuaded that ours is no wild-goose chase. Stand back Sir Ironical Sceptic; laugh if thou wilt. Thou wilt laugh on the other side of thy face one of these days, and we shall have the laugh of thee in those times. At any rate, if there be no heaven we shall be as well off as thou wilt be ; but, if there be a hell, where, O where, wilt thou be, and what will thy portion be ? So we even go on our own way confident and sure, nothing doubting; believing, as surely as we believe our own existence, that

> "Jesus, the Judge, will come
> To take his people up
> To their eternal home;"

and believing that one hour with him will be worth all the trials of the road; worth enduring ten thousand deaths, if we could endure them, in order to win it; and that, moreover, by God's grace we shall win it,

> "We shall behold his face,
> We shall his name adore,
> And sing the wonders of his grace
> Henceforth for evermore."

These daughters of Zelophehad, then, I hold up to your commendation and imitation on account of their faith.

But there was another point. Being thus sure of the land, and feeling certain about that, we must next commend them for *their anxiety to possess a portion in it.* Why did they think so much about it? I heard some one say the other day, speaking of certain young people, "I do not like to see young women religious; they ought to be full of fun and mirth, and not have their minds filled with such profound thoughts." Now, I will be bound to say that this kind of philosophy was accredited in the camp of Israel, and that there were a great many young women there who said, "Oh, there is time enough to think about the good land when we get there; let us be polishing up the mirrors; let us be seeing to our dresses; let us understand how to put our fingers upon the timbrel when the time comes for it; but as for prosing about a portion among those Hivites and Hittites, what is the good of it? We will not bother ourselves about it." But such was the strength of the faith of these five women that it led them to feel a deep anxiety for a share in the inheritance. They were not such simpletons as to live only for the present. They had outgrown their babyhood; they were not satisfied to live merely for the day. They knew that they would soon cross the Jordan, and that the tribes would be in the land, and so they began, as it were, like good housewives, to think about their portion where it would be, and to reflect that were they left out when the musterroll was read, and should no portion be appointed for Tirzah, and no portion for Milcah, and no place for any of the five sisters, they would be like beggars and outcasts in the midst of the land. The thought of all others having their plot of ground, and their family having none, made them anxious about it. Oh, dear friends, how anxious you and I ought to be to make our calling and election sure, and how solemnly should that verse of Wesley come home to our hearts,

> "But can I bear the piercing thought,
> What if my name should be left out
> When thou for them shalt call!"

Suppose I should have no portion in the skies! O ye foundations of jasper, ye gates of pearl, ye walls of chrysolite and all manner of precious stones, must I never own you? O troops of angels, and armies of the blood-bought, must *I* never wave the palm or wear the crown in your midst? Must the word that salutes me be that awful sentence, "Depart, ye cursed, into everlasting fire?" Is there no place for me, no room for me, in the inheritance of the saints? I do beseech you, never be satisfied till you can answer this question in the affirmative, and say, " Yes, I have a place in Jesu's heart; I have been washed in Jesu's blood; and therefore I shall be with Jesus where he is in his glory when the fitting time cometh." Oh, I would have you who are not sure about this, be as anxious as these women were. Let it press upon your hearts; let it even take the color from your cheek, sooner than that you should have a gayety and a mirth empty and frivolous, which will entice you down to the pit. Oh, do make sure work for eternity! Whatever else you trifle with, do seek to have an anchor that will hold you fast in the last great storm. Do seek to be affianced unto Christ, and grounded and bottomed upon his foundation—the Rock of Ages, where we must build for eternity. These women were taken up with prudent anxious thoughts about their own part in the land.

And let me say that they were right in desiring to have a portion there, when they recollect that the land had been covenanted to their fathers. They might well wish to have a part in a thing good enough to be a covenant-blessing. The land had been promised over and over again by divine authority; they might well wish to have a share in that which God's own lips had promised. It was a land to bring them into which God had smitten the first-born of Egypt, and saved his people by the sprinkling of blood; they might well desire a land which cost so great a price to bring them to it. Besides, it was a goodly land; it was the most princely of all lands; peerless among all the territories of earth. Its products were most rich. The grapes of Eshcol—what could equal them? Its pomegranates, its oil-olives, its rivers that flowed with milk and honey—there was nothing like it in all the world besides! They might well say, "Let us have a portion there!" And, my dear hearers, the heaven of which we have to tell you is a land so good that it was spoken of in the covenant before the world was. It has been promised to the people of God ten thousand times. Jesus Christ has shed his precious blood that he might open the gates of it, and bring us in. And it is a land—such a land—that, if you had but seen it, if you could but know what it is, you would pine away in stopping here; for its very dust is gold, its meanest joys are richer than the transports of earth, and the poorest in the kingdom of heaven is greater than he who is the mightiest prince in the kingdom of this world. O that your mouths were set a-longing after the feasts of paradise. O that ye pined to be where Jesus is; and then, surely, you would be anxious to know whether you had a portion there.

I hold these women up as an example, because they believed in the unseen inheritance, and they were anxious to get a portion in it:—

But I must commend them yet again for *the way in which they set about the business*. I do not find that they went complaining from tent to tent that they were afraid that they had no portion. Many doubters do that; they tell their doubts and fears to others, and they get no further. But these five women went straight away to Moses. He was at their head; he was their mediator; and then it is said that "Moses brought their cause before the Lord." You see, these women did not try to get what they wanted by force. They did not say, "Oh, we will take care and get our share when we get there." They did not suppose that they had any merit which they might plead, and so get it; but they went straight away to Moses, and Moses took their cause, and laid it before the Lord. Dost thou want a portion in heaven, sinner? Go straight away to Jesus, and Jesus will take thy cause, and lay it before the Lord. It is a very sorry one as it stands by itself, but he has such a sweet way of so mixing himself up with thee and thyself with him, that his cause and thy cause will be one cause, and the Father will give him good success, and thee good success too. O that some one here could breathe the prayer, if he has never prayed before, "Saviour, see that I have a portion in the skies. Precious Saviour, take my poor heart, and wash it in thy precious blood, and change it by thy Holy Spirit, and make me ready to dwell where perfect saints are. O do thou undertake my cause for me, thou blessed Advocate, and plead it before thy Father's face." That is the way to have the business done. Put it out of your own hands into the hands of the prophet like unto Moses, and you will surely speed.

Now, observe these women's *success*. The Lord accepted their plea, for he said unto Moses, "The daughters of Zelophehad speak right." Yes, and when thou criest to him, and when his dear Son takes thy prayer to him, God will say, "That sinner speaks right." Beat on thy breast, and say, "God be merciful to me a sinner;" and he will say, "That soul speaks right." Young women, imitate these five sisters now. May God the Holy Spirit bring you to imitate them by humbly offering your plea through the Mediator,

Jesus Christ, and God will say, " Ah! she speaks right; I have heard her; I have accepted her." And then God said that these sisters should have their portion just the same as the men had ; that they should have their share of land just as if they had inherited it as sons. And so will God say to every seeking sinner. Whatever may be the disability under which you labor, whatever bar there may have seemed to be to your claim, you shall inherit it among the children, you shall take your part and your lot among the chosen of God. Christ has set your cause before his Father, and it shall be unto you, poor sinner, according to your desire, and you shall have a part among the Lord's people.

I wish I had power to press this matter more immediately home upon you! Many of us who are now present are saved. It is a great satisfaction to remember how large a proportion of my congregation have come to Christ; but, oh! there are many, many here who are—well, where are they? They do not know that they have any inheritance. They cannot read their title clear to mansions in the skies, and, what is worse, they are unconcerned about it. If they were troubled about it, we would have hope; but no, they go their way, and, like Pliable, having got out of the Slough of Despond, they turn round and say to Christians, " You may have the brave country all to yourselves for me." They are so fond of present pleasures, so easily enticed by the wily whispers of the archenemy, so soon overcome by their own passions, that they find it too hard to be a Christian ; to love Christ is a thing too difficult for them. 'Ah! may God meet with you, and make you wiser! Poor souls, you will perish, some of you will perish while you are looking on at this world's bubbles and baubles! You will perish; you will go down to hell with this earth's joys in your mouths, and they will not sweeten those mouths when the pangs of hell get hold upon you? Your life is short; your candle flickers in its socket. You must soon go the way of all flesh. We never meet one week after another without some death occurring between. Out of this vast number surely it is all but impossible that we could all ever meet again. Perhaps before this day week some of us will have passed the curtain, have learned the great secret, and have looked into the invisible world. Whose portion will it be? If it be thine, dear hearer, wilt thou mount to worlds of joy, or shall—

> "Devils plunge thee down to hell
> In infinite despair?"

God make that a matter of concern with us first, and then may we come to Jesus, and receive the sprinkling of his precious blood; and thus may he make it a matter of confidence with us that we are saved through him, and shall be partakers with them that are sanctified!

II. With a view of giving the whole incident A PARTICULAR DIRECTION—

Does it not strike you that there is here a *special lesson for our unconverted sisters?* Here are five daughters, I suppose young women, certainly unmarried women, and these five were unanimous in seeking to have a portion where God had promised it to his people. Have I any young women here who would dissent from that? I am afraid I have! Blessed be God, for the many who come in among us—become solemnly impressed, and give their young days to Jesus; but there are some—there may be some here of another mind. The temptations of this wicked Metropolis, the pleasures of this perilous city, lead them away from their profession, and prevent their giving a fair hearing to God's Word. Well, but you are here, and may I, as a brother, put this question to you? Do you not desire a portion in the skies? Have you no wish for glory? Have you no longing for the everlasting crown? Can you sell Christ for a few hours of mirth? Will you give him up for a giddy song or an idle companion? Those are not your friends who would lead you from the paths of righteousness. Count them not dear, but loathe them, if they would entice you from Christ! But, as you will certainly die, and will as certainly live for ever in endless woe or in boundless bliss, do see to your souls. "Seek first the kingdom of God and his righteousness, and all other things shall be added to you." You have come fresh from the country, young woman, and, leaving your mother's care, it is very likely that you have begun to absent yourself from the means of grace, but I charge you not to do so. On the contrary, let this bind you to your mother's God, and may you feel that, whereas you might have neglected God's house hitherto and profaned God's day, yet henceforth, like the daughters of Zelophehad, you seek to have a portion in the promised land.

The subject bears another way. *Has it not a voice, and a loud voice too, to the children of godly parents?* I like these young women saying that their father did not die with Korah, but that he only died the ordinary death which fell upon others because of the sin of the wilderness; and also, their saying, "Why should the name of our father be done away from among his family because he had no son?" It is a good thing to see this respect to parents, this desire to keep up the honor of the family. I was thinking whether there may not be some here, some children of godly parents, who would feel it a sad thing if they should bring a disgrace upon the family name. Is it so, that though your father has been for many years a Christian, he has not one to succeed him? O young man, have you no ambition to stand in his place, no wish to let his name be perpetuated in the Church of God? Well, if the sons have no such ambition, or if there be none, let the daughters say to one another, "Our father never disgraced his profession, he did not die in the company of them that gathered themselves together against the Lord, but he served the Lord faithfully, and we will not let his name be blotted out from Israel; we will join ourselves to the people of God, and the family shall be represented still." But, oh! how I desire that the brothers and sisters would come together, and what a delightful thing it would be to see the whole family! In that household there were only five girls, but they all had their heritage. O father, would you not be happy if it should be so with your children? Mother, would not you be ready to say, "Lord, now lettest thou thy servant depart in peace, according to thy word, for mine eyes have seen thy salvation," if you could see all your children brought in? And why not, my brethren, why not? We will give God no rest until it is so; we will plead with him until they are all saved. And, young people, why not? The Lord's mercy is not straitened. The God of Abraham, of Isaac, and of Jacob, and your father's God, we trust, will be your God. O that you would follow in the footsteps of your parents so far as they followed Christ! These daughters of Zelophehad seem to me to turn preachers, and I stand here to speak for them, and all five of them say to you, " We gained our inheritance by seeking for it through a Mediator." Young women, brothers and sisters, you shall gain it, too, by seeking it through a Saviour.

And does not this text also speak to another class, to *orphans?* These good girls had lost their parents, or otherwise the question would not have arisen. Father and mother had gone, had passed away, and therefore they had to go to Moses for themselves. When the parents could not come to Moses for them, they came for themselves. Think of the skies a moment, some of you. Perhaps you were this morning in a very different place, but think of the skies a minute. No, I do not mean the meteoric stones; I do not mean the stars, nor yon bright moon; but I want you to think of your mother, who is yonder. Do you remember when she gave you the last kiss, and bade you farewell, and said, " Follow me, my children, follow me to the skies?" Think of a father who is there, his voice, doubtless, helping to swell the everlasting hallelujah. Does he not beckon you from the battlements of heaven, and cry, " Children of my loins, follow me as I followed Christ?" Some of us have an honored grandsire there, an honored grandmother there. Many of you have got infants there, young angels whom God lent you for a little time, and then took them to heaven to show you the way, to lure you to go upwards too. You have all some dear friends there with whom you walked to God's house in company. They have gone, but I charge you, by the living God, to follow them. Break not your households in twain. Let no solemn rifts and rents come into the family, but, as they have gone to their rest, God grant unto you by the same road to come and rest eternally too. Jesus Christ is ready to receive sinners; he is ready to receive you, and if you trust him, the joy and bliss which now your friends partake of shall be yours also. Daughters of godly parents, children of those who have gone before to eternal glory, I entreat you to look to Jesus; go and present your suit to him now. It shall surely prosper. If the question was once doubtful, it has now become " a statute of judgment." The Lord has commanded it. May God bless these counsels and exhortations to you for Christ's sake. Amen.

Black Clouds and Bright Blessings.

"If the clouds be full of rain, they empty themselves upon the earth."—ECCLES. xi. 3.

IT was raining very heavily when I was thinking over this text. The sharp crack of the thunder, and the quick flash of the lightning, seemed to be constant just where I sat. When I came here I found that you had not had a drop of rain, and the weather still continues hot and feverish. This seemed to me like an example and an illustration of the sovereignty of God's dispensations. True is it in the spiritual as well as in the natural economy, that one place is rained upon, and another is not rained upon. In one part of the church God's grace descends in a flood, while another part remains as dry and arid as the wilderness itself. Even under the same ministrations one Christian's soul may be refreshed till it becomes like a watered garden, while another may remain parched as the desert. He hath the key of the rain, and it is for us to ask him to give us of the dew and the rain of his Holy Spirit. Let us walk humbly with him, lest he should say of us, as he did to his Jewish vineyard of old, "Also I will command the clouds that they rain no rain upon it." We may stand up and look to the Most High, and learn our dependence upon him for spiritual blessings, just as the farmer, knowing his dependence for his harvest upon God, watches the sky and the clouds, for without the rain what can he do?

But, now, to come to the text itself: I purpose a meditation upon three of its practical uses. First, as *suggesting a comfort for the timid;* secondly, as *giving an argument to the doubting;* and thirdly, as *furnishing a lesson for the Christian.*

I. First, I think we may fairly use the text as a COMFORT FOR THE TIMID.

The clouds are black, they lower; they shut out the sun-light; they obscure the landscape. The timid one looks up and says, "Alas! how black they are, and how they gather fold on fold! What a dark, gloomy day!" What makes them black? It is because they are full, and hence light cannot pierce them. And if they be full, what then? Why, then it will rain, and then the hot earth will be refreshed, and every little plant, and every tiny leaf and rootlet of that plant will suck up moisture, and begin to laugh for joy. Out of the black sky comes the bright daisy, and the garden is painted with many colors, and the only palette that is used, is, after all, that black one, for the sky doth it by its rain.

Now, Christian, you too, are of a timid disposition, and every now and then your circumstances are not as you would like to arrange them. Losses come very closely upon one another. Friend after friend forsakes you. Sickness treads upon the heel of sickness. All things are against you, as against Jacob of old. The clouds are very black, but may they not be black for the very same reason as the clouds above you—because they are full? And is it not very possible that it will be with you as it has been often with God's saints, according to the hymn we sang just now—

> "Ye fearful saints, fresh courage take:
> The clouds ye so much dread
> Are big [aye, black] with mercy, and shall break
> In blessings on your head."

If the clouds were not black, you might not expect rain. If your afflictions were not grievous, they would not be profitable. If your adversities did not pain and trouble you, they would not be blessed to you. We have heard some people say—"If this trouble had come in such and such a shape, I would not have minded it." But God meant you to mind it, for it was in your minding it that it was blessed to you. "By the blueness of the wound," saith Solomon, "the hurt is made better." When the stroke causes black and blue, when really the spirit is thoroughly wounded, then the blessing comes. It is not merely said in the Scriptures that there is a needs-be for affliction. That is a great truth, but it is added then that there is a needs-be that the affliction should lower our spirit. Listen to the words—"Now for a season, if needs-be ye are in heaviness through manifold temptations." The needs-be is not for the temptation merely, but that ye be in heaviness feeling the temptation—not for the iron only, but for the iron entering into your soul. If the child liked the rod, it would be no chastisement; and if the Christian loved his affliction while he was in it, and it seemed joyous to him, then it were no affliction ; but it is the very sharpness of it, the vinegar and the gall, that is the medicine that produces the good effect. The blackness of the cloud proves its fulness, and its fulness brings the shower. I suppose we know this experimentally. As a church, we can look back upon mercies which God has given us in a very extraordinary manner. God intended that this house should be full of hearers every Sabbath-day for years. It is a very remarkable circumstance, and one that always astonishes me more, perhaps, than it does any of you, when I see the aisles and every place crowded Sabbath after Sabbath. But, how much of the success with which God has crowned our ministry, has been due to the most afflicting providence that ever befell a Christian minister or a Christian church? Was it not, dear friends—to allude to that sad event which is still upon the minds of some of us, and will be till we die, when the cry was raised, and death came into the midst of our solemn assembly—was it not due to that, to a very great extent, that the preacher became known, and that so he has had an opportunity of speaking to many more souls than otherwise would have listened to him, concerning the unsearchable riches of Christ? You will have found it so, I think, in your own private estate. A big wave has washed you on to a safe rock. A black life-boat has taken you out of a gay and bright, but leaky vessel, and brought you to your desired haven. You have been unburdened. If you have lost your riches, you have been better without them than with them. Your losses have, in the end, come to be practical gains. The good ship has gone across the waters more swiftly, when some of that which was but needless ballast, has been heaved overboard. Can you not affirm of your spiritual experience—certainly I can of my own—that the pelting showers and fiercer storms have been most soul-enriching? It is when one labors under a deep sense of sin; when perhaps one's hope is jostled to and fro like a reed shaken by the wind; when the spirit sinks and the soul is brought very low; that we learn to study the promises, find out their value, prove their faithfulness, and come to understand more than ever of the grace and goodness of a covenant-keeping God. "Before I was afflicted I went astray, but now have I kept thy word;" this is only another way of putting the same truth. The clouds were full of rain, but they emptied themselves upon the man who needed grace from on high.

Now, brethren and sisters, what has been true in the past, depend upon it, is true in the present. I do not know—how can I tell—what is your particular trouble; but you may well believe that he who appointed it, he who measured it, he who has set its bounds, will bring you to the end of it, and prove his gracious design in it all. Do not think that God deals roughly with his children, and gives them needless pain. It grieves him to grieve you. "He doth not afflict willingly, nor grieve the children of men." It is easy to have a faith that acts backwards, but faith that will act forwards from the point of your present emergency, is the true faith that you want now. Hath God helped you out of one trouble after another, and is it to be supposed that he will leave you in this? In six troubles he will be with you; yea, in seven there shall be no evil touch you. The particular water in which you now are struggling is intended and included in the promise, " When thou goest through the rivers I will be with thee, and through the floods, they shall not overflow thee." It is, I must confess, difficult sometimes to bring the promise down to the particular case, for unbelief fights hard against it; but remember, unless the promise be applied to the particular case, it is like the liniment which is not applied to the wound, or like the medicine that is not received by the patient. The medicine not received may be very potent, but the man cannot know its value; and the promise may be very sweet and precious, but it cannot comfort you unless it be applied. Do ask, then, for grace that you may believe while you are still under the cloud, black as it looks, that it will empty itself in blessed rain upon you.

So will it be on the largest possible scale in the whole Church of Christ. There are many clouds surrounding the church of God just now, and I must confess, that with all the religious activity there is abroad, there is very much to cause us great sorrow. The friends of evangelical opinions are few compared with the advocates of Broad Churchism and Romanism. The strength seems to be meanwhile on the wrong side, and the devil hath stirred up a fierce tempest, by reason of which some are alarmed. But we must not yield to fear. The Master knows. He understands that it is right for his soldiers to be sometimes rebuffed at Ai, though they have won Jericho, that afterwards they may search and find out the accursed thing, and stone the Achan that has brought upon them defeat. He will be with us yet, and the time shall come when we shall see that every cloud that was full of rain has emptied itself upon the earth.

II. Our second point is AN ARGUMENT WITH THE DOUBTING AND THE DESPONDING.

It is a law of nature that a full thing begins to empty itself. When the cloud gets full, it no longer has the power of retaining its fluid contents, but it pours them down upon the earth. When the river gets swollen, does it not rush with greater impetuosity towards the deep? And the ocean itself is continually emptying itself into the ocean that is above the firmament, that same ocean above the firmament emptying itself again, according to the text, upon the earth. As there is a circulation in the body, and every pumping of blood into the heart is accompanied by another pumping of it out again, so there is a circulation in this great world; everything revolving, and the whole machine kept in order, not by hoarding, but by spending; not by retaining, but by consecutively getting and giving.

Well now, dear friends, you may gather that when the cloud is full it is going to rain. I want you to draw an argument from this. *Our gracious God never makes a store of any good thing, but he intends to give it to us.* Just think for a moment of God, our gracious Father. He is love. His name is love. His nature is love. Love is God. "God is love." He is all goodness. He is a bottomless, shoreless sea, brimful of goodness. He is full of pardoning goodness to forgive sin. He is full of accepting favor to receive poor prodigals to his bosom. He is full of faithful goodness to watch over his dear children; full of bounteous goodness to bestow upon them all that they want. Now, if there be such a plenitude of goodness in the Father, it must be for some object—not for himself. Why should it be given to himself? It must be there for his creatures. Is it not written that he delighteth in mercy? We know that he maketh the sun to shine upon the evil as well as upon the just. Then I, even though I be evil, will hope that this store of goodness in the heart of the everlasting Father is intended, some of it, at any rate, to be poured out upon me, poor unworthy me. "If the clouds be full of rain, they empty themselves upon the earth," and if God be full of goodness, it is that he may spend that goodness upon the sons of men. But whither come those bright and sparkling drops, flashing like diamonds in the sunlight, turning to many colors, and forming the wondrous iris? Whither come ye, whither come ye, O ye bright and heaven-born drops of matchless rain, all pure and free from every stain; whither come ye? "We are come down to the black, hard, dusty earth; we are going to fall upon the desert or upon the sea; we descend on fields that ask not for us; we descend upon the soil that is chapped and needs us, but has not a tongue to speak for us, nor a heart to feel its need. We come down from our element in heaven to tabernacle among men, and to do them good." And so it is with the goodness of our blessed Father. If it be in him, it is there for the earth, for those who need it; for those who do not even feel their need, and whose need is, therefore, all the deeper; who cannot feel their need, and, therefore, have a need that is deepest of all needs. Oh! blessed goodness, that delights to spend itself upon the unworthiest of men!

Ah, troubled, doubting soul! think again; let me ask you this time *to muse a little upon Jesus Christ the Son of the Father.* Beloved, it is a part of our belief that "it pleased the Father that in him should all fulness dwell." We believe that in the atoning sacrifice there is a fulness of satisfaction made to divine justice; that there is a fulness of cleansing power in the precious blood; that there is a fulness of righteousness in Christ's holy life; a fulness of vivifying power in his resurrection; a fulness of prevalence in his plea; and a fulness of representation in his standing before the eternal throne to take possession of heaven for us. No one here, I think, looks upon Christ as a well without water, or as a cloud without rain. Now, dear heart, if thou believest Christ to be a cloud that is full of rain, for what reason is he full? Why, that he may empty himself upon the earth. There was no need that he should be a man full of sympathy except to sympathize with mourning men and women. There was no need that he should bleed except that he might bleed for you. There was no necessity that he should die except that the power of his death might deliver you from death. There was no need whatever that he should be a servant unless that his obedience might justify many. The fulness of his essential Godhead may be supposed to be there for himself, but the fulness of his mediatorial character is a mere waste, unless it is there for you. A man looking at the coal-mines of England, naturally considers that God made that coal with the intention of supplying the world's inhabitants with fuel, and that he stored it, as it were, away in those dark cellars underground for this favored nation, that the wheels of its commerce might be set in motion. Well, now, if I go to those everlasting mines of divine faithfulness and of atoning efficacy, which are laid up in the veins of Jesus Christ, I must conceive that there is a supply laid up for those who will require it; and so there is. Doubt it not; there is cleansing for the guilty, there is life for the dead, there is healing for the sick. If Jesus be full of power to save, he will save you. If you cry unto him, he will empty himself upon you.

To proceed yet further, I would ask the doubter to look *at the infinite fulness of power which is treasured up in the Holy Spirit.* It is a part of our conviction that there is no heart so hard that the Holy Spirit cannot soften it; no soul so dead that he cannot quicken it; and no man so desperately set on mischief that his will cannot be subdued by the effectual power of the Holy Ghost working in him. We believe the Holy Ghost to be no mere influence, no inferior or secondary power of moral suasion, but to be absolutely divine—a divine Being exerting irresistible force upon the mental powers of man. Well, now, if there be this might, surely when he appears in the character of a comforter and a quickener, his might is there to be exerted. Is thy heart hard? He will empty his softening influence upon it. Is it dead? His quickening power shall there find a congenial sphere. Art thou dark? Then there is room for his light. Art thou sick? Then is there a province for his healing energy. "If the clouds be full of rain, they empty themselves upon the earth;" and, if the Spirit of the living God be full of might and energy, it is that he may manifest it all in these poor, needy souls who desire to feel its power.

What a wondrous book this Bible of ours is. When you have read this Bible through a score of times, you may have only strolled over the surface, looked at the land, or ploughed at most the upper soil. If you take one passage, and dig deep for the treasure that coucheth beneath, you will find it inexhaustible. The Book has in it a matchless fulness. It were as possible to measure space, or to grasp the infinite in the hollow of your hands, as to investigate the entire compass of Holy Scripture. It is high; I cannot attain unto it. It is broad; I cannot reach its boundary. But oh, what an abundance of provisions, and what a fulness of comfort there are stored up in the promises of God's Word.

"What more can he say than to you he hath said;
You who unto Jesus for refuge have fled."

Now, what is this fulness in the Bible for? "If the clouds be full of rain, they empty themselves upon the earth." If the Scriptures be full of comfort, they are intended to be enjoyed, to be believed, to be fed upon by you. There is nothing to spare in this book. There is not too little, but rest assured, there is nothing too much. He that goeth out in the morning after this manna, though he gathereth his omer full, he shall have nothing over, and if he gathereth little, yet still he shall have no lack. There is enough for all, and all its fulness is meant to be used. I cannot amplify on this thought. I have not time to beat it out more, but I hope and pray it may be useful to some of you. You do not trust God, many of you, as you ought to do. You measure his corn with your own bushel.

You know that you would fail your fellow-men and you think that he will fail you. You know your own weakness and infirmity, and you imagine that he will be faint or weary. You know that you could not act very generously towards some who have been ungrateful and unkind to you, and you think he cannot. Remember the passage—"My thoughts are not your thoughts, neither are your ways my ways, saith the Lord. For as the heavens are higher than the earth, so are my ways higher than your ways, and my thoughts than your thoughts." You think about saving; he only thinks about giving. You take a delight in getting; he takes his delight in bestowing. Go to him! go to him! You would not need anybody to be long praying you to accept. Do not think that God needs much beseeching in order to give, for it is as easy for him to give as it is for you to accept; and, as accepting seems congenial to our nature, so does bestowing seem congenial to his. Go to him, and he will empty out his grace upon you!

III. THE TEXT FURNISHES A LESSON TO CHRISTIANS.

"If the clouds be full of rain, they empty themselves upon the earth." The drift of the passage is, of course, to be gathered from the connection, and it was intended by Solomon to *teach us liberality*. He says—" Give a portion to seven, and also to eight; for thou knowest not what evil shall be upon the earth. If the clouds be full of rain, they empty themselves upon the earth." By which he means to say—"If your pocket is full, empty it out upon the poor and needy; and if God has endowed you with much of this world's substance, look out for cases of necessity, and consider it as much the object of your existence to bestow help upon the needy, as it is the design in the creation of a cloud that it should empty itself upon the earth."

Do the clouds ever lose by emptying themselves? No doubt when the cloud has emptied itself out it is renewed, and still goeth on its course. At any rate, however it may be with the cloud, if it be dissipated when the rain descends, it is not so with the Christian man. God hath a way of giving by cart-loads to those who give away by shovel-fulls. If we give at the back-door—and I do not think we ought to give at any other door—he will be pretty sure to give in greater abundance at the window, and at the front door likewise. Says Bunyan:—

"There was a man, and some did count him mad,
The more he gave away the more he had."

Thank God for men of that sort. "There is that withholdeth more than is meet, but it tendeth to poverty;" and, on the other hand, that sentence which hath in it the nature of a proverb and a prophecy is often verified; "the liberal soon shall be made fat." I need not say much upon this to the members of my own congregation, with whom I am acquainted. Most of you, I believe, do empty yourselves upon the earth in proportion as God assists you, and enables you to give; but there are many persons in this land—I hope their number is on the decrease—worth thousands upon thousands a year, whose contributions to the cause of God are so utterly insignificant, that it is difficult to suppose that the love of Christ has ever gone far enough into them to thaw their hearts, for it has not even penetrated their pockets, making the gold to melt, and their riches to flow in liberality. I was spoken to by a brother minister not long ago, when I was preaching for him, and he said— "Do not spare them, sir; do not spare them; there is one pew there in front of the pulpit, where three men sit who are worth a million of money between them; our chapel is a thousand pounds in debt, and yet three of our members have a million between them." I said to him, "I think you ought not to 'spare them' yourself; I do not know why I should say it, only coming here to preach occasionally." "Well," said he, "but you can say, perhaps, what nobody else may." Really, it is a most horrible thing that there should be such positive covetousness allied with a profession of Christianity. Christian men—shall I call them so?— who, after all the plain precepts of Scripture, practise idolatry. They talk of being "stewards," but they act practically as if they were the owners. When a man once gets into the habit of giving to the cause of God, it becomes as much a delight to contribute of his substance as to pray for God's bounty, or to drink in the promise. How could I dare to exist if I did not do something for Christ? Not do something for Jesus? Were it not to rob me of the highest privilege which can be accorded to a man this side the grave? When I pray, I ask for something for myself; when I praise, it is but little I can render; but oh, to think that I, a poor creature of God's own making, should be able to give to him! It puts the creature in the highest conceivable light. It lifts him even above angels. There are works the laborious, disinterested, self-sacrificing Christian can do for Christ—

> "Which perfect saints above
> And holy angels cannot do."

Let the wealthy empty themselves upon the earth, and this shall be the way to fill themselves.

But, dear friends, though not many of us are intrusted with much wealth, we have other aptitudes to be useful. Some Christians *have a considerable amount of ability to serve the Lord.* They are, perhaps, able to speak for the Master. Now, I think that wherever there is some knowledge of God's Word, a personal acquaintance with its power, and a facility to speak, we should exercise our talent, if it be but one; and if we have ten, we should not keep one of the ten to ourselves. "If the clouds be full of rain, they empty themselves upon the earth;" and if a man be full of ability, he is the more bound to empty himself. If there is any minister who ought to work hard, it is the man who is successful. If there is a person living who ought to be always successful, it is the man whom God helps to preach with power. I say, if God makes me a full cloud, I must go on emptying. If he gives me a good store, I must take care that I scatter it. We must do, each man according to his ability, for God requireth not what a man hath not, but what he hath. Now, dear Christian friends, are you all, out of love for Jesus, doing what you can for him? Are you, whether you be big clouds or little clouds, trying to empty yourselves upon the earth? The nearest people of your acquaintance—your children, your kinsfolk, your neighbors—are you trying to show these the way of life—

> "Do you gladly tell to sinners round,
> What a dear Saviour you have found."

Though comparatively few of us have great genius, we all have some little capacity. Some Christians have a large amount of *experimental knowledge*. They are not eloquent, they are not educated, but they are wise. It has been our privilege to have met with those in the very humblest walks of life, whose experimental knowledge of divine things was very much more profound than would usually be found in a doctor of divinity; men and women who have learned their theology not in halls and colleges, but in courts and cellars; learned how to pray on bare knees; learned how to cry to the God of providence when the cupboard was empty; have tried the reality of religion in the hospital, and perhaps in the workhouse; some who have done business in the great waters, and have seen the works of the Lord, and his wonders in the deep.

It is a great treat to talk to some of those old saints. Their lips are like the lips of the girl in the fable, which dropped jewels. There is a savor, an unction, about what they say. It is not theory, but experience with them; not the letter, but the very soul, and marrow, and fatness of the truth. You do not find them looking to an arm of flesh, or talking about the dignity of manhood, or vaunting the excellence of mental power. They know of nothing except human weakness and nothingness; they trust in nothing but the divine arm, and the invincible strength of the Holy Ghost. Are there not some such in our midst? If you have any experience, let me say to you—do, as you have opportunity, tell it out; empty it upon the earth. If you have gained some knowledge of God, communicate it. If you have proved him, confess to a generation about you that he is a faithful God. I recollect in a time of great despondency deriving wonderful comfort from the testimony of an aged minister who was blind, and had been so for twenty years. When he addressed us, he spoke of the faithfulness of God, with the weak voice of a tremulous old man, but with the firmness of one who knew what he said, because he had tasted and handled it. I thanked God for what he had said. It was not much in itself. If I had read it in a book, it would not have struck me; but as it came from him, from the very man who knew it and understood it, it came with force and with unction. So you experienced Christians, if any others are silent, you must not be. You must tell the young ones of what the Lord has done for you. Why, some of you good old Christian people are apt to get talking about the difficulties, troubles, and afflictions you have met with more than about the succors, the deliverances, and the joys you have proved; not unlike those persons in "Pilgrim's Progress," who told poor Pilgrim about the lions, and giants, and dragons, and the sloughs, and hills, and all that could terrify and dishearten him. They might have mentioned all this, but they should also have told of Mr. Greatheart, and they should not have forgotten to speak of the eternal arm that sustains Christian in his pilgrimage. Tell the troubles, that were wise; but tell the strength of God that makes you sufficient, that is wiser still. Empty yourselves. If you have got experience, empty yourselves upon the earth.

I cannot particularize here what manner of endowment God has committed to any or all of you; but I think there is not one saint out of heaven but has his niche to fill, his particular work to do, and therefore some special talent intrusted to him. Do not hide it in the earth. Dig up that talent, and that napkin too, and go and put it out to heavenly interest for the benefit of others, and for the glory of your God. Herein is the folly of so many Christians, that, being wrapped up in the interest of their own salvation, and taken up with their own doubts and fears, there is little care they feel and little trouble they take for others. They never seem to empty themselves out into the world that is around them, and go forth into the world bigger than the homestead in which they live. But when a man begins to think about others, to care for others, to value the souls of others, then his thoughts of God get larger, then his consolations grow greater, and his spirit becomes more Godlike. A selfish Christianity! What shall I call it but an unchristian Christianity, a solecism in terms, a contradiction in its very essence. You do not find the men who are anxious after others so often troubled in mind as those who give no thought except to themselves. Mr. Whitefield, in his diary, has his times of depression, but they are comparatively few; and when he is going from one " pulpit-throne," as he calls it, to another and is preaching all day long, and is hearing the sobs and cries of sinners, and perhaps bearing the hootings and peltings of a mob; sitting down as soon as he has done in public to finish up his letters, or to devote an hour to prayer—why, he has not time enough to get desponding; he cannot afford space enough to be doubting his own interest in Christ. He is engaged in his Master's service, and has so much of the blessing of God upon it, that he goes right on without needing to stop. Christians! may you get into the same delightful state—warm with love to Christ, fervent with zeal for the spread of his kingdom. You shall not need then to ask any longer—

> "'Tis a point I long to know,
> Oft it causes anxious thought—
> Do I love the Lord or no,
> Am I his, or am I not?"

but you may give a practical answer to such scruples by saying—

> "There's not a lamb in all thy flock,
> I would disdain to feed;
> There's not a foe before whose face
> I'd fear thy cause to plead."

"If the clouds be full of rain, they empty themselves upon the earth."

Observe, lastly, when it is that the clouds do empty themselves. The text says, when they are full. This is a broad hint, I think, to the Christian; it tells him *when to work*. David was to attack the Philistines at a certain signal. "When thou hearest the sound of a going in the tops of the mulberry-trees, then thou shalt bestir thyself." Take this as. a divine signal; when you are full, it is time for you to set about doing good, emptying yourselves upon the earth. Mr. Jay tells young students—and there are some here—that they cannot always sermonize, but that there will come times when they can. "Now," says he, "when I find that the wind blows I put up the sails; I make hay while the sun shines, and get the outlines of my sermons when God assists me to do so, that I may have them in readiness, when, perhaps, the breeze may not seem to be so favorable, and my mind not so much upon the wing."

Do good to yourselves by storing up when you have

opportunity. But yet Christians have particular times when they feel fuller than at others. A sermon has warmed your heart; or you feel grateful, joyous, and zealous, on some other account. Well, perhaps, you will feel sick to-morrow; so you had better go and do some good to-day. "Nothing like the time present," is the world-old motto. "A bird in the hand is worth two in the bush," saith the proverb. Rest assured that a duty to-day done will be worth two duties saved for to-morrow. A word spoken for Christ to somebody before you go out of the Tabernacle may be timely, opportune, profitable; but, if you wait for season or circumstance to be more convenient, you may wait and wait till you are weary of waiting, but you might as well expect a lost hour to return as a lost opportunity. A Primitive Methodist brother said at one of the meetings lately, that the reason why the Primitive Methodists got on so was, that while other Christians were waiting for something to turn up, the Primitive Methodists turned it up themselves. It was a quaint thing to say certainly, but there is a great truth in it. Some Christian people are always biding their time and reserving themselves for a happy juncture. They want a fit occasion for doing good, and they mean to do something worthy of themselves when they get the opportunity. My brethren, you have always an opportunity if you will. How does Solomon put it? "Whatsoever thy hand findeth to do"—the first thing which comes—" do it with all thy might." I am ashamed to have to say as much as this in this vast City of London. Want work? Nonsense! Laziness! Want work in a city like London! A Christian woman want work for God in a city of three million inhabitants, with all its sickness and sorrow, its destitution and squalor! A Christian man not know what to do to serve his Master with all these courts, and alleys, and crowded houses; with all their filth and moral pollution, with all the thousands of gin-palaces that glare in the streets, and the crimes of drunkenness that darken the homes of the people! Nothing for a Christian to do! You are lazy, sirs; lazy, listless, sluggish, or else you would never raise such a question. It is not, "What should I do?" but "Where shall I begin doing it—which is the first point?" And I would say, begin at the point that is nearest to you. So they did when they built the walls of Jerusalem. Every man built opposite to his own house. There, you see, the advantage was he had not to walk two miles to his work at morn and then come back at night. He built opposite to his own house, so he was spared all that trouble. And when he had a little leisure time, when he went to his dinner, he could sit and look at his work, and think how to do it better next time. There was a further advantage in that. Much economy and great benefit would come of it were Christians to work near where they live, and take up that part of Christian service most congenial to their circumstances and to their tastes. "Whatsoever thy hand findeth to do"—next to thine own door —"do it with all thy might." Begin to do it; continue to do it, being always steadfast and immovable in the work of the Lord. But if there be a time when you shall specially and particularly labor for Christ, do it when you are full of his love. You have had a mercy lately—a great mercy; now is the time for liberality. You were spared from bankruptcy during the great crisis: consecrate to God what might have been lost. You feel full of love to Jesus; go, talk about Jesus to those who do not know him. You are full of zeal; let it manifest itself. You are full of faith; exercise it. You are full of hope; now go and lead others into the same hopeful state. Pray for a blessing upon others when you have had the best season of prayer, the sweetest period of communion at the Lord's Table, or when you have been well fed on the Word. "If the clouds be full, they empty themselves upon the earth."

God grant to those of you who have no rest, who are without God, and without Christ, that ye may know your emptiness; and then the Lord fill you with his own rich grace, as he is wont to do to all those that put their trust in him.

David's First Victory.

"So David prevailed over the Philistine with a sling and with a stone, and smote the Philistine, and slew him; but there was no sword in the hand of David."—1 SAMUEL xvii. 50.

CAREFUL perusal of the whole chapter will well repay your pains. I have selected a verse for convenience, but I want the entire narrative for a text. If you are well versed in the history, we shall have no need of any preface or exordium. So we shall proceed at once to regard David, in his conflict with Goliath, and his victory over him, first, as *a type of our Lord Jesus Christ*, and, secondly, *as an example for ourselves.* As that which is a type of the head always bears a relationship to the members, and as the members of Christ's mystical body now are, and shall yet more fully be, like unto himself, it is but one thought, after all, that we shall be following out in the meditation that lies before us.

I. Let us begin by calling your attention to the fact that David in this matter was A TYPE OF OUR LORD JESUS CHRIST.

The early fathers of the church were very great in

opening up typical analogies. So full, indeed, were they in their expositions, and so minute in their details, that at length they went too far, and degenerated into trifling. Origen, for example, very notably exceeded what can be regarded as wise interpretation in giving spiritual meanings to literal records. And others, who essayed to go yet farther than that great master of mysticism, very soon did much damage to the church of God, bringing precious truths into serious discredit. The study of the types of the Old Testament has scarcely regained its proper place in the Christian church since the days in which those gracious men, by their imprudent zeal, perverted it. We cannot, however, bring ourselves to think that a good thing ceases to be good because it has at some time been turned to an ill account. We think it can still be used properly and profitably. Within certain limits, then—limits, we suppose, which there is little danger of transgressing in these mechanical, unpoetic times—the types and the allegories of Holy Scripture may be used as a hand-book of instruction—a *vade mecum* of sound doctrine. Now, by common consent of all Evangelical Christians, David is accepted to be an eminent type of the Lord Jesus Christ. With regard to this particular transaction let us note, at the outset, that before he fought with Goliath, David was anointed of God. Samuel had gone down to Bethlehem and poured a horn of oil upon his head. The parallel will readily occur to you. Thus hath the Lord found out for himself one whom he has chosen out of the people. With his holy oil hath he anointed him. Upon Saul's head a phial of oil was poured—upon David's head a full horn of oil. This may perhaps be designed to contrast the brevity and scant renown of Saul's reign, with the length, and power, and excellence of the reign of David. Or, being interpreted spiritually, it may denote that the law, the old Judaism of which Saul is the type, had but a limited measure of blessing, while that of the gospel, which David represents, is characterized by its abounding fulness. Jesus, the antitype of David, is anointed with the oil of gladness above his fellows. Grace and truth came by Jesus Christ. The Spirit was not given by measure unto him. David was anointed several times—he was anointed, as you read in the chapter preceding our text, " in the midst of his brethren "— anointed, as you find in 2 Samuel ii. 4, by his brethren, the men of Judah—and anointed again, as you will observe in 2 Samuel v. 3, by all the elders of Israel. We will not go into that now, but it will suffice us to note that so was our Lord anointed of God, is anointed of his saints, and shall be anointed of the whole church. The Spirit of the Lord was upon him, and it was in the power of that Spirit with which he was anointed of the Father, that he went forth to fight the great battles of his church. At his baptism, coming up out of the Jordan, he was anointed by the Spirit as it rested upon him, descending out of heaven like a dove; and straightway he went, as he was driven, into the wilderness, and held that notable forty days' conflict with the arch-fiend, the dire adversary of souls. His battles were in the spirit and power of the Highest, for the might and majesty of the Eternal Spirit rested upon him.

See how the correspondence goes on. Our Lord was sent by his Father to his brethren. As David was sent by Jesse to his brethren with suitable presents and

11*

comfortable words, in order to commune with them, even so in the fulness of time was our Lord commissioned to visit his brethren. He remained concealed for awhile in the house of his reputed father, but afterwards he came forth, and was distinctly recognized as the sent One of God, bearing countless gifts in his hands, coming on an embassage of mercy and of love from God to those whom he was not ashamed to call his brethren. We have read how David was treated. His brethren did not receive him lovingly. They answered his unaffected kindness with unprovoked rudeness: bitter things did they lay to his charge. How truly does this answer to the manner in which our Lord, the Son of David, was abused. He came unto his own, and his own received him not. Though he came to them with words of tenderness, they replied to him with words of scorn. For his blessings they gave him curses; for the bread of heaven they gave him stones; and for the benedictions of heaven they gave him the spite of earth, the maledictions of hell! Never was a brother, "the first-born among many brethren," so ill-used by the rest of the household. Surely that parable of the wicked husbandman was fulfilled toward him. We know it is written that the vine-dresser said, "This is my son, they will reverence him;" but contrariwise they said, "This is the heir: let us kill him, and the inheritance shall be ours." Jesus was roughly handled by his brethren, whom he came to bless. David, you will remember, answered his brethren with great gentleness. He did not return railing for railing, but with much gentleness he endured their churlishness. In this he supplied us with but a faint picture of our beloved Master, who, when he was reviled, reviled not again. " Consider him that endured such contradiction of sinners against himself." His only reply, even to the strokes which were to effect his death, was, "Father, forgive them, for they know not what they do." " We hid as it were our faces from him; he was despised, and we esteemed him not." Yet for all that, no word of anger dropped from his lips. He might have said, " Is there not a cause?" Little spake he, however, in his own defence; he rather went about his life-work as zealously as if all who saw him had approved him. So David, being thus rejected of his brethren, became a type of Christ.

We pass on to observe that David was moved by an intense love of his people. He saw them defied by the Philistine. As he marked how they were crushed in spirit before their formidable enemies, a fervent indignation stirred his soul; but when he heard the terms of defiance, he felt that the God of Israel himself was compromised in this quarrel. The name of Jehovah was dishonored! That braggart giant who stalked before the hosts defied the armies of the living God! No wonder that the warm and devout heart of the brave young shepherd was moved with a mighty heaving. The passion of a warrior kindled in his breast at the sound of that profane voice of the uncircumcised Philistine, who could trifle with the honor of Jehovah, the God of heaven and of earth! A further motive was present to stimulate his patriotic ambition. How could David's bosom fail to glow with strong emotion when he was told that the man who should vanquish and slay that Philistine should be married to the king's daughter? Such a prize might well quicken his ardor. But with all these motives acting upon him, his determination to go forth and do battle with the champion of Philistia was prompt and resolute. Now in all this he plainly foreshadowed our Lord Jesus Christ. He loved his own: he was always ready to lay down his life for the sheep. But he loved his Father: "Wist ye not," he had said of old, "that I must be about my Father's business?" "The zeal of thine house hath eaten me up." And then there was the joy that was set before him that he should have the church for his spouse; that at the peril, not to say the price of his life, he should obtain her; that he should see of the travail of his soul in her, and should be satisfied. She was to be lifted up to his royalties, and to share his crown and throne. The new Jerusalem, the mother of us all, was to be unto Jesus the gift of God as his reward; and this inspired him, so he went forth and entered upon the battle for our sakes. Let us pause and bless his name that ever he should have loved the people, and that the saints should have been in his hands. Let us bless him that the zeal of God's house did eat him up,—that he consecrated himself so fully to the great enterprise. Above all, let us humbly and gratefully bless him that he loved us and gave himself for us. As a part of his church whom he had betrothed unto himself for ever, we are partakers in all that he did. It was for us that he fought the fight, for us he won the victory, for us he has gone into glory. And he will come by and by to take us up to behold that glory, and be with him where he is. While we see the type in David, let us take care not to forget to adore

Jesus himself, who is here mirrored forth to our minds in the achievement of our salvation.

I might, indeed, instance many further details in which David yet further became a type of our Lord. The whole narrative being full of minute particulars, supplies us copiously with points of analogy. But there is one thing I would have you specially observe.

Goliath is called in the Hebrew, not "champion," as we read it in the English, but the *middle-man*, the *mediator*. If you put the whole case fairly before your own minds, you will readily see the fitness of the word that is used. There is the host of the Philistines on the one side, and there is the host of Israel on the other side. A valley lies between them. Goliath says, "I will represent Philistia. I stand as the middle-man. Instead of all the rank and file coming forth personally to the fight, I appear as the representative of my nation—the mediator. Choose you a mediator who will come and contend with me. Instead of the battle being between the individuals of which the respective armies are composed, let two representative men decide in dread duel the question in debate." Now, it is exactly upon that ground that the Lord Jesus Christ fought the battles of his people. We fell representatively in the first Adam, and our salvation now is by another representative—the second Adam. He is the Middleman, the "one Mediator between God and man." In his love to us, and his zeal for the glory of God, we may view him as stepping forward into the midst of the arena which divides the camps of good and of evil, of God and of the devil, and there facing the defiant adversary, he stands to contend in our name and on our behalf, if we be in-

deed his people, that he may decide for us the quarrel
which never could have been decided by us. Personally,
we should, beyond a doubt, have been put to the rout.
But his one single arm is enough to win the victory
for us, and for ever to end the conflicts between heaven
and hell.

Mark well our warrior chief as he goes forth to the
fight. The son of Jesse rejected all carnal weapons.
He might have had them—they put the helmet on his
head, and the mail about his body, and they were about
to gird the sword upon his loins—but he said, "I cannot go with these, for I have not proved them." In
like manner the Son of David renounced all earthly
armor. They would have taken our Lord by force, and
made him a King, but he said, "My kingdom is not of
this world." Swords enough would have leaped from
their scabbards at his bidding. It was not alone Peter,
whose too-hasty sword smote the ear of Malchus, but
there were many zealots who would have been all too
glad to have followed the star of Jesus of Nazareth as
in former days; and yet more frequently in later days,
the Jews followed impostors who declared themselves
to be commissioned by the Most High for their deliverance. But Jesus said, "Put up thy sword into the
sheath. They that take the sword shall perish by the
sword." No doubt one of the temptations of the desert
was not only that he should have the kingdoms of the
world, but that he should have them by the use of such
means as Satan would suggest. He must fall down
and worship Satan: he must use the carnal weapon,
which would be tantamount to worshipping him.
Jesus would not have it. To this day the great fight of

Jesus Christ with the powers of darkness is not with sword and helmet, but with the smooth stones of the brook. The simple preaching of the gospel with the shepherd's crook of the great Head of the church held in our midst—this it is that lays low Goliath, and shall lay him low to the last day. Vain is it for the church even to think that she shall win the victory by wealth, or by rank, or by civil authority. No government will assist her. To the power of God alone she must look, " Not by might, nor by power, but by my Spirit, saith the Lord of hosts." Happy will it be for the church when she learns that lesson. The preaching of the cross, which is " to them that perish foolishness," is, nevertheless, to us who believe Christ, " the power of God, and the wisdom of God."

See, then, our glorious Champion going forward to the fray with weapons of his own choosing, and those such as human wisdom despises, because they do not appear to be adapted to the work. With great strength and power, nevertheless, did he go forth, for he went in the name of God. " Thou comest to me," said David, " with a sword, and with a spear, and with a shield : but I come to thee in the name of the Lord of hosts." Such, too, is the predominating influence which renders the gospel omnipotent. Christ is God's propitiation. God hath " set him forth to be a propitiation for sin." Christ is appointed of God, anointed of God, sent of God. And the gospel is God's message, attended with God's Spirit. If it be not, then is it weak as water—it must fail. But since the Lord has sent it, and he has promised to bless it, we may rest assured it will accomplish the ends for which it was ordained. "I come to thee in the name of the Lord of hosts!" These words might serve as a motto for all those who are sent of Christ, and represent him in the dread battle for precious souls. This was Christ's watchword, when for our sakes, and on our behalf, he came to wrestle with sin, to bear the wrath of God, and to vanquish death and hell! He came in the name of God.

Mark you well that David did smite Goliath, and he smote him effectually—not in the loins, or on the hand, or on the foot—but in a vital point he delivered the stroke that laid him low. He smote him on the brow of his presumption, on the forehead of his pride. I suppose he had lifted up his vizor to take a look at his contemptible adversary, when the stone sunk in which let out for ever that boastful soul. So when our Lord stood forth to contend with sin, he projected his atoning sacrifice as a stone that has smitten sin and all its powers upon the forehead. Thus, glory be to God, sin is slain. It is not wounded merely, but it is *slain* by the power of Jesus Christ.

And remember that David cut off Goliath's head with his own sword. Augustine, in his comment on this passage, very well brings out the thought that the triumph of our Saviour Jesus Christ is here set forth in the history of David. He, "through death, destroyed him that had the power of death, that is, the devil." "He death by dying slew"—cut off the giant's head with his own sword. The cross that was meant to be the death of the Saviour was the death of sin. The crucifixion of Jesus, which was supposed to be the victory of Satan, was the consummation of his victory over Satan. Lo, this day I see in our Conquering Hero's hand the grizzly head of the monster sin, all dripping with gouts of gore. Look at it, ye that once were under its tyranny. Look at the terrible lineaments of that hideous and gigantic tyrant. Your Lord has slain your foe. Your sins are dead; he has destroyed them. His own arm, single-handed and alone, has destroyed your gigantic enemy.. "The sting of death is sin, and the strength of sin is the law; but thanks be to God, which giveth us the victory through our Lord Jesus Christ." Blessed and magnified be his holy name. And when David had thus achieved the death of Goliath, he was met by the maidens of Israel, who came forth and sang in responsive verse, accompanied with the music of their timbrels and joyous dancings, "Saul hath slain his thousands, and David his ten thousands." So he had his triumph. Meanwhile, the hosts of Israel, seeing that the Philistine Giant was dead, took heart and dashed upon the adversary. The Philistines were affrighted and they fled, and every Israelite that day became a victor through the victory of David. They were more than conquerors, through him that had loved them and won the victory for them. So let us now bethink ourselves to be victors. Our Lord has won the victory. He is to his glory gone. The angels have met him on the way. They have said, "Lift up your heads, O ye gates; even lift them up, ye everlasting doors; and the King of glory shall come in." And they that have been with him have answered to the question, "Who is this King of glory?" They have said, "The Lord mighty in battle: He is the King of glory.

The Lord of hosts: He is the King of glory." And this day the feeblest believer triumphs in Christ. Though we should have been beaten, nor could we have hoped for victory—yet, now, through Jesus Christ our Lord, we chase our enemies; we trample sin under our feet; and we go from strength to strength through his completed victory. There is much room for you to think here. Will you think this over for yourselves? It is better I should not do all the thinking for you. You will find the analogy capable of much amplification. I have given you only just as it were a sort of charcoal outline—a rough draft. Make a picture of it at your leisure, and it may prove a beneficial study and a profitable meditation.

II. With much brevity let us now revert to David as AN EXAMPLE FOR EVERY BELIEVER IN CHRIST.

Above all things, it behooves us, dear brethren and sisters, to consider that if we are ever to do anything for God and for his church, we must be anointed with holy oil. O, how vain it would be for us to grow zealous with a sort of creature carnal fanaticism, and to attempt great things, in sheer presumption, which can only issue in utter failure. Unless the Spirit of God be upon us we have no might from within and no means from without to rely upon. Wait upon the Lord, beloved, and seek strength in his succor. There cannot come out of you what has not been put into you. You must receive and then give out. Remember how the Lord Jesus describes it:—" The water that I shall give him shall be in him a well of water springing up into everlasting life." And again, in another place, "he that believeth on me as the Scripture hath said, out of his belly shall flow rivers of living water."

You cannot do David's work if you have not David's anointing. When you remember that your divine Master tarried for the heavenly anointing, you can hardly expect to do without it. Be not so foolish. Christ went not to his public ministrations till the Spirit of God rested upon him. The apostles tarried at Jerusalem, and went not forth to preach till power was given to them from on high. The point, the prerequisite, the *sine quâ non* with us, is to have that power. O, to preach in that power—to pray in that power—to look after wandering souls in that power! Your Sunday-school work, your home missionary work, your every form of ministry for Christ, must be done in that power. Get ye to your knees. Get ye to the cross. Get ye to your Master's feet. Sit ye still in faith and hope, until he shall have given you the strength that shall qualify you to do the Master's work, in the Master's way, to Master's praise.

David, too, stands before us as an example of the fact that our opportunity will come, if our efficiency has been bestowed, without our being very particular to seek it. David fell into position. The place he was fitted to occupy, he was providentially called to fill as a great man in Israel. Little did he guess, when he went with the load of cheeses upon his shoulders, that he was ere long to be distinguished beyond all other men in Palestine. Yet it was so. Beloved, do not be in a hurry to look out for your sphere. Be ready for your sphere; your sphere will come to you. I speak to many dear young brethren who are studying for the ministry. Be prepared for any work rather than be looking out for some particular work. God has his niche for you. You will drop on your feet: depend upon that. Be ready. Your business is to be ready. Have your tools well sharpened, and know how to handle them. The place will come to you, the best place for you, if you are not so much looking after that which meets your taste, as after that which proves you to be a vessel fit for the Master's use. David finds his occasion. He has received the Spirit first, which is the main thing, and then he has found the occasion which calls out his credentials. These things being clear, I gather from David's example that when we feel a call from God to do something for him, and for his church, we need not wait until those whom we hold in respect coincide with us as to the propriety of entering upon the service. Had David said, " Well, I shall wait till Eliab, and Abinadab, and Shammah, my elder brothers, are all perfectly agreed that I am the man to fight Goliath," I suspect he would never have fought with Goliath at all. Great deference is due to the judgment of our seniors, but greater respect is due to the motions of the Spirit of God within our heart. I would to God there were more regard shown for those inward monitions among Christians than there is wont to be in these times. If thou hast a thought put into thy heart, or a charge sounded in thy conscience, obey it, man ; act up to it, though no one else perceives it or encourages thee. If God has shown thee his counsel, at your peril hide the presage or shrink from the performance. What! With the fear of God in our hearts, and a commission from God in our hands, shall we halt and hesitate and become the servants of men? I would rather die than have to come into this pulpit to ask your leave, or to get any man's consent, as to what I shall preach. God wots he will speak—what he hath to say to me, and by the help of his good Spirit I will deliver it to you as I hear it from himself. May this tongue be silent or ever it becomes the servant of man. David was of that mind. He felt he had something to do, and though he could listen to what other people had to say, yet they were no masters of his. He served the living God, and he went about the business intrusted to him undaunted by any judgment they might form of him. He that speaketh for God should speak honestly. Let others criticise and sift the chaff from the wheat. He must expect that. But as for himself, let him give out the pure wheat as he believeth it to be, and fear no man, lest he come under the condemnation of the God of heaven. Go, my brother, about thy business, if God give it thee to do. If I upbraid thee, what of that? I am but a man. Or if all those in whose good esteem you would gladly stand turn upon you with hard suspicions and cutting censures—they are but men, and to God alone is your allegiance due. Go thou about thy Master's work, as David did, with dauntless nerve but modest mien. He were an ill servant who, after once getting his Master's orders, should leave them unperformed, and excuse himself by saying, "I met one of my fellow-servants, and he said he thought I might be too bold in my adventure, and therefore I had better not attempt it." To your own Master you will stand or fall. Take care that you stand well with him.

Learn from David, too, to return quiet answers to those who would roughly put you aside from your work. Generally it is better to return no answer at all. I think David spake not so well by word as by deed. His conduct was more eloquent than his language. As he came back from the fight, holding up the giant's head, I could hope that Eliab saw him; and that Abinadab and Shammah came out to meet him. If they did, he might simply have held up the trophy, and allowed its ghastly visage to reply for him. It is not, they would think, after all, because of his pride or the naughtiness of his heart, or from an idle curiosity to see the battle, that he has come. They would perceive that he had come to do God's work in his own way: that God had helped him to gain the victory, rout the foe, and relieve the fears of Israel; and that through the man whom they despised the Lord had made his own name glorious.

Learn, again, from David's example, the prudence of keeping to tried weapons. I have often heard it spoken of as an unlikely thing that David should kill the giant with a stone. I think those who talk so miss the point. What missile could be handier or better suited for the occasion? If the fellow was tall, a sling would carry a stone high enough to reach him; and if he was strong, very strong, the sling would give such impetus to the stone that David could assail his adversary without getting within his reach. It was the best weapon he could have used. Oriental shepherds, if those of olden time were like those of modern days, had practice enough to make them proficient in slinging stones. They spend many hours both alone and with their fellows over feats of the sling. It is generally their best weapon for the protection of their sheep in the vast solitudes. I do not doubt that David had learnt to sling a stone to a hair's breadth, and not miss. As for the sword, he had never had one in his life; for there was neither sword nor spear found in the hand of any of the people that were with Saul and Jonathan, save that which was found with Saul and Jonathan his son. We are told as much as that in the thirteenth chapter. The Philistines had so completely disarmed the whole populace that they had not got any such weapons. With the use of them, therefore, David could not have been familiar. And as the coat of mail—a cumbersome, uneasy, comfortless equipment—the wonder to me is how the knights of old did anything at all in such accoutrements. No marvel that David put the thing off. He felt most at ease in his own shepherd's garb. Of course we are not going to infer that unsuitable instruments are desirable. We teach nothing so romantic or absurd. It well becomes us to use the most suitable tools we can find. As for those stones out of the brook, David did not pick them up at hazard; he carefully chose them, selecting smooth stones that would fit exactly in his sling—the kind of stone he thought best fitted for his purpose. Nor did he trust in his sling. He tells us he trusted in God, but he went to work with his sling as if he felt the responsibility to be his own. To miss the mark would prove his own clumsiness: to compass his aim would be of God's enabling. Such, my brethren, is the true philosophy of a Christian's life. You are to do good works as zealously as if you were to be saved by your good works, and you are to trust in the merits of Christ as though you had done nothing at all. So, too, in the service of God, though you are to work for God as if the fulfilment of your mission rested with yourselves, you must clearly understand, and steadfastly believe, that after all, the whole matter from first to last rests with God. Without him all you have ever planned or performed is unavailing. That was sound philosophy of Mahomet's when the man said, " I have turned my camel loose, and trusted in providence." " No," answered he, " tie your camel up and then trust in providence." Do the best you can and trust in God. God never meant that faith in him should be synonymous with sloth. Why, for the matter of that, if it is all God's work, and that is to be the only consideration, there is no need for David to have a sling. Nay, there is not any need for David at all. He may go back, lie on his back in the middle of the field, and say, " God will do his work : he does not want me." That is how fatalists would talk, but not how believers in God would act. They say, " God wills it, therefore I am going to do it "—not " God does it, and therefore there is nothing for me to do." Nay, " Because God works by me, therefore I will work by his good hand upon me. He is putting strength into his feeble servant, and making use of me as his instrument, good for nothing though I am apart from him. Now will I run to the battle with alacrity, and I will use my sling with the best skill I have, taking quiet, calm, deliberate aim at that monster's brow, since I believe that God will guide the stone and accomplish his own end." When you are bent on serving God give him your best; keep not back aught of nerve or muscle, aught of skill or sagacity you can dedicate to the enterprise. Say not, "Anything will do: God can bless my lack as well as my competency." Doubtless he can, but undoubtedly he will not. Be careful to do your best. David in his old age and his riper experience would not offer to God that which cost him nothing. Do not attempt to render unto God slovenly service, and flatter yourselves that he will bless it. He can bless it; but that is not the way in which he usually deigns to work. Though he often takes rough tools, he fashions them and polishes them for his use. He can convert rude men into able ministers of the New Testament. Think not, however, that his grace will excuse your presumption. But go with the instruments you have proved. When any of you working men attempt to preach the gospel of Jesus Christ, do not try the fine arguments that are often used to combat infidels. You will never manage them. They will be sure to embarrass you. Tell to your neighbors and comrades what you have felt and handled of the Word of Life. Declare to them those things that are written in the Scriptures. These texts are the smooth stones that will suit your sling. Keep to these things. Why, they tell us, now-a-day, that we ought to take up those arguments which are invented by modern philosophers, examine them, study them, and come forward on the Sabbath day and at other times to answer them; that we should use historical research and logical acumen to rebut infidel calumnies. Ah! Saul's armor does not fit us. They that like it may wear it; but, after all, to preach Christ and him crucified—to tell out the old, old story of eternal love and of the blood which sealed it, the manner of redemption, the truth of God's unchangeable grace—this is to use those stones and that sling which will surely find out the forehead of the foe.

Next, observe that from the work which David begun he ceased not till he had finished it. He had laid the giant prone upon the soil, but he was not satisfied till he had cut off his head. I wish that some who work for Christ would be as thorough as this young volunteer was. Have you taught a child the way of salvation? Do not leave off till that child is enrolled in the fellowship of believers. Have you faithfully preached the gospel to any congregation of people? Continue to instruct, counsel, and encourage them, until you see them established in the faith. Or if you have refuted a heresy, or denounced a vice, follow up the assault until the evil is exterminated. Not only kill the giant, but have his head off! Never do the work of the Lord deceitfully. Never spare a device of the devil pitifully. Bad habits and besetting sins should be levelled with a decisive blow. But let not that be enough. Give them no chance of recovering their strength. With humble penitence and earnest resolution, in reliance on God and detestation of the foe, see to it that the head shall be taken from the sin as well as the stone sunk in its forehead. In so doing you may look for help you had not reckoned on. You have no sword with you: you have not wanted to cumber yourself with one, even as David had no need to carry a sword in his hand, for Goliath was carrying a sword with him, which might well serve for his own execution. Whenever you serve God you strive against error; remember that every error carries the sword with which it will be slain. In maintaining the cause of truth, we need not be surprised if the fight be long; but we may always count on the pride of the adversary turning to his own hurt. The conflict will be shortened by himself. When the invaders, most of all, relied on the alliances they had formed, it often happened that Israel won the day through the Moabites and the Assyrians falling out among themselves. Very frequently it has been God's plan to let his adversaries turn upon each other and end the fight to his servants' comfort. Behold the giant's head taken off with his own sword. Let it be before your eyes for a sign. It matters not, brethren, though we should be in the minority on certain eminent matters, as we undoubtedly are. The question for you is, are you right? Are you right? The right is sure to win! Have you truth on your side? Have you the Bible on your side? Have you Christ on your side? Well, you may belong to a despised community; you may be associated with a very few and a very poor people. Flinch not—let not your heart quail. Had you no strength with which to overcome the adversary, excepting that which is promised by God, you have quite enough. But there lies in ambush, in the camp of your adversary, an assistance and an aid to truth that you have not perhaps thought of. The old dragons stings himself to death. As vice consumes the vitals of the man who indulges in it, so does error, in the long run, become its own destroyer. Full often truth shines out the more brightly from the very fact that an error has beclouded the world with its dense shadows. Go on, then! Strive with coolness and courage! Be not daunted by the comely face, the princely figure, or the battle array of your antagonist! Let not his vaunting words deter you. Call on the name of Jehovah, the Lord of hosts, and use, even in God's battles, those weapons which you have tested and proved. But take care to go through with God's work; do it thoroughly, looking unto Jesus, the author and finisher of your faith; so beloved, you may expect to go from strength to strength and bring glory to God.

I would we were all on the Lord's side, that we were all the soldiers of Christ. Do any here confess that they are not? Are there any of you that feel sin lying heavily upon you, and yet you fain would be at peace with God in fellowship with Jesus? Beloved, Jesus has never yet rejected one that came to him. It has never yet been said that his blood was not able to cleanse the vilest soul! Go to him. You cannot give him greater joy than by going to him and confessing your sin and seeking his mercy. He waits to be gracious. He slays sin, but he takes pity on sinners. He is ready to pardon them. He is the enemy of Goliath, but he sits on Zion's hill, glad to welcome the very poorest of the poor that come to him. If you are the worst sinner that ever lived, he is still able to save to the uttermost. If you have no hope and no confidence—if you feel as though sentence had gone forth that you should die for ever, your fears are no clue to God's counsels. He has not spoken the bitter things you have imagined against yourself. Give ear to what he has said—" Let the wicked forsake his way, and the unrighteous man his thoughts; and let him return unto the Lord, and he will have mercy upon him; and to our God, for he will abundantly pardon." Oh! to be on Christ's side, maintains the heart in calm and inflames the soul with joy, notwithstanding the pain that now tortures your nerves, or the shame that mantles your cheeks! But ah! to be on the other side—to be an enemy of Jesus—is a woe that blights all present joy, and a portent that augurs all future bane. The future, the future, the future! This is the worst of all to be dreaded. "Kiss the Son, lest he be angry, and ye perish from the way, when his wrath is kindled but a little. Blessed are all they that put their trust in him." The Lord give you, every one of you, to be thus timely wise, for his name's sake. Amen.

David and his Volunteers.

"And of the Gadites there separated themselves unto David into the hold to the wilderness, men of might, and men of war fit for the battle, that could handle shield and buckler, whose faces were like the faces of lions, and were as swift as the roes upon the mountains; Ezer the first, Obadiah the second, Eliab the third, Mishmannah the fourth, Jeremiah the fifth, Attai the sixth, Eliel the seventh, Johanan the eighth, Elzabad the ninth, Jeremiah the tenth, Machbanai the eleventh. These were the sons of Gad, captains of the host: one of the least was over an hundred, and the greatest over a thousand. These are they that went over Jordan in the first month, when it had overflown all his banks; and they put to flight all them of the valleys, both toward the east and toward the west."—1 Chronicles xii. 8–15.

DAVID, compelled to flee from his own country, and to hide himself from the malice of Saul, was eminently a type of our Lord Jesus Christ, who, in the days when he dwelt here among men, was despised and rejected of men. And at this moment it is well known to the true church of God, and it becomes palpably evident to every earnest believer in the gospel, that Jesus, the son of David, is not received, acknowledged, or tolerated in this present evil world. He has gone forth without the camp. All who would repair to him must go forth likewise, bearing his reproach. These eleven Gadites —all of them remarkable men—espoused the cause of

David when he was in his very worst condition; they left the ease and comfort, the honors and emoluments, of their own home to associate themselves with him when he was regarded as an outlaw under the ban of society. And to this day every Christian who is faithful to his profession must separate himself from his fellow men to be a follower of the despised Jesus. In that way, and with that faith which men still count heresy, must he join himself with that sect which is everywhere spoken against, running the gauntlet of the age, if he would espouse the cause of the Lord's anointed.

In tracing out the parallel, let me now draw your attention, first to the leader who commanded the voluntary homage of good and valiant men, and then to the recruits who joined themselves to him, of whom we find a graphic description in our text.

I. The leader, whom we regard as a type of our Lord Jesus Christ, was David, the son of Jesse; and in tracing out some points of analogy, we begin by noticing that, like David, our Lord was anointed of God to be the leader of his people. Hence the words of prophecy concerning him, "I will make an everlasting covenant with you, even the sure mercies of David. Behold, I have given him for a witness to the people, a leader and commander to the people." The Spirit of God is upon Jesus of Nazareth, for him hath God the Father anointed. "Unto him shall the gathering of the people be." We may well be ready to follow a leader whom God hath appointed and commended to us with such high praise. "I have laid help upon one that is mighty, I have exalted one chosen out of the people.

I have found David my servant; with my holy oil have I anointed him: with whom my hand shall be established: mine arm also shall strengthen him." The Lord in his own sovereignty, with wisdom and prudence, has been pleased to fix his choice upon the man Christ Jesus to be our Federal Head, our King, and our Commander. What other justification do we need for following Christ than that God himself thus sets him forth? To this choice of God our soul agrees. Never be afraid, young man, of acknowledging Christ. Never let any of us blush to own the blessed impeachment that we are followers of the Lamb. It is an honor to follow one who has the highest sanction of heaven in taking the command and exercising the authority that pertains to him.

Jesus was like David, too, in that he was personally fit to be a leader. David, alike by his character and his deeds of prowess, had become the foremost man of his times. So our blessed Lord, as to his person, is just such a King as one might desire to obey; and, as for his achievements, O tell what his arm hath done— what spoils from death his right hand won! Let his fame be spread over all the earth! He stood in the gap when there was none to help. He vanquished the foe who threatened our destruction. He set his people free. He led their captivity captive. In point of courage and in feats of war he so outstripped David that I may safely say David has slain his thousands, but Jesus his tens of thousands. He is a man of war. The Lord is his name. He hath defeated all the principalities and powers, and put to rout all the hosts of hell that came against his people. Therefore let him be acknowledged as King. Who else should be exalted among the people but he who hath done wonderful things for the people? No marvel that the men of Israel gathered around David with a glowing enthusiasm, and proved their patriotism by their allegiance to his sovereignty. Nor need we wonder that the children of God should shout —

> "All hail the power of Jesu's name!
> Crown him Lord of all."

Right well does he deserve all the homage we can ever ascribe to him.

But our Lord, though anointed of God and meriting the distinction which he gained, was, nevertheless, like David, rejected of men. Poor David! Saul thirsted for his blood, put him upon dangerous enterprises, in the hope that he might die; and when he saw that God was with him, he hated him yet the more, till he hunted him like a partridge upon the mountains. He could find shelter nowhere. If he went to the priests of Nob, the king came and slew all the inhabitants of the city; or if he went to Keilah, and fought with the Philistines and saved the inhabitants of Keilah, yet by and by they were willing to give him up to his enemies. He was safe nowhere. Now, our Lord Jesus Christ here upon earth was in like manner despised and rejected of men; nor has the offence of his cross ceased to this day. You may be a nominal Christian, and have the good esteem of all men; but if you are a true disciple of Jesus, obeying him from the heart, openly avowing his cause, and diligently testifying his name, you will meet with bitter hostility in all sorts of places and among all sorts of people. Rest assured that until Christ comes it will be true that if ye were of the world, the world would love its own, but because ye are not of the world, but Christ hath chosen you out of the world, therefore the world hateth you. There may be Christians placed in such sheltered nooks, and living among such godly families, that they do not come into collision with the outside world; but if you do come into connection with the world in any way, you will be sure to prove its enmity. As it is in rebellion against God, and hostile to Christ, it will be intolerant of you. So Ishmael persecuted Isaac even in Abraham's own household. So the seed of the serpent hates the seed of the woman. So, too, those that are under the law own no kindred with those that are the children of the promise. Marvel not then; it scarcely becomes you to murmur, though it sometimes appears to you a hard lot. Jesus Christ is still as a root out of a dry ground, without form or comeliness to the mass of mankind. True religion is not still to be found in fashionable circles; it finds little favor among the great and mighty, though to-day it does not hide its head in the clefts and caves of the rocks. While the violence of persecution is abated in its outward manifestations of terror, the malice out of which it grew still survives, and the people of God are harassed by it in a thousand ways. The iron is made to enter into their soul. Thus the cruel jealousy and the galling animosity with which David was driven forth, and hunted from place to place, find a counterpart in the treatment that Christ himself received, and that all his faithful followers have in their measure to endure. But notwithstanding the pains and penalties they incurred in those dark days,

the really good and pious people in Israel rallied to the
stand rd of David. I know it is said that those who
were in debt and discontented came to David. That
is quite true; and well it typifies the abject condition
of those poor sinners who come to Christ for refuge;
but many of those Israelites were reduced in circumstances and brought into debt through the bad government of Saul. Probably the very best people in the
country were to be found among those who gathered
around David; and certainly there was with David,
Abiathar the high priest. He came to David as the
representative of the godly, the puritanic party. With
David likewise there was Gad the prophet. And you
know how in the early days of David's persecution he
resided with Samuel the prophet of the Lord: so that
the gracious party was always on David's side. Does
not the like thing happen among those who ally
themselves with the Son of David at this day? Although
he whom we worship is despised and rejected of men,
yet unto you who believe he is precious. They that
fear the Lord love Christ and embrace his gospel.
Those that have a new heart and a right spirit are not
at all dubious which side to take. They have lifted
up their hands to the crucified One, and they are sworn
to do battle for his cause as long as they live. We
need not be ashamed to side with Jesus, for we shall
be in good company—not in the company of the nobles
of the earth, those who bear its titles, own its wealth,
or enjoy its empty fame, but in the company of the
pure in heart, of the heirs of the promises, of those to
whom God has been pleased to reveal himself, yea,
of the babes out of whose mouths he has perfected

praise. O we may be well content to cast in our lot with God's elect, be they who they may in the world's esteem, or be their lot what it may in their pilgrimage to the better country. With them would we be numbered; with them would we be associated; with them would we go. Let Christ's people be our people. Where they toil would we toil; with them would we live; with them would we die; with them would we be buried, in the glad hope that with them we shall rise again, to live for ever in the fellowship of the saints.

Mark one thing more. Despised as David was among men, yet, being anointed of God, his cause in the end was successful. He did come to the throne: and so it is with our Lord Jesus Christ. Notwithstanding all the opposition that still rages against his cause, it must prosper and prevail. He shall see his seed; he shall prolong his days, and the pleasure of the Lord shall prosper in his hands. Well may the enmity of the wicked provoke the irony of heaven. "Why do the heathen rage, and the people imagine a vain thing?" "He that sitteth in the heavens shall laugh: the Lord shall have them in derision." It is Jehovah himself who says it: "Yet have I set my king upon my holy hill of Zion." God's decree has placed him there. Shall the conspiracy, think ye, of kings and rulers unseat him? Nay, there must he sit, till all his enemies are beneath his feet. O it is good to be with Christ to-day, for then we shall be with him to-morrow. It is good to be with him in the pillory, for if we can bear the reproach we shall one day be with him on his throne to share the glory. If you will walk with Christ through the mire, when he goes barefoot, you shall be with him in the golden streets when he puts on the golden sandals, and the angels fall down and worship him. O, if you can foot it with him in his deeds of service, when he grows weary and footsore, you shall ride with him on his white horse of victory, when all the armies of heaven shall follow him in his great achievements. If you are with him in his humiliation, you shall be with him in his triumph. I think I have told you before, a little parable, which I will venture to repeat in this place. There was a certain king whose son was sent upon an errand to a far country, and when he came into that country, although he was the lawful prince of it, he found that the citizens would not acknowledge him. They mocked at him, jested at him, and took him and set him in the pillory, and there they scoffed at him and pelted him with filth. Now, there was one in that country who knew the prince, and he alone stood up for him when all the mob was in tumult raging against him. And when they set him on high as an object of scorn, this man stood side by side with him to wipe the filth from that dear royal face; and when from cruel hands missiles in scorn were thrown, this man took his full share; and whenever he could he thrust himself before the prince to ward off the blows from him if possible, and to bear the scorn instead of him. Now it came to pass that after awhile the prince went on his way, and in due season the man who had been the prince's friend was called to the king's palace. And on a day when all the princes of the court were round about, and the peers and nobles of the land were sitting in their places, the king came to his throne and he called for that man, and he said, "Make way, princes and nobles! Make way!

Here is a man more noble than you all, for he stood boldly forth with my son when he was scorned and scoffed at! Make way, I say, each one of you, for he shall sit at my right hand with my own son. As he took a share of his scorn, he shall now take a share of his honor." And there sat princes and nobles who wished that they had been there, ay! envied the man who had been privileged to endure scorn and scoffing for the prince's sake! You need not that I interpret the parable. May you make angels envious of you, if envy can ever pierce their holy minds. You can submit for Christ's sake to sufferings which it is not possible for seraphim or cherubim to endure.

II. Having thus drawn your attention to the Leader whom David the Son of Jesse prefigured, let me turn now to speak a little of those who gathered round him and enlisted in his service. The recruits who came to David were eleven in number. The first characteristic we read about them is that they were separated. "Of the Gadites, there separated themselves unto David," eleven persons. They were *separated*. Observe that. They separated themselves. They seem to have been captains of the militia of their tribe. The very least among them was over a hundred, and the greatest over a thousand. But they separated themselves from their commands over their tribes—separated themselves from their brethren and their kinsfolk. I dare say many of their friends said to them, "Why, what fools you are! You must be mad to espouse the cause of a fellow like David!" and then they would call David all manner of foul, opprobrious names. "Are you going to be among those who associate with him,—a troop of banditti,

—that ragged regiment?" I'll be bound to say they had terms for David and his men which, in ears polite, it would not be meet to quote. It is a mercy that the language of those men of Belial has not been recorded. But these men all said, "Yes, we will separate ourselves." And, for the matter of that, they did not merely tear themselves away from their friends, but from their kinsfolk too. David wanted their right arms and he should have them. He wanted valiant men, and they would go and fight for David, whatever fond connection should be sundered thereby.

Dear friends, in these times it is most important that everyone who is a Christian should understand that he must separate himself from the world. Ye cannot serve Christ and the world too. You cannot be of the world and of Christ's church. You may be nominally of the church and really of the world, but really of the world and really of the church you cannot possibly be. The Christian must differ from the world in many things. His language must not be the speech of Babylon, but the chaste, pure language which Christians use. His actions, his customs, his manners, his habits, must not be like those of other men. He is not to be full of affectation and eccentricity. He need not adopt a peculiar garb, or discourse in quaint phrases, or speak with an unnatural twang. All that may be mere formalism. Still there is ample room for separateness in that which meets the eye and addresses the ear of the observer. We need not display vanity in our attire. In dress Christians will be simple and chaste, not ornate and gaudy. In their speech, too, the children of God will certainly never use an oath or lend their tongue to the semblance of a lie; from foolish talking and jesting, which are not convenient, they will rigidly abstain. But the tongue of a believer, my brethren, ought to be as a fountain which sendeth forth sweet water; in his conversation there should be the meekness of wisdom: and when he cannot speak to profit, his silence may bear witness to his sincerity. But it is in his intercourse with the world that the Christian shows the moral force of his character. There it comes out because it cannot be hid. If his trade has become used to tricks and stratagems which will not bear the light, he cannot conform to them; he will shrink from them with abhorrence: he must keep a clean conscience. Other men may do the thing without compunction. It may have become "the custom." But no antiquity or universality of custom will authorize that which is obviously wrong: so he cannot do it and will not do it, for he is a Christian. He counts that a higher morality is required of him than of an ordinary man, and after this higher morality he seeks. From the world's religion the man of God will likewise stand aloof. He never asks himself what kind of religion does the present age consider most expedient. Nor does he wish to find out the fashionable taste in doctrine, or the order of devotion which is most agreeable to the undevout; but he seeks after God, he diligently inquires for God's truth, he joins himself to God's church and earnestly promotes its welfare. Moreover, he loves God's ways and desireth to be under the power of God's Spirit. After this manner he separates himself. Does not the church in these days need to hear sounded every day, as a thunder clap, that divine commandment—

"Come out from among them, and be ye separate, saith the Lord, and touch not the unclean thing; and I will receive you, and will be a Father unto you, and ye shall be my sons and daughters, saith the Lord Almighty"? O, the shameful conformity of some professors with the world. It degrades the church and debases themselves. God grant that we may be stanch in our nonconformity to the world! To whatever church we may belong, may we be "holy, harmless, undefiled, and separate from sinners." But, observe, that these people separated themselves unto David. You may separate yourself and not separate yourself unto Christ; and, if not, you only change from one form of worldly-mindedness to another. We are not to separate ourselves unto self-righteousness, or unto affectation, or unto a sect, but unto Christ. These people got away from their friends that they might get to David. We are to get away from the world that we may get closer to Christ. We often sing, "Oh, for a closer walk with God!" But if our walk is to be close with God, it must be a long way from the world. We must separate ourselves, by divine grace, unto Christ. And then, as you read that they separated themselves unto David in the wilderness, let me entreat you to ask yourselves if you are ready to take part with a rejected, crucified Christ. Tens of thousands would separate themselves to David if he were in Hebron on the throne of Israel. They would go there to crown David in the day of his prosperity; but the thing was to separate themselves unto David in the wilderness. That is the work of real grace in the heart which leads us to take sides with a despised Christ. O, it is a blessed thing when God teaches you to say, "I will follow the truth wherever it leads me. I will follow it, though some shall say to me, 'You are inconsistent.' I do not care about that. Though they shall say, 'Why, you are landed now in fanaticism.' I do not care about that. I will be a fanatic. If the truth leads me there, I will separate myself in the wilderness." Though they should tauntingly say, "You only go to some 'Little Bethel,' which is frequented by a few ignorant and vulgar people." Be it so. If Christ goes there, what matters that to us? If the truth should lead us down into the hovel, where we could only associate with the very lowest of the low, if they were the Lord's people, they should be our delight. I wish this spirit were in all Christians, that they would be loyal to truth and not pander to the world. Do not be everlastingly asking yourselves "What will so-and-so say? and what will so-and-so say?" Do the right, and fear not. Believe the truth: let what will come of it. Follow the straight line and do not trim your way. Go not round about for the sake of policy, but take sides with Jesus Christ in the day of scoffing, on the ground of principle. Do I speak to some men here who work in factories? O, own Christ when other men laugh at him. Stand up for Jesus when the whole shop is full of jesting and jeering against religion. If your religion is worth having, it is worth enduring a little banter for. He that is a friend must be a friend in need. If you would be a friend of Jesus you will defend his name when it wants a defender and everybody is raging at him. To come to the Tabernacle and join your fellow Christians in praising Jesus is very easy and involves no self-denial; but the thing is, you merchants, to praise Jesus among your fellow merchants who are ungodly,—to bear witness, you working men, among others who fear not the Lord,—to separate yourselves unto David in the wilderness,—to cleave to Christ where he is scoffed at and despised. That is a true Christian. I beseech you, test yourselves by this; for if you are ashamed of him in this evil generation, he will be ashamed of you when he cometh in his glory. But if you, out of a pure heart, can confess him before a godless world, he will acknowledge you in the day when he cometh in the glory of his Father, and all his holy angels with him. O, for grace to be separate in this way!

Note, next, about these men that they were men of might. It is said of them that they were men of might whose faces were like faces of lions, and they were as swift as the roes upon the mountains. All that came to David were not like that. David had some women and children to protect, but he was glad to receive others that were men of might. Now there came to Jesus, the greater David, in his day, the weak ones of the flock, and he never rejected them. He was glad to receive even the feeblest; but there did come to our Lord and Master eleven men who, by his grace, were like these Gadites. Truly, I may say of his apostles, after our Divine Lord had filled them with his Spirit, that they had faces like lions and feet like hinds' feet, so swift were they for service and so strong for combat. How wondrously they ran to and fro to the very ends of the earth, like the roes of the mountains; and how bravely they faced persecution and opposition, like lions that could not flinch from their prey; and what grand works they did for David! Would to God we were like them, beloved! The grace of God can make us like them. The grace of God can make us brave as lions, so that wherever we are we can hold our own, or rather can hold our Lord's truth, and never blush nor be ashamed to speak a good word for him at all times. He can make us quick and active too, so that we shall be like the roes upon the mountains. I am afraid that often we are like the ass that coucheth down. We need the whip and the spur to make us move. We are like bullocks unaccustomed to the yoke of service. Yet it ought not to be so. Loved as we have been with such great love, and having tasted, as some of us can testify, of such dear favors from our Lord, being indulged with such intimate fellowship with himself, and sustained as we are now with such joy and peace in him, we ought to serve him with celerity and activity, with courage and confidence. We really should outvie the lion for his bravery, and the hinds and the wild goats of the rock for their swiftness. I pray it may be so. May God send to this church men—and women too—of this order, strong in the Lord and in the power of his might, to whom the joy of the Lord shall be their strength, who shall go about their Father's business with all their might—that might which is given them of God—and do great exploits for David while he is in the wilderness and needs their aid.

But it is worth noticing that they were men of war, inured to discipline—men fit for the battle, that could handle shield and buckler. Now there are some men of might who do not seem to be good men of war, because they cannot keep rank. What exploits they may do they needs must do alone, for they cannot march with the army. There are some brethren I know who are most excellent people as individuals, but they seem never to be meant to march in the ranks; they must everyone of them lead—they feel they must, they cannot be second to anybody; neither can they be under any discipline or rule. Instead of taking their place in Christ's church, they seem to consider themselves independent of the church and its organization. Howbeit, the men Christ wants in the church—and I pray him to multiply their number in our midst, and enlist all of us among them—are such as can keep step, observe the rule, and preserve order in the march, or in the fight for the service of the Lord. Men who can smite the foe, who can handle the sword and buckler, and ward off the arrows of the enemy, who can use the shield of faith and withstand the assaults of the adversary: we want these. May God teach us how to keep our places and to do our work. Some men have swords, but their swords seem to be more dangerous to their friends than to their foes. That is a kind of people one wishes to keep clear of. They are, no doubt, very zealous, but if they had a little more love as well as a lot of zeal, and were endowed with a capacity for fellowship, it would greatly improve their character. This, however, seems to be their defect. They have such an excess of individuality, and they are withal so exclusive, that we can hardly imagine how they could pray—" Our Father which art in heaven," or recognize anybody else as belonging to the family of the Most High. God make us men of might, but may he also make us men of discipline. While we keep our place, and do our own work, may we delight to see others do their share of the work too. When we smite the foe may we delight to see others use the weapons of Christian warfare with skill and success. Do not shrink from the drill or revolt against discipline, for it is a great trait of a good soldier that he should know how to keep rank. These Gadites likewise furnish us with a noble example of strong resolution. When the eleven men determined to join David they were living the other side of a deep river, which at that season of the year had overflowed its banks, so that it was extremely deep and broad. But they were not to be kept from joining David, when he wanted them, by the river. They swam through the river that they might come to David. O, I would like to hold up my Master's banner, and be his recruiting sergeant to-night, if I could entertain the hope that out of this company there would come men of such mettle whose hearts the Lord has touched to join themselves to the Lord, and fight for his cross, whatever might impede and stop their way. Do you stand back and shrink from avowing your attachment to the standard of God's anointed because it would involve a loss of reputation, displeasure of friends, the frowns of your associates in the world, or the heart-breaks of anguish of those you tenderly love? Know, then, that our Lord is worthy of all the troubles you incur and all the risks you run; and be assured that the peace which a soul enjoys that once joins Christ in the hold, and abides with him in the wilderness, well repays a man for all that he has to part with in getting to his Lord and Master. We have known some of the rich that have joined Christ's church that have had to swim through overflowing rivers of contumely; the unkindness they have braved has indeed been cold and chilling. We have known many a poor woman who has had to suffer from her husband's brutality, and many a poor man who has had to run the gauntlet of a thousand cruel tongues. But who is afraid? Once see the King in his beuty; and your fears will vanish like smoke. Did you ever see his face bestained with spittle, and black and blue with the blows of mailed hands? Did you ever see that head surrounded with the thorn crown, and mark the painful agony that was upon his visage, more marred than any man's? And have not you said, "Saviour, since thou didst endure all this for me, there is nothing that I will count hard to endure for thee. I will count shame for thee to be my glory, and thy reproach shall be greater riches to me than all the treasurers of Egypt"? Have not you said that? If you have said so from your very soul, God the Holy Ghost writing it upon your heart, I know you have resolved to endure any pain or shame if you could but get to your Lord and stand side by side with him. They swam the river to get to David. O, believer, swim the river to be with Christ!

Now, it would appear that after they had got across the river they were attacked, but we are told that they put to flight all them of the valleys both toward the east and toward the west. They were men of such resolution that if they had to fight to be on David's side they could fight; and, notwithstanding the opposition of those on the right hand and the opposition of those on the left, still push their way, lion-like men as they were, through all the forces that would impede them. O ye that love the Lord and Master, I beseech you in this evil day, this day of blasphemy and rebuke, stand not back: be not craven. Cast in your lot with him and with his people. Come to the front, hide not away like cowards; for this is the day when he shall be accursed that comes not to the help of the Lord, to the help of the Lord against the mighty! See you not everywhere how truth is fallen in the street—how the old idols of Rome are once more set up in the high places of this land? The whole nation seems to have gone after the idols which our fathers removed. O ye that love Christ, come out and separate yourselves from all acquaintance, all association with this evil thing. Come and join yourselves unto the Son of God by a holy covenant. If he be your beloved, and if his grace be in your heart, fear not. What have you to fear? Greater is he that is with you than all they that are against you. Fear not. The battle is not yours, it is the mighty God's. If truth be with you, you must conquer. If Christ the incarnate truth be with you, you are already more than a conqueror through him that has loved you. Never be ashamed, never turn aside from him who gave himself for you. Be steadfast, immovable. For this steadfastness you need to pray much and often to God, for many are the seductions of the world.

> Can ye cleave to your Lord, can ye cleave to your Lord,
>   When the many turn aside?
> Can ye witness that he hath the living word,
>   And none upon earth beside?
>
> Do ye answer we can, do ye answer we can,
>   Through his love's constraining power?
> But do ye remember the flesh is weak,
>   And will shrink in the trial hour?
>
> Yet yield to his love, who around you now
>   The bands of a man would cast;
> The cords of his love, who was given for you,
>   To his altar binding you fast.

Do examine yourselves. Prove your own hearts. Consider what manner of men ye ought to be. Let the precepts admonish you. Let the *esprit de corps* stimulate you. Never let the disciples of Christ fall behind followers of David in warmth of attachment, or in order of service. The nearer you get to the person of your Lord, the more you will catch of his spirit. Methinks, beloved, you need direction more than exhortation. The more you live under his eye, and the oftener you listen to his voice, the better, truer, nobler men you will prove now, and the happier recognition you will find in the day of his appearing.

www.ingramcontent.com/pod-product-compliance
Lightning Source LLC
Chambersburg PA
CBHW032105220426
43664CB00008B/1145